EDMUND S. WEHRLE

BRITAIN, CHINA, AND THE ANTIMISSIONARY RIOTS 1891-1900

UNIVERSITY OF MINNESOTA PRESS

Minneapolis

PRINTED IN THE UNITED STATES OF AMERICA AT THE
NORTH CENTRAL PUBLISHING COMPANY, ST. PAUL

Library of Congress Catalog Card Number: 66–15064

PUBLISHED IN GREAT BRITAIN, INDIA, AND PAKISTAN BY THE OXFORD
UNIVERSITY PRESS, LONDON, BOMBAY, AND KARACHI, AND IN CANADA BY
THE COPP CLARK PUBLISHING CO. LIMITED, TORONTO

FOR MARY WEHRLE

Preface

IN the shadow of the vast expansion of European control overseas
which occurred in the last half of the nineteenth century, a massive expansion of Christian missionary work took place. This study
seeks to explore the relationship between these two developments —
movements so parallel that the missionary has often been regarded as
simply another agent of his nation's imperial aspirations. In a sense this
was true. It was but natural that expansion overseas was a total affair;
it was the extension of an entire civilization with its political forms, its
economic methods and technology, and its religious beliefs. From this
point of view, then, the historian would depart from reality if he sought
to isolate national imperialism from religious expansionism.

Nonetheless these movements did, in fact, differ in the aims which
they pursued. Of course, this need not have precluded close cooperation; but, in the case of Great Britain which we shall bring under study
here, it was not considered proper for the government to grant direct
support to the missionary and most missionaries rejected on principle
any direct government support. For the missionary, the task of spreading
the Gospel was not to be tarnished by amalgamation with that necessary
evil of the sinful world — state power. For the nineteenth-century liberal, government was a limited power always to be hedged about with

restraint, and to extend its duties was to damp down the creative spirit of the individual who was, in the final analysis, responsible for the achievement of domestic prosperity and overseas power.

Naturally there was a certain self-deception here. Indirect assistance and cooperation were expected in this strange governmental-missionary relationship. Direct aid would be forthcoming when an emergency arose. And there was always a strong case for national support when the missionaries of a competing power were the recipients of special favor from their home government. But the reluctance to establish formal lines of cooperation was real and based on historical precedence, for Britain through most of the nineteenth century preferred to stand clear of any commitment — commercial or religious — which might extend its direct political responsibility. This was the era that British historians John Gallagher and Ronald Robinson have called one of "informal imperialism," for indirect control of an area of imperial interest was preferred to political involvement.

In a limited sense, this period might also be called an age of irresponsibility; at least, this descriptive term invariably comes to mind when one ponders Anglo-Chinese-missionary relations in the 1890's. The British Foreign Office declined to assume full control and responsibility for its nation's missionaries in China. The missionary community continually overlooked its responsibility as the acts and mere presence of missionaries created a series of diplomatic incidents. And the Manchu Government, admittedly enfeebled, denied responsibility for the actions of its people throughout its far-flung domain. Each stood ready to justify its narrow conception of responsibility; yet, in reality, each simply lacked the will or perhaps the power to undertake extensive and all-embracing duties.

Another theme encompassed in this story is that of the increasingly tense struggle between the great European Powers for position in China as the time for the supposed partition of China grew closer. At that moment in history world politics and missionary politics became almost completely intermixed. An understanding of how this came about is basic for a properly balanced view of the siege of the foreign legations in Peking during the Boxer rising. In a sense, this study may be regarded as an analysis of a series of antimissionary riots in China, climaxed by a massive antimissionary riot, the Boxer rising of 1900. In the period under study, the decade from 1891 to 1900, British missionaries were most often victimized and therefore British policy was most often at issue. But the other Powers were increasingly drawn in as their ambitions and interests in China increased. So two intensified trends are evident: an increasing frequency in antimissionary riots and increasing intensity of the struggle among the Powers in China. Both of these tendencies come together in the European phase of the Boxer rising.

This study is based on material drawn from two basic sources: the Public Record Office in London and various British missionary archives. I wish to express my thanks to the staff at the P.R.O. for the careful consideration they gave to me; transcripts of Crown-copyright records in the Public Record Office, London, appear by permission of the Controller of H.M. Stationery Office. Equally helpful were Miss Irene M. Fletcher, archivist at the London Missionary Society, Miss Rosemary Keen, archivist at the Church Missionary Society, and the librarian at the Society for the Propagation of the Gospel in Foreign Parts. I also thank Dr. John F. A. Mason who generously allowed me to consult the Salisbury Papers housed at Christ Church, Oxford, and Lord Salisbury who has graciously permitted me to draw quotations from his grandfather's papers.

This is primarily a study concerning the deeds of British statesmen and missionaries and my research is basically confined to Western sources related to these two factors. For the equally significant Chinese side of the story I have been forced to rely upon Western translations and the findings of scholars who have labored among the available Chinese source materials. I have especially profited from the work of Chester Tan, Jerome Ch'en, and Victor Purcell whose studies have drawn material from the valuable collections published since 1951 by the Chinese People's Republic. Chief among these was I-ho t'uan tzŭ liao ts'ung k'an (Source Materials of the Boxer War), Shanghai, 1951. *The Papers on China*, based on the work done in the East Asia Regional Studies Seminar at Harvard, were most helpful and are an ever increasing source of knowledge based on Chinese sources. My thanks are due to Professor John K. Fairbank who was generous in sending me certain valuable essays from that seminar.

The writings of Paul A. Cohen in his articles and in his recently published book, *China and Christianity*, have been of incalculable value. He has traced out the pattern of antimissionary agitation through a detailed study of Chinese materials. His work, concentrating on the 1860's, throws much light on the happenings of the 1890's.

Both English and American scholars have been kind in offering their advice and assistance in the preparation of this study. In Great Britain, Professors C. L. Mowat of the University College, North Wales, G. S. Graham of the Institute of Historical Research (London), and W. G. Beasley of the School of Oriental and African Studies (London) gave counsel during the research stages of this study. At Cambridge, Dr. Victor Purcell was kind enough to discuss his extensive studies of the Boxer rising, but his excellent study, *The Boxer Uprising*, was published too recently to be used extensively in this work. In the United States, Professor John Clive of the University of Chicago provided invaluable and patient direction in style and form, as did Professor Stephen Hay, also of Chicago. I profited from the suggestions concerning this manuscript offered by Professor Robert H. Ferrell of Indiana University and Dean Paul A. Varg and Professor Kwan-wai So of Michigan State University. Any sense of the nature of foreign policy shown here was learned from Professor M. A. Fitzsimons of the University of Notre Dame. Finally, my wife has offered maximum sympathy and advice during the difficult moments of synthesis involved in the preparation of this work.

E. S. W.

University Heights, Ohio
December 7, 1965

Key to Spelling and Abbreviations

For the romanization of Chinese place names, whenever possible I have followed *China (Gazetteer No. 22): Official Standard Names Approved by the United States Board on Geographic Names* (Washington, D.C.: Department of Interior, 1956). In certain exceptional cases, I have relied on G. M. H. Playfair, *The Cities and Towns of China: A Geographical Dictionary* (Shanghai, 1910). As a guide for standard usage in Chinese and Manchu personal names, I have used whenever possible Arthur Hummel (ed.), *Eminent Chinese of the Ch'ing Period*, 2 vols. (Washington, D.C.: U.S. Government Printing Office, 1943–44).

A.F.R.	Archibald Little (ed.). *Anti-Foreign Riots in China.* Shanghai: North China Herald, 1892.
B.D.O.W.	G. P. Gooch and Harold Temperley (eds.). *British Documents on the Origins of the War, 1898–1914,* Vols. I and II. London: H. M. Stationery Office, 1927.
C.M.S./G1/CH2	Reports and letters of the missionaries of the Church Missionary Society in Central China. Contained in boxes in C.M.S. House, London.
D.D.C.	French Ministry of Foreign Affairs. *Documents Diplomatiques Chine* ("Livres Jaunes"). Series 1894–98, 1898–99, and 1899–1900. Paris: Imprimerie Nationale, 1898–1900.
D.D.F.	French Ministry of Foreign Affairs. *Documents Diplomatiques Français, 1871–1914* (1ʳᵉ serie 1871–1901).

	Vols. VIII and IX. Paris: Imprimerie Nationale, 1938–39.
F.O. 17/–	British Foreign Office Ministerial reports and correspondence concerning China affairs at the Public Record Office, London.
F.O. 27/–	British Foreign Office Ministerial reports and correspondence concerning France at the Public Record Office, London.
F.O. 65/–	British Foreign Office Ministerial reports and correspondence concerning Russia at the Public Record Office, London.
F.O. 228/–	British Foreign Office Consular reports and correspondence concerning China affairs at the Public Record Office, London.
G.P.	J. Lepsius, A. M. Bartholdy, and F. Thimme (eds.). *Die Grosse Politik der Europäische Kabinette, 1871–1914.* Vol. XIV. Berlin: Deutsche Verlagsgesellschaft für Politik und Geschichte, 1924.
L.M.S./NC and /CC	Reports and letters of the London Missionary Society in North China and Central China at L.M.S. House, London.
P.P.	British *Parliamentary Papers* (Blue Books). Various series of printed Foreign Office correspondence concerning China, 1891–1901. London: H. M. Stationery Office, 1891–1901.
S.P.G.	The letters and reports of the missionaries of the Society for the Propagation of the Gospel in Foreign Parts at S.P.G. House, London.
F.R.U.S.	United States Department of State. *Papers Relating to the Foreign Relations of the United States, 1891–1901.* 13 vols. Washington, D.C.: Government Printing Office, 1892–1902.

Table of Contents

BRITAIN, CHINA,
AND THE ANTIMISSIONARY RIOTS

Whilst it is not right to do evil that good may come, still God often brings good out of evil, as the following will clearly prove: . . . War may compel strong foreign governments to open the door and to give freedom and security to the missionary and his converts . . . Hear the words of Bishop Moule: — "It is probable that in consequence of the exclusive policy of China and her intolerable arrogance, nothing but a series of humiliating defeats such as she experienced in 1841–42 and 1858–60, could have opened her brazen gates and have brought to the more amenable and friendly common people the blessings of honest commerce and Christian truth."

Rev. W. Laycock in the
Church Missionary Intelligencer, December 1890

But now if a Boniface or a Columba is exposed to these martyrdoms, the result is an appeal to the Consul and the mission of a gunboat. . . . I must not conceal from you that at the Foreign Office the missionaries are not popular.

Lord Salisbury, British Prime Minister, speaking before the bicentennial meeting of the Society for the Propagation of the Gospel, *ca.* 1900

CHAPTER I

Introduction

Lord Curzon, Britain's blunt-spoken Indian viceroy, once remarked that his nation's China policy was "a riddle unsoluble by man."[1] It was indeed a riddle. The puzzling factor was why the Foreign Office in the second half of the nineteenth century supported certain interests in China which apparently ran contrary in purpose to one another. On the one hand, statesmen in and out of Parliament constantly reiterated the view that Britain's primary concern in China was commercial. Perhaps Lord Clarendon put it most clearly in 1870 when he declared that "British interests in China are strictly commercial, or in all events only so far political as they may be for the protection of commerce."[2] On the other hand, when we examine the actual history of Anglo-Chinese relations since the 1860's we discover numerous diplomatic initiatives which run counter to a policy of keeping hands off politically. This was increasingly the case by the 1890's. In that decade, British gunboats were rushed to quell local outbreaks; British consuls exercised pressure in legal suits and property transactions; and British ministers acted to obtain the

---

[1] J. D. Hargreaves, "Lord Salisbury, British Isolation and the Yangtze Valley, June–September, 1900," *Bulletin of the Institute of Historical Research*, XXX (1957), 70.

[2] N. A. Pelcovits, *Old China Hands and the Foreign Office* (New York: American Institute of Pacific Relations, 1948), p. 85.

[3]

dismissal of Chinese officials as high as the rank of governor-general. Almost without exception, such political involvement had its origin in disturbances stemming from the missionary movement in China.

The first continuous and systematic missionary effort undertaken by Europeans in China was begun by the Jesuits in the late sixteenth century. Their knowledge of science and astronomy had captured the imagination of the Imperial court, but before Catholicism had firmly established itself the early spirit of accommodation subsided both in Rome and Peking. Imperial persecutions in the eighteenth century forced the relatively few Christians to disperse into isolated communities. Not until the middle years of the nineteenth century was the missionary drive resumed. This time it was the ships and guns of the commercially aggressive European Powers which opened the way for missionary penetration. The French exercised a sudden new concern for the security of the Catholic missionaries, for their safety had become an aspect of national prestige. But it was the British who led the way in seeking commercial privileges, and with the British came the first Protestant missionary groups in China.

There were two ways in which the Protestant and Catholic missionaries gained influence in China and both involved clinging to the coattails of a militant Britain and France. Initially, they shared in the benefits of the political and commercial concessions forced from China by way of a series of treaties imposed upon China by armed action and thus aptly described as the "unequal treaties." The first of these, the Treaty of Nanking, was dictated by Britain after she defeated China in the Opium War (1839–1842). By its terms the island of Hong Kong was ceded to Britain and five ports were thrown open to her trade and residence.[3] What was open to the trader was open to the missionary, and thus the Protestant missionary movement began its expansion in China. Privileges in the treaty ports were soon requested by other Western Powers and China offered no resistance to these claims. By way of a supplementary treaty in 1843, the British added the most-favored-nation clause which stated that any concession which China might grant to another Power would also fall to them. Accordingly, when the United States gained extraterritorial rights from China in a treaty signed in 1844, like privileges fell to Britain. Henceforth, civil and criminal cases involving Britishers (including missionaries) in China would be tried before consular courts.

Recurring friction between Britain and China led to a renewal of warfare in 1856. This time Britain was joined by France. By 1858 both Powers were able to wring further concessions from a defeated China; in addition, the United States and Russia joined with the victors in drawing up the Treaties of Tientsin. Now the Yangtze River as well as eleven more treaty ports were to be open to Western commerce; trade in opium was legalized and the West was able to set the Chinese tariff at a low fixed rate. Most significantly, diplomatic representatives of the West were to be provided with residences in Peking. At this point a second brief flurry of hostilities broke out and as a result of this additional concessions were extracted from China by way of the Conventions of Peking (1860).

As has been indicated the missionaries were the indirect beneficiaries of these treaty provisions, but at the same time they received direct support in most of the treaties cited above. Following the British Treaty of Nanking, the French in 1844 induced the Chinese to issue an edict of toleration for Chinese Christians. Missionary work beyond the treaty ports remained illegal, but the more audacious missionaries were encouraged to push ahead. More extensive concessions were forthcoming in the Treaties of Tientsin: the toleration of Christianity was confirmed, missionaries were permitted to preach and practice Christianity throughout the Empire and the Chinese Government was to be responsible for their protection.[4] By implication the Western Powers might intervene to see that this protection was, in fact, provided. Furthermore, when the Conventions of Peking were being drawn up, the French managed to place an even more extensive concession in the Chinese version of the French convention. It authorized French missionaries to rent and purchase land in the interior of China and erect buildings thereupon. This clause was later contested by the Chinese, but the right was confirmed in the Berthemy Convention drawn up between France and China in 1865.[5] According to the most-favored-nation clause this right was passed on to British Protestant missionaries, but, as we shall see, it was not re-

---

[3] For a more detailed summary of the treaties touched upon here in the text see Li Chien-nung, *The Political History of China, 1840–1928*, trans. Ssu-yü Teng and Jeremy Ingalls (Princeton, N.J.: D. Van Nostrand Co., 1956), Chapters 1 and 2.

[4] Chao-Kwang Wu, *The International Aspect of the Missionary Movement in China* (Baltimore: Johns Hopkins Press, 1930), pp. 26 and 250.

[5] *Ibid.*, pp. 29–30.

garded as a clear-cut treaty provision until the legal basis of this claim was clarified in 1903.[6]

In a sense, the British Government established these rights for British missionaries and then stepped aside, as if to indicate that the missionaries might make of them what they would. Apparently there was a reluctance on the part of British officials to seek enlargement or even clarification of the established missionary privileges. Thus, Sir Thomas Wade, the acting British minister, instructed his consuls in 1870 not to sanction permanent residence by missionaries outside treaty ports.[7] And throughout the decade of the 1890's the British Foreign Office turned aside the pleas of missionary groups for official support of their efforts to move to the interior by arguing that it was inexpedient to claim the right of inland residence under the most-favored-nation clause. Once such residence was established, however, it was deemed proper for British authorities to defend this *de facto* property right, and in numerous cases consuls argued for the validity of contracts of sale obtained in inland areas by missionaries, even after the Chinese authorities sought to block their execution.[8] But in no way did British officials encourage or look with favor upon the territorial bridgeheads established by missionaries beyond the confines of the treaty ports.

Clearly, Britain's primary interest in China *was* commercial. It wanted the Manchu regime to keep an open door for the trade of all — which meant, in practice, continued economic dominance by Britain. There was no desire on Britain's part to undertake the expense or risk the danger involved in the creation of an "Indian Empire" in the Valley of the Yangtze. The result was that China provided a classic example of that type of "informal imperialism" which characterized nineteenth-century British economic expansion from South America to Asia. In a recent study John Gallagher and Ronald Robinson have aptly characterized this type of imperialism: "It is only when and where informal political means failed to provide the framework of security for British enterprise (whether commercial, or philanthropic or simply strategic) that the question of establishing formal empire arose."[9]

The crucial question then became how any given nation or region might best be integrated into Britain's expanding economy.[10] As we have seen in the case of China, it was necessary to engage in two sizable wars in order to force open this potentially great market and investment area. Once this was done, Britain was satisfied with a settlement which opened certain ports to her trade in particular and, as soon followed, to world trade in general. This system of treaties also provided for a mechanism which, it was hoped, would work to guarantee the security of that trade: a British representative was henceforth to be accredited to and accepted by Peking, British consuls were set up in the treaty purts, and Her Majesty's Navy secured a stronghold in Hong Kong. However, the most characteristic feature of this system of informal empire was to be seen in the establishment of the Imperial Maritime Customs Service in the 1850's and 1860's. Its organization was worked out principally under British supervision and while it remained part of the Chinese bureaucracy its top staff positions fell to Europeans. Britain, as the leading trading nation in China, filled most of these positions including that of inspector-general. In this position Sir Robert Hart did much to maintain the integrity of the Service.

Once having established this framework of loose control, it became of vital importance for Britain to sustain the Manchu dynasty. However reluctantly, that regime was Britain's ally in maintaining the minimum of security necessary for profitable trade. So it was that the British, soon after 1860, supported the dynasty militarily against the Taiping Rebellion – this, in spite of the pseudo-Christian origin of the rising.

Clearly, the Middle Kingdom for all its past Imperial greatness had come upon troubled times. Even a hasty sketch of the principal features of the Chinese governmental structure must reveal the sources of the decay that had set in by the mid-nineteenth century.[11] One weakness was perhaps inevitable. The Manchu or Ch'ing dynasty was made up of foreign conquerors who had swept down upon China

---

[6] *Ibid.*, p. 34.

[7] *Ibid.*, p. 32.

[8] Kenneth S. Latourette, *A History of Christian Missions in China* (New York: Macmillan, 1929), p. 418.

[9] John Gallagher and Ronald Robinson, "The Imperialism of Free Trade," *Economic History Review*, 2nd Series, VI (1953), 13.

[10] *Ibid.*, p. 5.

[11] My description of the condition of the Manchu regime in the last half of the nineteenth century is based largely on material found in Franz H. Michael and George E. Taylor, *The Far East in the Modern World*, revised edition (New York: Holt, Rinehart, and Winston, 1964), pp. 20–44.

and established themselves as a dominant caste and ruling house in 1644. They were never fully accepted by the Chinese and any weakness or incapacity of rule would easily excite the undercurrent of Chinese opposition to the dynasty.

On the surface all remained in order. The Emperor was supreme as the "Son of Heaven" whose command was the law and who alone was to worship at the Temple of Heaven in Peking. The central apparatus of government was still intact, from the Grand Council whose function it was to advise the Emperor on policy to the six administrative boards whose function it was to carry out the Emperor's decisions. The central government still made appointments to the various administrative positions throughout the eighteen provinces of China. There were governors in each of the provinces of China and the majority of the provinces were grouped into pairs over which a governor-general presided with elements of the Imperial Army at his disposal. From these lofty positions down to that much overworked official, the magistrate of the district or *hsien*, the dynasty extended its power of appointment and control. Promotion through the various civil service ranks was based on examinations controlled by the government and success was determined by a narrow and rigidly conceived formal essay in which one sought to demonstrate his unflinching adherence to the neo-Confucian orthodoxy preached by the Manchu. Finally, before 1861, foreign affairs so little concerned the dynasty that their conduct was relegated either to that branch of the government which dealt with China's outer dependencies or to the provinces, which were free to carry out certain limited policies of their own.

Behind this façade of order and uniformity, however, an almost irreversible institutional deterioration had set in. So evident had the government's weakness and corruption become that by the mid-nineteenth century there was a widespread popular belief that the regime had lost the "mandate of heaven" which sanctioned its rule. With the death of the pleasure-loving Hsien-feng Emperor in 1861, chief authority fell into the hands of the Empress Dowager, who maintained her position either as regent or as the power behind the throne until her death in 1908. Her corruption-ridden court did much to weaken the Empire, but the chief weakness ran deeper and was one which the bureaucratically oriented Chinese dynasties had faced in the past. The vast centralized network of administration which appeared to be so comprehensive amounted to little more than a rope of sand if it failed to command the allegiance and support of the scholar-gentry class or *literati*. This elite was made up of those who had passed the various governmental examinations and thus were well versed in the Confucian classics.

Degree holders supplied the personnel for the various levels of the bureaucracy, but the majority of this group held no official office. It was their duty to perform the multitude of essential tasks on the local level of government. They presided over the settlement of civil disputes; they supervised the management of vital public works such as irrigation; and they were the government's tax collectors.

It required continuous discipline to keep this unofficial bureaucracy in line. By way of its position as tax collector it imposed an increasingly heavy tax burden upon the peasant, thereby providing for itself a larger surplus over that amount which it was required to return to the central government; and, at the same time, it sought to reduce the size of the central levy by a variety of excuses. Through the nineteenth century this evil increased as the Manchu house began to sag under the weight of its own vast administrative and territorial expanse. The overtaxed peasant grew restive and the dynasty looked in vain for adequate revenue to bolster its position. It became more and more difficult for the regime to secure prompt and complete compliance with the edicts and directives which continued to flow forth from Peking. When the central government most needed to reassert its authority power tended to revert to the provincial level.

These weaknesses were compounded by the military and economic impact of the forces of the West. The Imperial Army was easily outclassed by the modern arms of Britain and France, and the opening of China to cheaply produced factory imports threw large segments of the economy into disarray. Perhaps the chief evidence of the incapacity of the Manchu was its inability to adopt those reforms which would enable it to effectively oppose the West. Some changes of form, however, were imposed upon China. The conduct of foreign affairs was placed in the hands of the Tsungli Yamen which was created as a result of the Treaties of Tientsin.[12] The Emperor appointed its members from

---

[12] Pao Chao Hsieh, *The Government of China, 1644–1911* (Baltimore: Johns Hopkins Press, 1925), pp. 238–240.

officials already assigned to the six administrative departments. It was controlled by a board of three to seven supervising ministers headed by a Manchu prince. In its operation it failed to satisfy completely the Western Powers, for its members proved to be most adept at evading responsibility and avoiding clear-cut statements of policy.

In another area Chinese administrative practice and British needs appeared to complement each other more adequately. China showed a remarkable adaptability in accepting cooperative management of certain aspects of its trade with the British. John K. Fairbank has studied the historical development of this peculiar flexibility. He observed that in Chinese relations with the barbarian conquerors of past ages a pattern emerged involving the creation of a joint administration, a mixed bureaucracy of Chinese and non-Chinese which he referred to as a "synarchy."[13] But, as Fairbank put it, in the nineteenth century Sino-foreign rule was "left standing on one leg."[14] British-led participation was confined to the interests of the treaty ports with the Imperial Maritime Customs Service and beyond that to a concern for the missionaries. Britain declined to follow the Chinese lead and join in a form of joint control in Peking. According to Fairbank, this refusal was based on the British assumption that such joint participation in government might delay the moment when China would come of age and take its place in the family of nations. A mature China devoted to free trade would, of course, provide Britain with a larger and more secure market for her products.

Aside from such long-range speculations, any joint administration in Peking would be costly and dangerous; therefore, for the moment, Britain preferred to limit herself to the predictable gains of informal imperialism. She had a skeleton force of political and military representatives on the spot to reinforce the security provided by the Manchu Government. As things stood, Englishmen might obtain political redress for treaty violations by appeal to the British minister in Peking or through his consuls in the treaty ports. Military assistance might be obtained from the highly maneuverable fleet of British gunboats with their landing companies of bluejackets. This force was adequate to guarantee the British freedom for commercial and religious endeavors.

There was of course no reason for British statesmen to think that such informal control could continue indefinitely; nor could they assume that China would emerge in the foreseeable future as a self-sustaining nation devoted to the principles of free trade. They were aware that as the strength of other European Powers in China grew the need to formalize their dominion would increase. Still, such political involvement was to be put off as long as circumstances permitted; there was even a strong possibility that the creation of a full-scale empire in China would ultimately be rejected as too great a strain on the British Empire as a whole. Nevertheless, the frequent hostilities provoked by missionary activities led the British toward increased political commitment.

If missionary activity threatened to disrupt the loose sort of control requisite for informal empire, why were the missionaries granted the indirect support of the British Government? Various explanations suggest themselves. First, Lord Salisbury, who as Conservative Prime Minister was his own secretary of state for foreign affairs, and the other hard-minded diplomats at the Foreign Office were not devoid of an idealistic bent. Both Salisbury and his successor as foreign secretary, Lord Rosebery, were believing Christians, and neither would be inclined to inhibit unnecessarily the expansion of their faith. Not only was it Christianity which was expanding, it was civilization; at least, so it appeared to the late-Victorian mind.

Second, there was a practical political reason for not limiting missionary work. The nonconformist churches, who had sent the largest missionary force to China, constituted a well-organized political force which carried considerable weight at election time. Whitehall could no more ignore their frequent petitions than it could ignore those of the commercial interests of Manchester. Equally important, the Church of England, in a less flamboyant but possibly more direct way, was able to bring pressure upon the Foreign Office by way of its many connections at the higher level of government.

Finally, the ideology which inspired the concept of informal imperialism was not simply economic; it was a more general social and political philosophy. The free play of British trade, politics, and religious ideas had in the nineteenth century created what amounted to

---

[13] John K. Fairbank, "Synarchy under the Treaties," in *Chinese Thought and Institutions*, ed. John K. Fairbank (Chicago: University of Chicago Press, 1957), p. 205.
[14] *Ibid.*, p. 227.

a new empire overseas. To inhibit the working of any one of these factors, to bind the initiative of any Englishman, no matter what his cause, was possibly to cripple that peculiar genius which had built this new empire. In short, this liberal empire was to embrace freedom for religion as well as freedom for trade; to reject one was to reject the other.

British diplomacy was, then, obliged to construct a China policy out of two disparate aims: to preserve the informal, essentially non-political nature of British influence in China and at the same time to allow missionaries the freedom they demanded, which carried with it the danger of incidents requiring political intervention by British officials. The British were largely successful in fulfilling this difficult assignment through most of the nineteenth century. But the moment of testing for the dual policy did not arrive until the last decade of the century. It was not until then that the size of the English missionary movement assumed challenging proportions throughout China. It was not until then that the varied activities of the missionaries brought them into the more remote provinces where their safety was increasingly dependent upon political intervention by Britain. Nor did Chinese resistance to the ever growing encroachments of the West reach its height until late in the 1890's, and this resistance often struck at the weakest but most obvious manifestation of foreign influence, the missionary.

Statistics explain, in part, the reason for the increasing number of diplomatic incidents caused by missionary activities. In 1858, the year when the toleration clause was written into the treaties, there were only eighty-one Protestant missionaries in China.[15] At that stage, all of them resided in the four southern coastal provinces which constituted the center of British influence. From that time on, missionary work increased until, just before the decade of the 1890's, there were 1296 Protestant missionaries in China, about 55 per cent of whom were British.[16] But the real onrush came after 1890. Protestant missionaries more than doubled their number in the next decade, reaching a total of 2818 by 1900, more than half of whom were British.[17] By 1890 these missionaries had established residence in all the provinces of China with the possible exception of Hunan; after 1890, they intensified their efforts as the number of mission stations rose from 132 in 1881 to 498 in 1900.[18]

[12]

The missionaries came to China organized in self-reliant and zealous groups. The China Inland Mission, created by Hudson Taylor for the specific purpose of doing evangelical work in the interior of China, was the largest single missionary group in China. It was affiliated with no denomination, but its membership had grown to include 784 workers by 1900.[19] The C.I.M. was particularly aggressive in its assault on the pagan customs of the Chinese. This recklessness made it the target of frequent attacks by the Chinese, yet its constitution generally forbade the calling in of the British authorities to redress grievances it suffered.

The Church Missionary Society, associated loosely with the Church of England and low church in orientation, constituted the second largest British missionary group in China. This organization did considerable work in the southern coastal region and in the area of the Yangtze Valley. By 1900 it had 189 members throughout China.[20] Generally, it accepted the authority of the Anglican bishops in China; but, just as in all the mission societies, its individual membership exercised a remarkable freedom of decision and there was no clearly recognized chain of command. The Society for the Propagation of the Gospel in Foreign Parts was a second Anglican mission organization in China. Although it had only twenty-nine members there in 1900, they were generally well educated and influential.[21] This society tended to have a closer relationship than the others with the British authorities, and its methods of evangelization were marked by a more conservative temper.

The London Missionary Society, an agent of the Congregational

---

[15] Latourette, *A History of Christian Missions in China*, p. 405. The scope of Roman Catholic missionary work might be gauged from the fact that there were 720,540 Catholic converts in 1901, as compared with 131,404 Protestant converts in 1904. In 1913 there were 1365 Catholic priests of foreign extraction at work in China. Their labor was concentrated among Christian communities, and they placed less emphasis on higher education and changing the social structure than the Protestant missionaries. See Kenneth S. Latourette, *A History of the Expansion of Christianity*, Vol. VI: *The Great Century in Northern Africa and Asia, 1800–1914* (New York: Harper and Brothers, 1944), pp. 293, 277, and 338.

[16] Latourette, *A History of Christian Missions in China*, p. 406.

[17] Gilbert M'Intosh, *The Chinese Crisis and Christian Missionaries: A Vindication* (London: Morgan and Scott, 1900), pp. 89–90.

[18] Latourette, *A History of Christian Missions in China*, p. 407.

[19] M'Intosh, *loc. cit.*

[20] *Ibid.*

[21] *Ibid.*

churches, did extensive work. In 1900 it had 120 workers in China.[22] Originally situated in the southern provinces, it had expanded into central and northern China. Large-scale operations were also carried on in China by the Methodist Episcopal Missionary Society and the Baptist Missionary Society, as well as by twelve other British societies large and small.[23]

It was not, however, the size or variety of missionary groups so much as what they said and did that gave rise to hatred and misunderstanding. Without a doubt, the special convictions which animated the British missionary contributed to the strife between him and the Chinese. For the most part, the missionaries were drawn from the middle class. Few had received a university education, but many were trained at those church colleges which produced the majority of nonconformist clergymen. Women carried a heavy share of the missionary burden in China; in 1900, fully half of the Protestant missionary community were either single women or wives of missionaries.[24] The missionary's knowledge of China was usually acquired after his arrival, and this seldom was sufficient to moderate his disdain for things Chinese. He little understood native standards of conduct, which he dismissed as pagan and evil. He was all too ready to identify the dirt, suffering, and disease endemic to China with moral corruption. It was partly as a result of this disdain, this attitude of moral superiority, this ignorant rejection of native institutions that a deep opposition to the missionary grew up in the hearts of countless Chinese — which propagandists could play upon in inciting violence against the missionary.

In addition the missionaries advocated a new system of values which had deep social and political implications; this was the primary reason for the fierce opposition of the Chinese gentry and official class. To preach the concept of the one God was to question the semidivinity of the Emperors and undermine the Confucian system of ethics. To reject ancestor worship seemed to be a condemnation of all forms of filial respect. To demand that Christian converts not participate in village religious festivals and theatricals appeared to be an attack on the communal structure of rural China. In the best of times and by the most persuasive of advocates the implantation of Christianity in China would have been a formidable task. Not only did its doctrine give offense to Chinese values, but it came as an ideology imposed by the aggressive barbarian. Then, too, the tactics of evangelization employed by the missionaries caused additional irritation.

For most of the Protestant missionaries the first task of Christianization was, simply, to bring the Word of God to the heathen who was otherwise doomed to eternal perdition.[25] Emphasis was therefore placed on reaching as many Chinese as possible with the good Word. Journeys deep into the interior, visits from village to village, and street preaching marked this phase of activity. The Christian message was, oftentimes, lost in a garble of half-mastered Chinese dialect; the fleeting visit of a missionary was simply a matter of passing curiosity to isolated villagers; but to men and women intent on spreading the Word with all too little regard for how it was assimilated, these were secondary considerations. The Word was also passed about in tracts distributed among the Chinese or in Bibles carried into the interior and sold by colporteurs. Here again there was ground for misunderstanding. Passages from the Old Testament, which were often distributed without commentary, might not only confuse the Chinese but, in certain cases, be interpreted as attacks upon the public order. Indeed, the Foreign Office specifically cautioned the missionary societies about the dangers in distributing tracts without commentaries.[26]

By and large, evangelization was carried out from a mission compound, which was quickly constructed once property was obtained within a treaty port or in some city in the interior. The compound normally consisted of a chapel, a preaching hall, a school, possibly a hospital, and the residences of the missionaries. This group of buildings might be surrounded by a high wall; but, in most cases, the preaching hall was set apart in the main street of the town.[27] In some ways, then, the missionaries in their European houses and gardens were isolated from the Chinese, and in other ways they were in close contact with the people by way of the preaching hall.

It was from these centers that the missionaries would fan out across the countryside, visiting villages near and far. There they would seek to lay the foundations for new Christian communities. If possible, a

---

[22] *Ibid.*
[23] Foreign Office Report, March 1893. F.O. 17/1171.
[24] Latourette, *A History of Christian Missions in China*, p. 407.
[25] *Ibid.*, p. 416.
[26] Gardner to Jervoise, Hankow, Oct. 26, 1891. F.O. 17/1128.
[27] Latourette, *A History of Christian Missions in China*, p. 418.

native pastor was appointed to guide each group between visits by the missionary. In turn, these communities might later form the basis for new mission stations.

Such operations presented numerous occasions for conflict with the local authorities. There was violent opposition to the purchase of land by missionaries for homes or religious chapels. There was resentment when the missionaries claimed that by the toleration clause their converts were exempt from giving the customary contributions to local religious festivals. There was fear that the mission schools with their foreign studies and new ideas would undermine the traditional system of education upon which the rank and authority of the gentry-official class was based. But the most irksome cause of dispute was the interference by missionaries in cases of law involving their converts.

The missionaries claimed that Chinese officials brought pressure on the converts by way of the courts. If accused of a crime the convert, it was said, could expect swift condemnation in a Chinese court; if, in turn, the convert brought suit against the neighbor who molested him, he might be sure he would lose. It became common for the missionary to intervene in defense of his convert; and, in case of necessity, the support of the foreign consul would be brought into play. This proved to be so effective that often the simple transmission of a missionary's calling card to the local yamen would assure victory for the convert. The Chinese authorities claimed that this had become a great abuse. The worst elements in society, it was asserted, came to embrace Christianity in order to secure the support of the missionaries in court.

In a recent study concerned with the missionary movement in China in the 1860's, Paul A. Cohen has demonstrated that the most serious and widespread abuse committed by the Catholic missionaries was their interference in local affairs on behalf of their converts.[28] To an increasing extent by the 1890's, the British consuls found themselves drawn into similar disputes on behalf of the Protestant missionaries and their converts. As one consul with many years of experience in China put it: "It is their [the consuls'] duty to insist on the observance of the treaty according to which 'persons teaching or professing the Christian religion shall . . . be entitled to the protection of the Chinese authorities . . .' Consequently any direct prohibition of Christianity, any punishment of a man for being a Christian, and destruction of mission property, the publication of blasphemous or obscene books and placards, stirring up people against Christians, and even the forcible compulsion of a convert to contribute to idol ceremonies, call for official remonstrances, but complaints that a convert when a plaintiff never gets justice, but when he is a defendant has to give satisfaction whatever the facts of the case may be — such complaints I say are refused a hearing." [29]

Accordingly, even though the consuls refused to accept any wholesale condemnation of Chinese treaty violations, they stood ready to support the missionaries upon specific appeal. But this support was often reluctantly rendered. Missionary cases were burdensome and prolonged affairs. At times it was necessary to call for the intervention of British gunboats to quell unrest and violence. All this interfered with the tranquillity necessary for trade, and entailed the sort of political interference which the consuls were instructed to avoid if possible. Here was the problem: British consuls were expected to aid their nation's missionaries in China, and yet, at the same time, they were instructed to remain aloof from Chinese affairs. Of course, if both injunctions were to be absolutely followed, the consuls would face a hopeless dilemma. In practice, it was up to the consul to seek out a workable middle ground between these conflicting principles.

At stake in this game of missionary diplomacy was Britain's lucrative position in China. If full-scale political intervention was necessary to protect the missionaries, then the other European Powers would enter the scramble; and, in all probability, this would begin the partition of China. The English might emerge with a formal political empire on the Yangtze, but the rest of China would be divided into spheres closed to her trade. If Britain could maintain the *status quo*, she could continue to dominate the trade and politics of the Yangtze area and simultaneously enjoy the privileges of an open door to trade throughout China. Whatever else transpired, British interests centered upon the Yangtze; it was therefore paramount for Britain to support the Manchu dynasty which had come to accept British pre-

---

[28] Paul A. Cohen, *China and Christianity: The Missionary Movement and the Growth of Chinese Antiforeignism, 1860–1870* (Cambridge, Mass.: Harvard University Press, 1963), pp. 131–148.

[29] C. J. R. Allen, "A Layman's Defense of Missions in China," *Mission Field*, XLVI (January 1901), 26.

eminence there. But, as we shall see, political difficulties and missionary disputes arose to weaken the understanding between Britain and the Manchu house. When this happened events moved rapidly toward a crisis. Through all these political difficulties, however, Britain declined to spell out her vaguely defined prerogatives in China, for the existing situation fostered advantages in trade and allowed the British to avoid the expenses of direct government and the risks of defense. Britain had everything to gain by keeping things quiet in China.

The last decade of the nineteenth century was a period of pronounced danger for the survival of Britain's informal empire. In 1893, Lord Rosebery noted the source of this danger; he explained to the Chinese minister in London that the only matter which threatened the perfect harmony of Anglo-Chinese relations was the missionary disputes.[30] But this problem grew worse as antiforeign hatred was stirred up after the Chinese collapse in the Sino-Japanese War of 1894–1895. Next the missionary cause became deeply involved with imperialist politics, starting with the German seizure of Kiaochow in 1897. Finally, the missionary movement acted as a catalyst in drawing the Boxers into the siege of the legations in Peking.

It will be necessary, then, to evaluate British policy against the interplay of complex political and religious factors. The crucial question must be whether the ideal of noninvolvement, however successful had been its application in semicolonial affairs through most of the nineteenth century, was not incompatible with the new forces rising within the dynamics of imperialism. In particular, one must ask if this attitude of partial commitment was not inescapably opposed to the driving force and total engagement of the Christian missionary movement in China.

---

[30] O'Conor to Rosebery, Peking, Jan. 27, 1894. F.O. 17/1227.

CHAPTER II

The Riots of 1891: A Pattern Set

THE preceding chapter has described something of the nature of the informal imperial control exercised by Great Britain in China. By the summer of 1891 the interests fostered by this control — commercial and missionary — were threatened by a widespread rising of the Chinese populace along the Yangtze River; it was an unofficial challenge to informal empire. The Chinese authorities appeared to be helpless in the face of this near rebellion. The British were momentarily thrown back upon their own resources. They sought to implement those weapons which in the past had speedily put down sporadic antimissionary risings. But whether traditional methods — techniques designed to control a situation without involvement in the situation — could cope with risings on such an enlarged scale or of so complex an origin was another question.

The Nature of the Riots

The British had never found it necessary to analyze the forces which opposed their informal dominion in China. If missionaries were attacked, it was considered to be a case of local native obstreperousness — the quick dispatch of gunboats to the scene, along with diplomatic pressure at Peking, invariably put the trouble to rest. As for the outbreaks in 1891, the officials at the Foreign Office in a somewhat bored gesture had at first grouped them all under the nondescript term "riots." But these uprisings differed from those of the past. While the weapons of informal imperial control might blunt their impact and halt them temporarily, they were too extensive and deeply rooted to be so easily subdued.

In July 1891, just after the worst period of the riots, the Foreign Office grew alarmed at a newspaper story which attributed them to a great revolutionary upsurge. No indication of this sort had reached Whitehall officially; but Sir John Walsham, Britain's minister in China, was notoriously lax in channeling information. Since Walsham's opinions could not in any case be rated expert, Lord Salisbury telegraphed his minister instructing him to sound out Sir Robert Hart for his evaluation of the riots.[1] Hart had been forty years in China and, as head of the Chinese Imperial Customs Service, had the reputation of being Britain's foremost authority on the Celestial Empire. His promptly telegraphed reassurances were sufficient, at least for the moment, to return the Foreign Office to its previous mood of bland optimism.

Hart sharply opposed those who attributed the riots to a revolutionary movement. He admitted that certain factors in the riots supported the contention that they were part of a plan, but this illusion, in his view, probably resulted from the circumstance that discharged soldiers had taken common action in seeking by lawless deeds to recreate a need for their own employment; perhaps, Hart suggested, they hoped that fear of military action by the Western Powers in revenge for the abuse of missionaries would lead to their recall.[2] This was probably one cause of the riots, but not, he insisted, the only one: the imprudent act of a single missionary could spark violence among the normally quiet and law-abiding Chinese, as could a rumor that the kidnappings which plagued their land were planned behind the high walls of the missionary compound.[3] Hart was fully aware of the peculiar burden of imperialism which Britain bore in China. Accepting these limitations — or as he put it, "short of full force, ruling that is" — he suggested that British policy regarding the riots should be "firm, patient, tactful." [4]

If Hart's diagnosis of the riots was correct his formula for retaining Britain's informal position in China was also sound. But Hart's thinking was too much entrenched in the past for him to understand the future which was developing around him in China. For a thousand miles up the Yangtze River, the heartland of British interest in China, the Western missionaries were beset by burning and looting. Eleven full-scale assaults and more than twice that number of incidents involving, for example, the destruction of an isolated chapel or residence took place in the summer of 1891. French Catholic properties suffered the heaviest damage but the British paid dearly with the death of two British subjects.

Attacks on missionaries were nothing new, it is true. Recently our understanding of the recurring outbursts of anti-Christian violence has been increased considerably by the research into Chinese sources carried out by Paul A. Cohen. In his *China and Christianity*, he has demonstrated that there was an anti-Christian tradition in China running back at least as far as the early seventeenth century. This was based upon an opposition to any creed or philosophy which sought to challenge the orthodoxy of Confucianism, and just as Buddhism was condemned as a heterodox doctrine, so many of the same denunciations were employed against Christianity.[5] With the Treaties of Tientsin (1858) and the Sino-French Convention of Peking (1860), by which the foreign missionary was given permission to live, own property, and preach in the interior of China, opposition to Christianity reached a new level of intensity. Henceforth, according to Cohen, the purpose of anti-Christian literature was no longer primarily to educate against Christianity, but rather "overwhelmingly propagandistic" and designed to incite mass action against missionaries and converts.[6] In the 1860's, as Cohen amply documents, there was a sharp increase in the number of riots and incidents involving disputes with Christians, culminating in the disastrous Tientsin Massacre in 1870.[7] Outbreaks continued spasmodically in the 1870's and 1880's. Then came the great surge of new missionaries, especially British, into China and the greatly increased opportunities for friction. By 1891 it

---

[1] Salisbury to Walsham, Tel., London, July 29, 1891. F.O. 17/1126.
[2] Walsham to Currie, Tel., Peking, July 29, 1891. F.O. 17/1126.
[3] Hart to Walsham, Peking, Aug. 1, 1891. F.O. 17/1127.
[4] *Ibid.*
[5] Paul A. Cohen, *China and Christianity*, pp. 3–60.
[6] *Ibid.*, pp. 44–45 and 58.
[7] *Ibid.*, *passim*. At Tientsin, on June 21, 1870, a dispute arose between the Catholics supported by the French consul and the local Chinese. Rioting followed which led to the death of thirty to forty Chinese converts and twenty-one foreigners. *Ibid.*, p. 233.

should have been clear that the burgeoning antimissionary outbursts presented a challenge of new dimensions. It was a challenge Hart apparently did not recognize.

Evidence of the intensity of antimissionary feeling may be found in the flood of rumors, pamphlets, and posters which circulated freely along the Yangtze Valley and which did much to solidify the opposition of the Chinese masses to the missionaries. To explore the ideas they reflected is to enter a world of primitive superstition and violence, but only in this way, perhaps, may we gain some understanding of the fierce and reckless abandon of many of the attacks on missionaries.

The Chinese villager was possessed of a dark and distorted image of the Western missionary. This image, in an extreme form, can be reconstructed by an examination of one of the most widely circulated antimissionary pamphlets, entitled *The Devil Doctriners Ought to Be Killed.*[8]

The pamphlet began with a moralistic defense of the traditional religions of China. From of old, it announced, there were three religions promulgated in China — Confucianism, Taoism, and Buddhism. Then the Devil Doctriners (Christians) came; they castigated our teachings of filial respect; their Devil Book (Bible) attacked the worship of the earth, the sun, and the moon: "deities great and small the Devil's Book attacked them in a heap." Such charges were put into verse for better remembrance:

> They do not respect heaven and earth
> The Emperor or their Relatives;
> They never burn joss sticks in the temples
> Their families do not erect ancestral temples . . .[9]

Along with these charges the pamphlet emphasized the evil in the religion of Westerners. They worshipped a chief Devil, Jesus, whose wicked life led to His execution in an ancient kingdom. Were they not, it asked, more stupid than pigs to worship such a one (great play was made over the phonetic similarity in Chinese of the word for Lord and the word for pig)? Then it charged that the leading doctrine of the Devil's religion was that however great a crime was committed it was redeemed by the worship of Jesus; this led to a consideration of the morality of the missionaries.

The supposed vile deeds of the missionaries and their converts were dwelt on at length. Wives, daughters, and children were warned that they were in constant danger from the strange drugs and wild lusts of the missionaries. Children were warned that during sleep the missionaries were liable to appear, pluck out their eyes, and use them to manufacture precious metals. Young men and women were warned that their vital bodily parts were sought after by the missionaries for use in the concoction of their mysterious drugs.

The fate awaiting converts, despicable as they were, was described as one of misery. The chief missionary was said to order each convert family to put aside a daughter for his personal pleasure. Among the converts themselves, fathers, mothers, sons, and daughters were permitted to intermarry freely. After depicting these offenses in elaborate detail, the pamphlet writer summed it all up: "I am a man of seventy-five years of age, but never [have I] heard of cuckolds committing sodomy or copulating with their own daughters. . . . Ought they not to die a myriad deaths?" [10]

Finally, the missionaries were linked with the efforts of foreign Powers to gain control of China. The missionaries, the pamphlet charged, were responsible for the Taiping Rebellion, and since then their subversive activities had continued. They were, in effect, "an internal force to cooperate with the outer force in obtaining possession of China's rivers and hills. The Prince gives the head missionaries large sums of money and a free hand in doing their business." Then the text and verses concluded with this admonition:

> Fathers and elder brothers teach this song;
> By this act of virtue become happy
> Lads and boys learn this song;
> To prevent disaster and avoid disorder.
> Where it is found the devils are many;
> Then you must take and exterminate them.[11]

---

[8] Pamphlet enclosed and translated in Gardner to Salisbury, Hankow, Oct. 6, 1891. F.O. 17/1127. This pamphlet is no doubt a short adaptation of the *Pi-hsieh shih-lu* (A True Record to Ward off Heterodoxy) which was translated by the missionaries as *Death Blow to Corrupt Doctrines*. Paul A. Cohen has subjected the *Pi-hsieh shih-lu* to careful analysis, and he has indicated that it was a version of the *Pi-hsieh chi-shih* (A Record of Facts to Ward off Heterodoxy). Using internal and external evidence, Cohen tentatively concluded that this pamphlet was first written in 1861 by a Hunanese. Gardner in the dispatch cited above indicated that the *Devil Doctriners Ought to Be Killed* was composed by a Hunanese. Cohen, *China and Christianity*, pp. 45–58 and 277–281.

[9] Pamphlet. F.O. 17/1127.   [10] *Ibid.*   [11] *Ibid.*

This was powerful propaganda, and the riots themselves testify to its effectiveness. Here was a danger that could not easily be controlled by Britain's indirect jurisdiction in China. There were sufficient grains of truth amid the calumnies of this literature to ensure ready acceptance of the whole. Normal evangelical activity had already made the missionary an aggressor in the minds of many Chinese: the missionary had condemned the Confucian ancestor ritual, so basic to the Chinese household; his new religion was a stark challenge to the cherished beliefs of an entire society; his habits and dress were strange and frightening; and worst of all was his real and almost inevitable connection with the Western imperialists. It would not be too much to say that the riots found their most basic impulse in the natural resistance of Chinese society to forces which seemed to attack the traditional order. This fear and hatred was usually latent, but it could be brought to the surface by disruptive incidents or a sudden emotional upsurge, or by calculation, if certain groups sought to aggravate it for their own ends.

Sir Robert Hart had underestimated the depth and fury of China's opposition to the missionaries; he may well have been equally wrong in dismissing the element of premeditation in the 1891 outbreaks. The path and character of the riots tend to support the hypothesis that there were two separate movements afoot—at times intertwined but possessed of distinctive purposes.

Traced on a map the riots form two divergent lines: the first thrusting down in a north to south direction along the Grand Canal; the second, less distinct in pattern, moving up the Yangtze River from east to west.

Observers at the time were in particular agreement that the Grand Canal riots, which began on May 10, were premeditated. Auguste M. Colombul, a Jesuit stationed in riot-ridden Kiangsu Province, noted: "It seems very much as if these deeds were committed by men obeying a word of command in an organized scheme — by a band which has travelled from Chinkiang to Tangyang [Tan-yang] along the Grand Canal, and next to Wusieh [Wu-hsi] along the same channel. These evil-doers have evidently orders to do what they have done — destroy so many schools without taking lives." [12] And British Acting Consul-General Mowat agreed that the same group of rioters had hit the various ports along the Grand Canal.[13] The riots along the Grand

Canal, then, were carried out by a relatively small group who worked methodically from port to port. Their object was simply the destruction of mission property. The lives of missionaries were not threatened; violent placards and sudden rumors played a secondary role in these attacks. And Roman Catholic (French) property was the principal target.[14]

The second line of riots began at Wu-hu, 300 miles up the Yangtze River and far from the Grand Canal. It was evidently a far less controlled movement. Preceded by rumors of the bewitching of children by Catholic missionaries, the first riot, on May 12, burst forth when a woman appeared at the gates of the Catholic mission at Wu-hu demanding her missing child. It then followed an erratic pattern — a mob gathered and destroyed the Catholic mission, moved on to invade the British consulate, and was only broken up when it faced a well-organized defense at the customs' compound.[15] Posters had been distributed before this riot began and the disturbances that followed, spreading from Wu-hu along the Yangtze, were invariably preceded by the dissemination of provocative pamphlets and posters. On May 16, seventy-five miles further up the Yangtze from Wu-hu, an attack on the British China Inland Mission compound seemed directly attributable to these pamphlets. Not until mid-June did this series of riots, pushing even further up the Yangtze, burn itself out.

Certain broad and tentative generalizations may be offered concerning the nature of this dual movement. The Grand Canal riots were, for the most part, carried out by the Ko-lao hui — a secret society dedicated to the overthrow of the Manchu and the restoration of the Ming dynasty.[16] The detached air its members displayed while carrying out their devastations would not have been found in avid xenophobes. Père Leveille, the French Jesuit missionary at Tan-yang, was able to pass unharmed through the mob which was destroying his church and school; in fact, one of the rioters told him that they

---

[12] A.F.R., p. 38.

[13] Mowat to Walsham, Shanghai, June 10, 1891. P.P., China No. 3 (1891), Enclosure 2 in No. 20, p. 25.

[14] A.F.R., pp. 28–29 and passim.

[15] Walley to North China Daily News, Wu-hu, May 14, 1891. A.F.R., p. 14.

[16] F. L. Masters, "An Account of Chinese Secret Societies," Chinese Recorder and Missionary Journal, XXII (May 1891), 268. Also see L. F. Comber, Chinese Secret Societies in Malaya (Locust Valley, N.Y.: Augustin Incorporated, 1959), p. 1.

meant him no harm, that their sole aim was the destruction of his buildings.[17] Further evidence of their purpose may be found in the posters distributed at the riot which subjected the local *taotai* (government official in charge of civil and military affairs over two or more districts) to scurrilous abuse and made threatening allusions to a recent uprising in Kwangtung. Some attacks along the Yangtze were also inspired by the Ko-lao hui. The attack at Wu-hu, according to Rev. John Walley of the Methodist Episcopal Mission there, was one of these.[18] The propaganda posters distributed at Wu-hu would seem to support this view since they urged that the attack be limited to the Catholic (French) Mission properties, and especially had warned against attacking the Chinese Imperial Customs Service (British) area.

The motive of the Ko-lao hui, one may speculate, was devious but single-minded. By encouraging attacks on missionaries the society played upon widespread antiforeign feeling, but the ultimate objective was thereby to involve the Chinese Government in disputes with the European Powers. This might lead to war and bring about the collapse of the hated regime. Such was the official explanation given by the Chinese ambassador in London, and many Western experts agreed.[19] As for concentrating on the French missionaries, they were more numerous and — most significantly — there was a greater chance of baiting the French into renewing their recently terminated war (1884–1885) with China.[20] At that time the English benefited by a friendship based on mutual accommodation with the Chinese regime, and provoking them into a controversy with the Manchu was evidently not considered likely. In spite of the hard feelings caused by the missionary riots, this friendship remained basically intact through the early 1890's owing to the fact that British interests were especially tied to the retention of a strong Manchu dynasty.[21]

Assuredly members of the Ko-lao hui played a prominent part in the uprisings. Some may have been carried out by them alone; other riots which appeared to be spontaneous may have been influenced by them. In addition there is evidence to support the contention that a large number of riots were traceable to some other group that was inspired by patriotism rather than rebellion. It must be kept in mind that most of the pamphlets scattered along the Yangtze Valley were patriotic, not revolutionary. The inflammatory *The Devil Doctriners Ought to Be Killed* preached the duty of Emperor worship; and a memorial by certain Hunan gentry, distributed in poster form, urged the defense of the Emperor in the face of the missionary assault, a totally orthodox sentiment.[22] Furthermore, the pattern of attacking only the French was continually disregarded along the Yangtze River. Although Ko-lao hui posters instructed the mobs attacking Wu-hu to confine their attack to the Catholic (French) mission, in fact the mob invaded the British consulate and was only turned away from the compound of the British-controlled Chinese Imperial Customs Service at bayonet point.[23]

This fierce orthodox patriotism could be traced to one province: Hunan. It was the virtual homeland of Chinese patriotism, south of the Yangtze and far secluded from the eastern coast. Only the most determined merchant or missionary had penetrated into this isolated province and few had dared to remain. From Hunan had come the stubbornly loyal soldiers who had broken the back of the Taiping Rebellion almost half a century before. Since the 1860's, it had been from Hunan that antimissionary literature was spread into other provinces.[24] And now testimony from up and down the Yangtze Valley singled out the Hunan rowdies as the instigators of the riots: at Wu-hsüeh, where two British lives were lost, the Hunan men were said to be the ringleaders; at Nanking, discharged Hunan soldiery were responsible for desecrating the Western cemetery.[25] Such instances could be multiplied many times. But, most significantly, Hunan, as the center for the production and distribution of the antimission-

---

[17] Allen to Walsham, Tel., Chih-chiang, May 25, 1891. F.O. 288/1064.

[18] Walley to North China Daily News, Wu-hu, May 14, 1891.

[19] Sanderson to Walsham, London, Sept. 24, 1891. F.O. 17/1127. Also see "The Present State of Troubles in China and Their Cure," Chinese Recorder and Missionary Journal, XXII (November 1891), 525. This article claimed that the secret societies hoped to "raise between China and the West a strife that cannot be settled without war. Their hope is that being between the two they may secure profit from them both."

[20] An editorial in the Chinese Recorder summed it up in this manner: "The program calls for a decisive movement against French Catholics in the hope of involving the Government in serious complications with a foreign power, when the long sought opportunity of bringing in a native dynasty may present itself." Chinese Recorder and Missionary Journal, XXII (July 1891), 337.

[21] Waddington to Ribot, London, Aug. 8, 1891. D.D.F., VIII, No. 475, pp. 638–639.

[22] Gardner to Salisbury, Hankow, Oct. 26, 1891. F.O. 17/1128.

[23] Walley to North China Daily News, Wu-hu, May 14, 1891.

[24] Cohen, China and Christianity, p. 48.

[25] A.F.R., pp. 25–40.

ary literature, was tending to assume command of the antimissionary drive.

The spirit of the Hunanese resistance was solely antimissionary; that is, when the Hunan men devastated mission compounds, they concealed no ulterior motives. They regarded missionary penetration as the vanguard of Western domination and saw the missionaries as purveyors of heresy. Slanderous and salacious as most of the anti-missionary propaganda was, its source was the literary class and it defended the traditional values of Chinese society. An anti-Christian compact drawn up in 1891 by some gentry and officials of Hunan testified to the intensity of their dedication and, incidentally, gave no indication of opposition to the dynasty. It urged that, as an Imperial policy, all Chinese be made to offer sacrifices in the temple to the spirit of the Master, Confucius; those who refused would be driven from Hunan. It called on Peking to punish any Chinese officials who were of "the Jesus pig squeak"; and it pledged that they would fight for the Emperor if the Western Powers resisted this move.[26] Obviously the Hunan men would never join the Ko-lao hui in betrayal of a dynasty which they supported.

Apparently, then, there were two different movements — with separate, even conflicting objectives — underway. However, cooperation on certain limited objectives was possible. The plans of both called for attacks on the missionaries, and the Hunan men, even if they were not heretical members of a secret society, were willing to partake in a movement directed against the foreigners. If these speculations are correct, the two movements were united operationally during the 1891 riots. British diplomacy, therefore, was confronted with a situation of great complexity. Understanding of the nature of these riots was called for, as well as a firm and decisive leadership by Britain.

Efforts to Quell the Riots

Since 1885 Sir John Walsham had been Great Britain's minister in China. Urbane in manner, the Walshams had the reputation of being charming hosts: Sir John, tall and slight; and Lady Walsham, "young looking, fascinating" and a born "Ambassadress."[27] Sir John, known as a hard worker, one who kept all the details of legation work in his own hands, was the successor to a line of brilliant representatives — Alcock, Wade, and Parkes — but he was unable to carry on the tradition.

He had attempted to impose the manners of European diplomacy on the Tsungli Yamen; he failed in this, and he was equally unsuccessful as a practitioner of European statecraft. He was plagued by indecision and tended to let his correspondence go unanswered.[28] He earnestly probed the problems before him, only to leave them unresolved. It was to this man in 1891 that the task of piloting Great Britain through the crisis in the Yangtze Valley fell.

The first wave of riots, early in May, was barely sufficient to gain the attention of the Foreign Office. Walsham's cabled opinion that fresh outbreaks were unlikely was certainly reassuring.[29]

But on June 5 after rioters at Wu-hsüeh killed two British subjects the riots became the foremost concern of British policy in China.[30] The brutality of the murders was particularly shocking. When a Chinese Christian porter was found transporting four infants by cart to the Catholic mission at Kuikiang, the hasty conclusion of the populace was that the missionaries intended to make medicine out of the infants. A mob gathered and in rage turned on the Wesleyan mission in town. So fierce was their attack that three lady missionaries fled the mission, but they were intercepted in the streets and beaten, only escaping through the intervention of friendly Chinese. Across town the Reverend Mr. Argent, a Wesleyan missionary, and Mr. Green, of the Chinese Imperial Customs Service, saw flames rising from the mission compound. Fearing for the ladies' safety they rushed toward the compound, but ran headlong into the hysterical mob, intent upon killing. After a brief struggle both Green and Argent lay dead — their heads crushed between heavy stones.[31]

Walsham had at his disposal the traditional weapons of British informal empire: the gunboat and diplomatic pressure. In the circumstances the gunboat was his most immediately effective weapon, and cries rose for its use. Shanghai's *North China Daily News* urged that

---

[26] Gardner to Salisbury, Hankow, Oct. 19, 1891. F.O. 17/1128.

[27] Edgar T. S. Dugdale, *Maurice de Bunsen, Diplomat and Friend* (London: John Murray, 1934), p. 101.

[28] *Ibid.*, p. 100.

[29] Walsham to Salisbury, Tel., Peking, May 16, 1891. *P.P.*, China No. 3 (1891), No. 2, p. 1. In this telegram Walsham attributed the riots to scandalous accusations against the missionaries.

[30] Gardner to Salisbury, Tel., Hankow, June 10, 1891. F.O. 17/1126.

[31] Hill to Gardner, Wusih (Wu-hsüeh), June 9, 1891. F.O. 17/1126; and *A.F.R.*, p. 30.

half the North China Squadron be sent up the Yangtze.[32] Rev. T. Stevenson from Shanghai pleaded with Sir William Harcourt, a leading member of the Liberal party in Parliament, to use his influence with the government to see that "we should never be left without a gunboat."[33] An occasional missionary was more blunt; Rev. W. E. Macklin called for authorities to send "a few gunboats to Nanking, and order the Viceroy to stop the nonsense in his district, with the alternative of a bombardment. . . . Our government should get some good magic lanterns, and show some of the pictures of gunboats to the officials. It might save the expense of manufacturing war vessels."[34]

But gunboats could not be everywhere at once. Vice-Admiral Sir Frederick Richards, in command at the China Station, was hard pressed; he had five to six gunboats available to cover the nine treaty ports on the Yangtze. Some assistance might be forthcoming from the other European Powers and from the handful of gunboats of the Chinese Imperial Navy, but that could not be relied upon. By the middle of May, Richards faced the difficult problem of meeting almost simultaneous calls for assistance from virtually every treaty port on the Yangtze.[35] The consuls faced no easier decision in attempting to assess the imminent danger in their own community relative to the crises brewing in other treaty ports. The difficulties confronting Consul Ford at Wu-hu exemplified the situation. On May 16 there was fear of riots at nearby Yu-ch'i chen but so perilous were conditions at Wu-hu that he dared not request that the two Chinese gunboats which protected his port proceed to Yu-ch'i chen. On the other hand his fears were not so great that he felt justified in calling for British aid from Hankow which was also threatened by the possibility of riot. This dilemma was resolved on the following two days when news arrived that mobs were gathering at An-ch'ing.[36] Admiral Richards had no choice but to order all available gunboats to that port.

Whitehall was aware of its limited power in China. An estimate by the Admiralty of the forces available in China led Sir Thomas Sanderson, the permanent undersecretary at the Foreign Office, to conclude that it was essential to avoid the necessity of active measures in China.[37] Further, General Edward Chapman, director of military intelligence, informed Sanderson that there were no troops available for China, if any should be wanted.[38] The Foreign Office was about to inform Walsham of Britain's weak military posture in China when

Salisbury killed the dispatch with the comment that Walsham "is not fit to be trusted with such discouraging information." [39]

There was one obvious solution to this problem. Britain might call on the other Western Powers to increase their naval contribution in China waters. But the whole rationale of informal empire went against this solution; it would throw out of balance the delicate control exercised by Britain in China. When the Admiralty suggested that Germany might increase her naval force in China, Salisbury sarcastically offered it a lesson in power politics: "The admiralty must remember that if we press the various powers to increase their naval forces in China and other foreign centers, we shall persuade them to increase their navies, which I do not suppose we altogether desire." [40]

So much for effectiveness of the gunboat. It could dominate a limited disturbance; but there were insufficient gunboats available to quell a continually expanding crisis. Britain's success in controlling the situation in 1891 therefore depended on damping down the riots as soon as possible and for this the British turned to diplomacy.

The diplomacy of informal empire was the diplomacy of the carefully posed *threat*. It was bolstered by gunboat action, the show of force, the demonstration; but such maneuvers were primarily a reminder of the darker fate which lay in store if current demands were not complied with. Wrangling, arguing, and cajoling also played their part, but it was the threat that bore the brunt of the attack. And after that there was the *renewed threat*, a weapon liable to rapid dulling

---

[32] Clipping from June 9, 1891, edition found in F.O. 17/1126.

[33] Stevenson to Harcourt, Shanghai, May 22, 1891. F.O. 17/1126.

[34] Macklin to Barr, in Vice-Admiral Richards to Admiralty, China Station, July 29, 1891. F.O. 17/1127.

[35] Dugdale, *Maurice de Bunsen*, p. 97. Confidential Report by the Admiralty, Oct. 16, 1891. F.O. 17/1128. Richards to Admiralty, China Station, June 19, 1891. F.O. 17/1128. In this last report Richards mentioned the following numbers and nationalities of foreign ships then in the Yangtze River: 4 French, 2 American, 2 Russian, and 1 Spanish.

[36] Ford to Mowat, Wuhu (Wu-hu), May 16, 1891, and Tisdall to Richards, Wuhu (Wu-hu), May 18, 1891. *P.P.*, China No. 3 (1891), Enclosures 5 and 9 in No. 14, pp. 7 and 8.

[37] Minute by Sanderson to Confidential Report by the Admiralty, Oct. 16, 1891. F.O. 17/1128.

[38] *Ibid.*

[39] Minute by Salisbury to Confidential Report by the Admiralty, Oct. 16, 1891 F.O. 17/1128.

[40] Minute by Salisbury, Foreign Office, Aug. 22, 1891. F.O. 17/1126.

by overuse. The use of the threat called for a trained and subtle hand, for to follow through on the threat was to chance toppling the house of cards — forces would be unleashed which might crush the type of informal control desired and substitute for it actual empire or chaos.

The first move in the game of threat came when Walsham joined with the other representatives in Peking "in urging upon the Yamen immediate adoption of most stringent measures to protect foreigners against these repeated outrages." [41] This pressure was seemingly successful. On June 13, the official *Peking Gazette* carried an Imperial edict which strongly condemned all attacks on missionaries and called on the proper authorities to protect foreigners and severely punish those who incited people against them. Missionary interests greeted this edict as the best proclamation of its kind ever issued in China. They admitted that its influence was partially diminished since the Chinese officials knew that it had been obtained by foreign pressure. Still, they felt that in quieter times it would become an edict of toleration for Christianity. [42]

Having successfully wrested the edict from the Tsungli Yamen, Walsham considered that victory was his. He informed the Foreign Office that nothing was so distasteful to the Chinese as recognizing the rights of foreigners, and that Chinese authorities had always tried to conceal from their people the granting of such rights. [43] Now, he noted confidently, these concessions were to be publicized. Walsham had overlooked the comment of his predecessor, Sir Harry Parkes, on dealings with the Tsungli Yamen. The former minister had declared that extracting concessions from the Yamen was "like trying to draw water from a well, with a bottomless bucket." [44] Indeed, Walsham's bucket had held little water. In the disaffected areas the edict was either not distributed or appeared in abridged form, and few rioters were captured and punished. [45]

There was need for the British to reinforce their demands. On July 11, Sir Thomas Sanderson, the permanent undersecretary at the Foreign Office, came down hard on the Chinese minister in London through his British secretary, Sir Halliday Macartney. He insisted that Macartney impress upon the Chinese minister that "serious danger" might arise out of the attacks on missionaries. He pointed to the "strength and importance of the feeling in favor of missionaries in this country." Referring to the protection which the French Government gave to its missionaries, he emphasized "that if public opinion once became alarmed and indignant in France and England, a cry for intervention might arise which would have very embarrassing and even serious consequences."[46] Then, at a later interview, Sanderson insisted that British interests in China were larger than those of any other nation, and he implied that these interests entailed an equivalently large concern for the British missionary. The Chinese should not assume, he concluded, that they might halt the intrusion of "any foreign movement or institution" by a resort to popular outbreaks or violence.[47]

It fell to Walsham to press home these threats. On July 27, he reported to the Foreign Office that peace was not assured nor had the edict been published in all the provinces. As a result, the British, French, and German ministers in Peking asked their governments to disregard the assurances of the Chinese ministers and to approve their continued joint protestations.[48]

This approval was forthcoming and on August 12 and again on August 25 the nine foreign representatives in Peking — from Belgium, France, Germany, Great Britain, Italy, Japan, Russia, Spain, and the United States — demanded that adequate safeguards be forthcoming and that the guilty be punished. This twice-renewed threat was met by an evasive rejoinder. The Tsungli Yamen argued that several had already been punished, and that others who joined in the riots were merely the foolish and ignorant who could not be punished; as for the edict, there were unavoidable delays in its publication.[49]

However, on September 2, there was a serious outbreak at I-ch'ang,

---

[41] Walsham to Salisbury, Tel., Peking, June 21, 1891. F.O. 17/1126.

[42] Report by Rev. W. Brereton to S.P.G., Tientsin, June 30, 1891. S.P.G., Series D, 1891, No. 16. As experienced a missionary as Rev. Griffith John regarded the edict as a "splendid document" granting "fullest tolerance." John to Thompson, Hankow, Aug. 29, 1891. L.M.S./CC/16.

[43] Walsham to Salisbury, Tel., Peking, June 21, 1891. F.O. 17/1126.

[44] Henry Norman, People and Politics of the Far East (New York: C. Scribner's Sons, 1895), p. 501.

[45] Tsungli Yamen to Foreign Representatives, Peking, Sept. 3, 1891. P.P., China No. 1 (1892), Enclosure 1 in No. 110, pp. 85–86.

[46] Salisbury to Walsham, Foreign Office, July 22, 1891. F.O. 17/1126.

[47] Ibid.

[48] Walsham to Salisbury, Tel., Peking, July 27, 1891. P.P., China No. 1 (1892), No. 1, p. 1.

[49] Tsungli Yamen to Foreign Representatives, Peking, Sept. 3, 1891. Loc. cit.

on the Yangtze River. And in Manchuria Dr. James Grieg, a medical missionary of the Presbyterian Church of Ireland, was nearly beaten to death.[50] Now it was necessary to edge toward fulfillment of the threat. By September 12 the foreign representatives broke off further negotiations with the Chinese on the antimissionary riots, and informed the Tsungli Yamen that they would report to their governments the failure of these negotiations and recommend a new policy toward China.[51]

But within the self-imposed limits of informal empire what new policy could there be for Britain? What new demands could be made? How could Britain enforce these demands without jeopardizing her delicately balanced relationship with the Manchu regime? It was a situation with which the listless Walsham was ill equipped to deal. Nevertheless, on September 9, he joined with the entire diplomatic body in drawing up recommendations to meet the China crisis. These were bundled into a protocol. And the ministers' respective home governments were notified that a new China policy had been devised.

Since Walsham partook in the preparation of this protocol and approved the final draft, it might be assumed that its recommendations would be conducive to fostering Britain's long-range objectives in China. Let us see if an examination of the protocol itself supports this assumption.

First, the protocol attributed the riots to the hostility of the masses toward the missionaries. But it surmised that the Tsungli Yamen was using the outbreaks to force negotiations with the West that would curtail the treaty rights of missionaries — in fact, that would subject the missionaries to restrictions neither provided for nor intended in the treaties. As an immediate remedy it urged the stationing of men-of-war at the open ports on the Yangtze River and at Canton and Shanghai, along with an increase of the European naval force.[52]

Then it took up the problem of the many missionaries scattered throughout the Chinese Empire, beyond the reach of the men-of-war. Their safety, it argued, depended entirely on bringing the Chinese Government to comprehend fully that it would be held responsible for their protection. This would be accomplished when the Chinese Government was made to recognize that the foreign Powers had both the will and the force to extract from them this required protection for their nationals.

Next the protocol boldly registered an even broader claim. It held it to be the duty of the Powers to protect "such part of the native population, as through confidence in the stipulations of the treaties have adopted and profess the Christian religion."[53] In short, it was the duty of the Powers to make it incumbent upon the Chinese regime to stamp out religious persecution.

Finally, the protocol struck its only realistic note in positing the need to meet the Chinese request for negotiation of a change of status for the missionaries and missionary establishments. But then it buried this beneath a list of nearly prohibitive prerequisites: that effective measures first be taken against the offending *literati*, that the outstanding missionary cases be settled, and that the provincial officials be instructed to observe all treaty rights especially those regarding freedom of religion for Chinese converts.

Nothing could have been more destructive of Britain's informal control in China than an attempt to follow through on this mandate to protect missionaries far in the interior, as well as their converts. One must assume that Walsham either was totally ignorant of the grand design in Britain's China policy, or, more likely, was swamped in the conference by those nations which saw in the close defense of missionary rights no impediment to their imperial ambitions.

The protocol's sole note of realism — the suggestion that the treaty rights of missionaries be re-examined — was muted by the insistence that first these treaty rights be properly promulgated and enforced. Only the most naive could imagine that, if this was accomplished, the European Powers would voluntarily submit to negotiating some of these rights away. In substance, then, the protocol amounted to an enlarged and formalized presentation of the demands previously made upon the Tsungli Yamen. It was an inflated, unrealistic, and farcical form of threat. That Walsham, as spokesman for the principal European Power in China, would permit a protocol so contrary to the general policy of his government to pass with his assent demonstrated his incapacity.

---

[50] A.F.R., pp. 43–44 and 56.
[51] Foreign Ministers to Tsungli Yamen, Peking, Sept. 10, 1891. P.P., China No. 1 (1892), Enclosure 3 in No. 110, pp. 88–89.
[52] Protocol of Sept. 9, 1891. P.P., China No. 1 (1892), Enclosure 4 in No. 110, p. 89.
[53] *Ibid.*

It is not difficult to imagine the consternation caused at the Foreign Office by the arrival of Walsham's protocol. No record of this reaction, however, is to be found among the Foreign Office papers collected at the Public Record Office. As a matter of fact, if one accepts the evidence collected in the Parliamentary Blue Book, the protocol did not even arrive in London until mid-November, over two months after its conception in Peking. There are two possible explanations for this mysterious delay.

The first explanation rests on the hypothesis that, in fact, there was no delay. It is not impossible to surmise that Walsham immediately telegraphed the essence of the protocol to London on September 9, but that the Foreign Office, dismayed by its overwhelming demands, chose to assume the pretense of awaiting its arrival by normal mail. Such a contention would be supported by the logical supposition that Walsham would have telegraphed home the import of such a vital document. There is, furthermore, evidence that the Foreign Office was aware in October, a month before the recorded arrival of the protocol, of at least certain of its provisions; namely, the recommendation that men-of-war be permanently stationed at the Yangtze treaty ports and at Canton and Shanghai, with the strengthening of the China Squadron as a possible further measure.[54] If this hypothesis is true, Whitehall was providing itself with an excuse for its hesitancy to act in China. Thus, when the French were urging joint action late in September, Salisbury agreed that such action was required but must be delayed until the arrival of the recommendations from Peking.[55]

On the other hand, there is evidence that the Foreign Office was honestly awaiting the arrival of the protocol. On September 21, the Chinese minister in London, implying that the disturbances had been quelled, asked what more Whitehall required of his government. The British in reply only reiterated the basic need of security for foreigners, and that same day the Foreign Office telegraphed Walsham to send on the recommendations of the representatives and details on any new demands which might be pressed on the Chinese.[56] Again on October 2, when the Chinese minister noted that the dispatch of a large portion of the Chinese Imperial fleet to the Yangtze River meant additional security for foreigners, Walsham was telegraphed for his views.[57]

Walsham dispatched the protocol by mail steamer on September

30. The Parliamentary Blue Book indicated it reached London on November 16. That same day, oddly enough, Walsham telegraphed an explanation of his tardiness which may have applied to the delayed arrival of the protocol.[58] He pleaded that uncertainty about the extent of the risings and about the real attitude of the Chinese Government had made him hesitate to draw conclusions, and so he had withheld his advice as long as possible. If one accepts the view that the protocol was actually not received in London until mid-November, the mystery lies not in Walsham's conduct, but in the tolerant acceptance of it by the Foreign Office.[59] There are three possible explanations for its ready acceptance of his delay.

First, hopes were high that the Chinese imbroglio was mending itself. The presence of gunboats on the Yangtze River was having its effect. And a British military directive, permitting bluejackets to land and fire on Chinese mobs if European lives were in danger, had put the Chinese on the defensive. On September 1, the Chinese minister had urged that this directive be withdrawn, arguing that the Chinese were capable of protecting the foreigners.[60] Continued assurances of this sort may have led the Foreign Office to believe that the worst was over in China and that the need for action on the protocol was not urgent.

Second, one must assume that the proposal received in October, that men-of-war be stationed at the Yangtze treaty ports and at Canton and Shanghai, was sent by telegraph from Peking apart from the full protocol. Since this new suggestion went exactly counter to basic policy at Whitehall, the Foreign Office may have felt that, if the

---

[54] Confidential Report by the Admiralty, Oct. 16, 1891. F.O. 17/1128.

[55] Salisbury to Trench, London, Sept. 22, 1891. *P.P.*, China No. 1 (1892), No. 53, p. 38.

[56] Salisbury to Walsham, Tel., London, Sept. 21, 1891; and Foreign Office to Sieh Ta-jen, Sept. 21, 1891. *P.P.*, China No. 1 (1892), Nos. 51 and 50, p. 37.

[57] Salisbury to Walsham, London, Oct. 2, 1891. *P.P.*, China No. 1 (1892), No. 71, p. 47.

[58] Walsham to Salisbury, Tel., Peking, Nov. 16, 1891; and Walsham to Salisbury, Sept. 30, 1891. *P.P.*, China No. 1 (1892), Nos. 112 and 110, pp. 95 and 84.

[59] The Foreign Office had grown to expect Walsham's delays. In October 1891, Sanderson remarked in a minute to Salisbury that Walsham's advice might be sought on keeping a gunboat at Tientsin for the winter, but that one could not be certain that he would reply. Sanderson's Minute to Confidential Report by the Admiralty, Oct. 16, 1891. F.O. 17/1128.

[60] Salisbury to Walsham, London, Sept. 12, 1891. *P.P.*, China No. 1 (1892), No. 34, p. 28.

protocol merely enlarged upon such advice, it might just as well be delayed.

Finally, the delayed arrival of the protocol supplied the British with a handy excuse to delay decisions pending among the European Powers concerning intervention in China. The significant element here, whatever the strange machinations underway in Whitehall, was that Britain was desperately trying to put off any decisive move in China.

It must be noted, however, that Walsham was obviously incapable of carrying out even this negative policy. As one missionary with long experience in China put it: "Sir John Walsham should go home to his estates. . . . China is clearly not the place for him." [61] But even with the imprudent Walsham in charge in Peking, there was every expectation that the combined weight of the Western Powers would force the Chinese Government to suppress the riots quickly. And there is little doubt that that would have been the case had the European Powers been able to unify their China policies.

The Riots and European Entanglements

The attitudes assumed by the European nations concerning the riots were in large part determined by their power positions and ambitions in China. England and Germany came to occupy a middle ground with respect to their readiness to bring pressure on the Chinese. France was more radical and urged decisive action, while Russia was a conservative force, always emphasizing restraint and compromise. But all this was made clear only as the crisis developed in the last half of 1891 and the Powers were forced to take up basic positions.

By 1891 Great Britain had enjoyed more than a decade of good relations with China. In part this was the work of Marquis Tseng, China's progressive minister to Great Britain until 1885. In part it was due to China's hope that Britain would oppose Russia and France, who were closing in along the borders of China. For England good relations with a relatively strong China meant not only a large area open to the inroads of commerce but a solid block opposing Russia's extensions to the north.[62] Up to the time of the riots both had benefited from this understanding: in 1891 the right of China to place consuls in British colonial ports was recognized; and China had added

Chungking to the list of treaty ports. This drift toward rapproche-
ment was momentarily cut short by the antimissionary outbreaks and
the threatening attitude which Britain thereupon necessarily assumed.

As early as July 1891 it had become clear that increased diplomatic
pressure on the Tsungli Yamen was essential. Britain realized that she
could best preserve her position as China's friend by cloaking her
action in the form of joint pressure by the Powers. Late in July, Salisbury declared himself willing to join in a collective demarche at
Peking to assure the security of foreigners in China.[63] Paris quickly
assented to this. Russia avowed that she too was ready to join but
had yet to receive notice from London of this proposed move — even
at this early stage, Russia while declaring her desire to go along with
the Powers found reason for delay.[64]

As already indicated, it must remain a moot point whether Britain
was immediately aware of the extensive demands contained in the
September 9 protocol of the ministers at Peking. But it was soon after
that date that the British grew lukewarm about action in China. After
the foreign representatives broke off negotiations with Peking on September 12, it was the French who assumed the lead in pushing for
active measures. On September 14 they called for common action by
the Powers. However, their request excluded and ignored the pro-
crastinating Russians.[65]

Immediately the British became suspicious of the French motive.
Salisbury instructed Sanderson to keep from the French the fact that
Vice-Admiral Richards had been granted permission to land and fire
on the Chinese in certain circumstances. And regarding the French
call to action in China, Salisbury commented suspiciously: "I fancy
M. Ribot is not singleminded in this matter." [66] Britain, joined by
Germany, sought to delay the French request for action. Britain ex-
plained that she thought it best to await the reception of advice from

---

[61] Wilson to Thompson, Chungking, May 31, 1891. L.M.S./CC/6.
[62] Waddington to Ribot, London, Aug. 8, 1891. *D.D.F.*, VIII, No. 475, pp. 638–
639.
[63] *Ibid.*
[64] Kotzebue to Ribot, Paris, Aug. 10, 1891. *D.D.F.*, VIII, No. 484, pp. 645–646.
[65] Ribot to Representatives at Berlin and Washington, Tel., Paris, Sept. 14, 1891.
D.D.F., IX, No. 11, p. 15. Also see Andrew Malozemoff, *Russian Far Eastern Policy,
1881–1904* (Berkeley: University of California Press, 1958), p. 51.
[66] Minute by Salisbury, Foreign Office, Sept. 5, 1891. F.O. 17/1127.

her representatives in Peking; [67] and Germany explained that she had insufficient forces in China to act.[68]

Clearly, Germany hastened to assume an attitude conducive to the protection of her long-range interests in China. Continuation of the type of informal control which Britain fostered in China was also pleasing to German trading interests. It was not surprising that Sir Edward Malet, British ambassador to Germany, reported on October 20 that Baron Hatzfield, the German ambassador to Britain, had expressed views which coincided with Britain's China policy.

Hatzfield granted that it was necessary to impose reasonable indemnities on China for the missionary outrages, but he warned of increasing these to a point which might imperil the stability of the Manchu regime. There was nothing that Britain or Germany might gain by coercion, he estimated, which would "outweigh the dangers resulting from the overthrow of the present dynasty in China." [69] The Russians would be quick to seize the opportunity given by such actions to establish supposedly friendly relations with the Chinese Government; this, Hatzfield concluded, would not be consistent with the continued independence of China, and, while French wishes should be acceded to as far as possible, Britain and Germany should never go to the extent of coercing China without the active concurrence of Russia.[70]

At about the same time Baron von Marshall, the German secretary of state, was even more explicit in explaining his fears of French policy. France, he told Malet, was seeking to punish China on account of the barren results obtained from her last war with China; now France was attempting to exploit her tempting position on the southern borders of China. As far as action by Germany was concerned, there was no intention of "pulling chestnuts out of the fire for France." [71]

By November Britain and Germany had agreed on a common policy regarding China. They would only take action in conjunction with all the other Powers in China. Of course, that especially meant Russia. They concluded that the crisis in China was passed. However, if necessity arose they would consider the recommendations sent by the representative body in Peking. And they would only exert further pressure on China to obtain adequate indemnities for those who suffered in the riots, most of these being missionaries.[72]

By mid-November the protocol had officially arrived in the European capitals. Action could no longer be delayed on its recommendations. France led the way in an effort to secure joint action in support of its recommendations. But the British bluntly replied that they could not go as far as the recommendations in the protocol for protecting native converts. To ease their reply they noted that the situation in China seemed to be improving.[73]

M. de Giers, the Russian foreign minister, answered the French plea by urging the need for a prudent policy in China. In a conversation on November 21 with Ribot, the French foreign minister, the Russian warned that the missionaries must be prevented from venturing inland, lest they involve their governments in grave embarrassments. He pointed out that while China must be convinced that the European Powers were acting in accord common action was, in fact, extremely difficult to obtain.[74]

Early in December a sudden outbreak in Manchuria, which as it happened the Chinese handily put down, gave the French a last opportunity to call for common action by the Powers. In particular the French urged that the various naval commanders in the Far East consult in regard to common needs.[75] Britain and Germany answered by reiterating their optimistic view that China could control the riots.[76] Russia, in her reply, noted that she had approved the participation of her representative in drawing up the protocol of September

---

[67] Constant to Ribot, London, Sept. 18, 1891. *D.D.F.*, IX, No. 16, p. 18.

[68] Herbette to Ribot, Berlin, Sept. 18, 1891. *D.D.F.*, IX, No. 15, pp. 17–18.

[69] Malet to Salisbury, Berlin, Oct. 20, 1891. F.O. 17/1128.

[70] *Ibid.*

[71] Malet to Salisbury, Berlin, Oct. 17, 1891. F.O. 17/1128.

[72] Dufferin to Malet, London, Nov. 3, 1891. F.O. 17/1129.

[73] Lytton to Salisbury, Paris, Nov. 21, 1891. F.O. 17/1129.

[74] Memorandum by Ribot, Nov. 21, 1891. *D.D.F.*, IX, No. 76, pp. 111–114.

[75] Ribot to Ambassadors in London, Berlin, Washington, St. Petersburg, and Rome, Tel., Paris, Dec. 2, 1891. *D.D.F.*, IX, No. 88, p. 134. It was also possible that by late November Russian pressure on the French had caused them to draw back from their forward policy in China. About that time the French minister instructed the Catholic missionaries at I-ch'ang to accept a compromise indemnity for their losses. British Consul Everard at I-ch'ang commented on this change of front: "This sudden change on the part of the French minister looks as if the French Government had decided to follow in the steps of Russia, and not put pressure on the Chinese Government." Everard to Walsham, Ichang (I-ch'ang), Dec. 1, 1891. F.O. 228/1066.

[76] Herbette to Ribot, Berlin, Dec. 7, 1891. *D.D.F.*, IX, No. 95, pp. 148–150. Salisbury to Egerton, London, Dec. 4, 1891. F.O. 17/1129.

9, but she explained that she was "disturbed" by certain "menacing formulas" in the protocol.[77] As for present action, Russia could only recommend prudence. Unofficially the Russians sought to undermine France's forward policy. The Russian ambassador in Berlin pointed out to the French ambassador that to move against China would merely serve the interests of England; and he asserted that the British were setting the stage for a coup similar to their strike in Egypt. But he insisted that France could halt all this by a categoric refusal to accept all proposals.[78]

Any determined action by the Powers seemed to face an inevitable veto. One final example of British caution revealed just what weight the missionary interest carried when balanced on the scales of power politics. On December 17 a note by the Chinese minister in London had implied that the responsibility for the protection of native Christian converts fell solely on the Chinese Government. Officials at the Foreign Office were about to dispute this point since the toleration clauses in the treaties had given the foreign powers a certain responsibility in this area. Salisbury cut short this move. He reminded his underlings that they must consider any objections raised in the light of the power alignment in China; in his own words: "I think I would not raise the question of the native Christians at this stage. We shall do no good and furnish a handle to the French."[79]

As 1891 drew to a close the winter winds had cooled the passion of riot that blazed through central China. It was fortunate that this was so, since the need to threaten China with ever more formidable retribution if the riots were not suppressed had raised the possibility of large-scale intervention by the Powers. While allowing the threat to stand, Britain, Germany, and Russia hastily retreated from actual implementation. France stood alone in advocating positive action. This neutralized any effective cooperation by the Powers, an inability that might prove to be dangerous if internal unrest continued to mar the China scene.

The Crisis Sets a Pattern

The Chinese Government was not unaware of this disunity in the Western front. In spite of this, the Chinese authorities acceded to European demands, and in their own good time took action against the rioters. This was the absolutely vital element. Gunboats and threats could never put down a massive rising of the Chinese people, but the Manchu regime was still able to command sufficient obedience to control the situation. The Manchu leaders were willing to comply with European pressure for many complex reasons. Vice-Admiral Richards gave as good an explanation of their motives as any: "The Government at Peking are endeavouring, quite as much on their own account as for any regard to foreigners, to act in conformity with treaty obligations." [80]

Peking acted against the risings because they constituted as much a threat to the Chinese regime as to the foreigner. Still, the action was of a slow and halting nature. This was, partly, because there was no warm feeling for the missionaries in Peking; and, partly, because it was not wise to suppress quickly a movement so popular with the people. Indeed, the regime no doubt desired to foster among the masses a hatred for and mild opposition to the foreigner.

But the cautious reaction of the Manchu regime was also due to the complex nature of the movement confronting them. One group of riots, those evidently of secret society origin, were suppressed as swiftly as possible and their instigators sought out. In October 1891, Consul T. L. Bullock reported that the high authorities were giving their full attention to tracking down the Ko-lao hui men.[81] On the other hand Chinese officialdom was slow to move against those outbreaks inspired by patriotism and in large part finding their origin among the Hunan men. This was why Walsham had to report that the Tsungli Yamen would act only under the strongest pressure and then "most unwillingly and most ungraciously." [82] All this meant that in the total picture Chinese action against the rioters was uneven, and appeared inexplicable to some. Because of this confusion no meaningful explanation of the riots of 1891 was readily apparent to the British officials — and they felt no need to seek enlightenment since the gunboat and the threat had, for the time being, moved the Manchu Government to action, and the riots were being suppressed. The

[77] Montebello to Ribot, Tel., St. Petersburg, Dec. 7, 1891. *D.D.F.*, IX, No. 93, p. 146.
[78] Herbette to Ribot, Berlin, Dec. 8, 1891. *D.D.F.*, IX, No. 97, pp. 152–154.
[79] Minute by Salisbury, Foreign Office, Dec. 18, 1891. F.O. 17/1129.
[80] Richards to Admiralty, Yokohama, Nov. 10, 1891. F.O. 17/1112.
[81] Bullock to Walsham, Kiukiang, Oct. 2, 1891. F.O. 228/1060.
[82] Walsham to Salisbury, Peking, Sept. 30, 1891. F.O. 17/1128.

experience with the 1891 riots left the British no better prepared than before to deal with future outbreaks of a similar or possibly larger nature.

The solution for the 1891 riots amounted to a compromise. It was not a written agreement; rather it was no more than an implicit understanding between the British and Chinese governments. It was something like an agreement between two fighters to pull their punches for the next few rounds. For their part the Chinese authorities were able to reduce the thunderous clamor of rioting to a dull hum, though occasionally a sharp call to violence broke through the undercurrent of murmured hate. The British simply had to learn to live with these outbursts, as did the other foreign groups, even if they didn't learn to understand the complex struggle which underlay the specific incidents. This permitted British informal empire to stumble along for at least another decade in China.

CHAPTER III

Efforts to Control the Missionaries

THE great rush to the new missionary frontier of China that took place in the 1890's was instigated by men like Hudson Taylor, the leader of the China Inland Mission. Speaking at the Shanghai Missionary Conference of 1890, he had called for 1000 new missionaries in the next five years. The riots of 1891 only added urgency to the call and through the decade well over 1000 new Protestant missionaries streamed into China.[1]

To British diplomats, anxious to preserve the calm essential for their informal dominion in China, this presented 1000 new occasions for riots and the accompanying danger of involvement for the British Government.[2] Consequently, British officials faced a twofold challenge: to compel the Chinese to subdue their obstreperous subjects; and to seek to control the methods and movements of their own missionaries. This chapter discusses those efforts to control missionary

---

[1] Latourette, *A History of Christian Missions in China*, p. 414.
[2] Bishop Charles Scott of the S.P.G. was aware of this growing danger. The rapid increase in the number of missionaries, he wrote, "who travel or reside inland, and the steady growing influence of the missions seem to me to account in the most natural and straightforward way for the multiplication of the instances of friction between the Chinese and the Foreigners." Scott to Tucker, North China, Dec. 1892. S.P.G., Letters, 1892, No. 14.

activity which at times became as vexing a task as suppressing anti-foreign violence itself.

Missionary Ardor

The encounter of missionary and diplomat pitted men of burning ardor against men of slow deliberation. It was a conflict of enthusiasm against sophistication, of dedication against detachment. But the odds against the dispassionate diplomats rose steadily. Once the missionaries, some independent and some affiliated with denominational groups, began to pour into China, the studied cautions of the Foreign Office would have little effect upon the movement as a whole.

A typical representative of the new and zealous missionary contingent was Rev. J. Haywood Horsburgh of the Church Missionary Society. His determination overrode the warnings of Foreign Office officials, the doubts of his own society, and the opposition of the Chinese themselves. His was a new approach to mission work in China. He would operate on very simple lines: The missionaries would abandon the custom of occupying a walled mission compound. Rather, they would live in Chinese houses, wear Chinese dress, eat Chinese food, and, spending as little as possible, seek to identify themselves with the Chinese people.[3] By 1891 Horsburgh had convinced the C.M.S. to support his project in the establishment of a new mission in Szechwan, far in the interior of China.[4]

But accusations soon were heard concerning Horsburgh's supposed imprudence. The first cry came in 1892 as his party was on the last lap of its journey up the Yangtze River. He had so arranged his transportation that five women missionaries, unaccompanied by any male missionary, traveled by junk on the turbulent Yangtze between I-ch'ang and Chungking. The British consul had warned against taking such risks, and the *South China Daily Mail* picked up the story, declaring that the group should never have been allowed passage.[5] In a confidential letter to the C.M.S. in London, Bishop Moule of the Mid-China Mission deplored Horsburgh's tactics; he pointed out that Szechwan was in a critical and dangerous state, and that such procedures went contrary to the cautions advanced by Lord Salisbury and the Archbishop of Canterbury.[6]

Having arrived in Szechwan, Horsburgh faced the determined opposition of the Chinese authorities from the governor-general to the local magistrates. The Chinese officials feared to allow open riots such as those of 1891; they demonstrated a staunch and unyielding determination to prevent the missionaries from settling in any previously unoccupied cities. In fact, this seemed to be the semiofficial Chinese policy toward missionaries throughout China. Horsburgh found that his party was free to join the China Inland Mission groups at residences in those cities which they already occupied. His missionaries were free to dwell in villages in the countryside; and they might itinerate through the country, making short sojourns in the otherwise forbidden cities. But any attempt to push further was opposed. In a few instances, Chinese officials were able to force a withdrawal from the smaller missionary stations by means of prolonged legal disputes over property rights and various forms of noncooperation. The new Chinese tactics turned the tide of the missionary advance. By 1892 three to four cities in Szechwan previously occupied by the China Inland Mission had been abandoned because of official opposition.[7]

Such setbacks were not due to the timidity of the missionaries. At Sung-p'ing Rev. W. W. Cassels had refused to be ejected from his residence. He stayed within as Chinese rioters came and removed the tiles from his roof. The deluge of rain which followed did not budge him; finally the Chinese broke in and carried him out. Still, it was noteworthy that they were careful not to do Cassels bodily harm or to destroy his movable property.[8] Horsburgh was aware of such obstacles, but he was undaunted. The Lord had brought him to Szechwan, he said: "when human powers are determined to keep Him out, we have a good indication I think that we will roll away the stone . . . as soon as we are ready."[9] Horsburgh called for more men to follow him to the interior, and this in spite of his bishop's request

---

[3] Eugene Stock, A History of the Church Missionary Society (London: C.M.S., 1916), III, 577.

[4] Ibid.

[5] Moule to Fenn, Foochow, May 12, 1892, with enclosed clipping, South China Mail, May 9, 1892. C.M.S./G1/CH2/P2, 1892, No. 140.

[6] Ibid.

[7] Verden to Fenn, Chungking, March 19, 1892. C.M.S./G1/CH2/P2, 1892, No. 112.

[8] Horsburgh to Fenn, Ch'eng-tu, Aug. 29, 1892. C.M.S./G1/CH2/P2, 1892, No. 182.

[9] Ibid.

that recruiting be halted. If men would not come he called for women; and if the educated would not come he called for the good of spirit.[10]

Not until 1894 did Horsburgh's relentless efforts to gain lodgment in certain parts of Szechwan succeed. Then he was able to establish C.M.S. residencies in four previously untouched cities: Hsin-tu, Chung-pa, Mien-chu, and Mien-yang. This was done against the steady opposition of the mandarins, but Horsburgh had gained a footing, and he called for more workers to fill the newly won openings.[11] The following year, in the face of rioting and unrest, the members of Horsburgh's Interior Evangelical Mission joined in a petition for twelve more volunteers to bring the word of God to six more "dark and sad towns."[12] In the same message they announced that their intention was to push still deeper inward to Tibet and elsewhere.

Horsburgh's methods — his haphazard adoption of Chinese ways, his encouragement of itineration by unaccompanied female missionaries — were so unconventional that Bishop Moule soon asked the C.M.S. in London to be relieved of responsibility for him.[13] Certainly such tactics risked incidents which might embroil the British with the Manchu regime. The really remarkable fact was that, at least until 1895, Horsburgh's group provoked no such incidents.

The riots of 1895 which swept Szechwan only indirectly touched Horsburgh's mission; none of its dwellings, though invaded, were pulled down or pillaged.[14] In a confidential report, which by indirection revealed the more cautious and tolerant aspects of his methods, Horsburgh singled out the narrow approach of the China Inland Mission as largely contributing to the riots. He granted that the mere presence of missionaries in China created a sore, but he argued that the C.I.M. managed to irritate this sore rather than soothe it.[15] Doubtless he was referring here to the C.I.M. predilection for vehement attacks on the rites and superstitions of the Chinese. That the C.M.S. group under Horsburgh emerged virtually unscathed from the Szechwan riots offers some testimony, at least, to the success of his methods. Even as the riots grew and the British consul declared Chungking to be unsafe for missionaries, Horsburgh called for substantial reinforcements and he declared that there would soon be "wider openings and a still greater need."[16]

Whitehall Rejects Controls

Such enthusiasm was extreme even among missionaries, but it dramatized a general attitude which, for the calmer custodians of British diplomacy, was a constant irritation. The riots of 1891 had supplied British officials with an occasion for reassessing their missionary policy in China. Advice of all kinds, foolhardy and learned, public and private, general and detailed, poured into the Foreign Office. It was up to Whitehall to formulate a policy, keeping in mind all these varied interests.

First to balk at the prospect of safeguarding an ever expanding missionary effort was the naval commander at the China Station, Vice-Admiral Sir Frederick Richards. In a stinging protest, he declared that it was not enough that he had to provide for the safety of the twenty-four treaty ports, but now he was to look after the missionaries as well, missionaries whose special aim seemed to be to escape the limits of the designated ports. Once out, they refused to accept the risks involved but were the first to clamor for gunboats. England, Richards went on sarcastically, having removed the beam from her own eye, had now turned her missionaries loose to pluck the mote from the eye of China; but, in so doing, the missionaries chose to obey neither the cautions of the British consuls nor the norms of discretion. Lastly, Richards urged that the actual rights of missionaries outside treaty ports be settled, and that some check be put on missionaries who felt free to reject the advice of British consuls and then looked to the same consuls for protection.[17]

---

[10] Horsburgh to Fenn, Mencheio (Mien-chu), July 26, 1893. C.M.S./G1/CH2/P2, 1893, No. 189. Also see Vaughan to Baring-Gould, Blackheath, May 10, 1894. C.M.S./G1/CH2/P2, 1894, No. 100.

[11] Horsburgh to Wigram, June 9 and Sept. 15, 1894, Mien Chuh Hsien (Mien-chu Hsien). C.M.S./G1/CH2/P2, 1894, Nos. 163 and 216.

[12] Interior Mission to Wigram, Ch'eng-tu, May 1895. C.M.S./G1/CH2/P2, 1895, No. 147.

[13] Moule to Fenn, Hankow, Dec. 12, 1892. C.M.S./G1/CH2/P2, 1892, No. 19.

[14] Horsburgh to Baring-Gould, Kuan Hsien, June 19, 1895. C.M.S./G1/CH2/P2, 1895, No. 219.

[15] Ibid.   [16] Ibid.

[17] Richards to Admiralty, China Station, July 27, 1891. F.O. 17/1127. In 1892 Vice-Admiral E. R. Fremantle, who had replaced Richards, sustained his judgment. He urged that missionaries not be permitted to advance into the interior without approval of the British consul. Fremantle to Admiralty, China Station, May 20, 1892. F.O. 17/1147. The duties of the commander at the China Station had increased as new treaty ports had been opened from time to time after the Treaties of Tientsin.

Similar, but more detailed, comment came from Christopher Gardner, British consul in Hankow. This aggressive defender of what he regarded as the British cause in China energetically boosted both missionary and mercantile interests. But at the same time he insisted that more peaceful conditions would prevail if the following six injunctions could be urged upon the missionary societies:

1. If less reticence were observed at what goes on in orphanages and in schools. [That is, if Chinese officials might be granted freer access to inspect these schools.]

2. If the Bible Societies would refrain from flooding the country with uncommented books of the Bible such as Joshua-Judges, Ruth, and the Song of Solomon, etc.

3. If Chinese prejudices and superstitions were more considered in the forms and heights of buildings erected.

4. If missionaries would refrain from meddling in pecuniary disputes between Christians and non-Christian natives.

5. If missionaries would attack heathen prejudices and superstitions with courtesy and without violence.

6. As a rule the Elder Missionaries of all denominations are moderate and temperate. With regard to the Catholics if there was a vicar-Legate in Peking his influence would be useful in inculcating prudence.

With regard to Protestants greater difficulty exists but the influence of the Foreign Office on the Societies at home is great, and the personal influence of the consuls who are generally middle-aged men on the heads of missions out here is not small, and could be exerted beneficially.

I should like consuls to have more power to refuse passports or withdraw them from persons of known indiscretion. . . .

[Lastly] female missionaries travelling together with unmarried male missionaries gives rise in the Chinese mind to the idea that we practice promiscuous intercourse.[18]

In a second report to the Foreign Office in January 1892, Gardner felt it necessary to deprecate the tendency of British missionaries to push beyond the safety of the treaty ports. Demands by certain missionaries that their right of residence should be extended to the interior of China had led Gardner to emphasize that this would place the missionaries beyond the protection of British power. He argued that, even though the missionaries freely assumed this risk, Britain could not allow her countrymen to be murdered or outraged, and that such incidents endangered the lives of the missionaries and merchants in the treaty ports and also threatened the growth of British trade.[19]

The most precise and penetrating analysis of British policy appeared in an article by Rev. G. T. Candlin in the *Manchester Guardian,* which was passed on to the Foreign Office. Candlin blamed the riots on the "ill-defined relation between the missionaries in China and the Chinese government." The solution, he proclaimed, was to make clear just what these rights were; thus, the vague status of the missionary's claim to reside in the interior should be replaced by an absolute right guaranteed by China and properly promulgated for all to know; but at the same time, the equally fuzzy claim of the missionary to protect his converts should be dropped.[20]

As we sum up the proposals presented to the Foreign Office, two general principles emerge: there was the demand that the indiscretions of the missionaries be checked; and there was the admonition that the right of missionaries to reside in the interior be clarified, that is affirmed or denied, with the less drastic suggestion that some limiting principle be set upon the issuance of passports to the missionaries.

Now just what the Foreign Office proceeded to do with these suggestions is curious and revealing. Gardner's six points had dwelt on the indiscreet conduct of missionaries. The Foreign Office had these printed and distributed to the headquarters of the various mission societies in Great Britain, tactfully suggesting that they be taken as a rule of conduct.[21] But Gardner's lengthy suggestions concerning greater Foreign Office and consular guidance of the missionaries were dropped as was his suggestion that consuls be given greater power to refuse passports to missionaries. No hint was included of Gardner's later suggestion that mission residence in the interior should be prohibited, a point which Vice-Admiral Richards had also emphasized. Nor did the Foreign Office seek to clarify the right of residence in the interior as the Reverend Mr. Candlin suggested.

The obvious conclusion that the Foreign Office was reluctant to reexamine the treaty status of missionaries in China, or to increase its con-

---

[18] Gardner to Gervoise, Hankow, Oct. 26, 1891. F.O. 17/1128.

[19] Gardner to Salisbury, Hankow, Jan. 28, 1892. F.O. 17/1146.

[20] Cutting from the *Manchester Guardian.* Enclosed in Angur to Salisbury, London, Jan. 13, 1892. F.O. 17/1146.

[21] Landen to Archbishop of Canterbury, London, Jan. 13, 1892. F.O. 17/1146.

trol over the movements of missionaries, was supported by the observations which the Foreign Office made concerning Candlin's article. Sir Thomas Sanderson, undersecretary of state for foreign affairs, thought it a "sensible paper" but "not practicable"; and Lord Salisbury commented that it "hardly lay within the field of practical politics."[22]

Why this reluctance to establish clearly the missionary's right to permanent residence in the interior? Why the hesitancy to extend control over the movements of missionaries?

The answer seems to lie in the fact that both efforts would have transgressed the limited sort of control which Britain sought to impose upon China. If Britain formalized permission for her missionaries to reside in the interior, it was likely that this would accelerate the sweep of missionaries into the heartland of China, and thereby increase the likelihood of collision between Great Britain and China. If Britain extended official control over the action of her missionaries, strict limitations on their activities would provoke the powerful missionary societies. Then too, effective control of missionary activities would necessitate the creation of an ever expanding consular force to keep pace with the ever expanding missionary community in China.

The Foreign Office's determination to preserve the obscurity of the missionary's status was successful in the sense that it avoided a blunt insistence by the missionary societies that Britain claim full use of a prerogative which was technically hers. As has been previously shown, Britain possessed the privilege of missionary residence in the interior, inasmuch as this right was won by France in 1860 and, in turn, fell to Britain under the most-favored-nation clause.[23] While British missionaries had taken up residence in the interior and continued to do so, Britain never formally asserted this right, the chief reason no doubt being its wish not to encourage this practice by the missionaries. Yet neither did Britain desire to abandon this latent right which, after all, might be useful in the future, and to reject such a privilege would bring a storm of protest from the politically significant missionary groups at home. Thus mission policy was allowed to stumble along; confused and contradictory, it posed a threat to rationalized diplomatic dealings with China.

Efforts to Control Missionaries before the Sino-Japanese War

Aloof as the Foreign Office chose to stand from any form of missionary control, developments in 1892 pointed with increasing urgency to the need for some regulations. Fukien Province on China's southeast coast was perhaps the foremost area of concentration for English missionaries. In its Chien-ning Prefecture determined Chinese resistance had turned away efforts by Catholic and by American Protestant missionaries to establish themselves, but by 1892 elements of the C.M.S. led by Dr. John Rigg had won a foothold in three heretofore untouched towns. Resistance was obviously brewing against these inroads. The British consul in Fukien and Archdeacon Wolfe of the C.M.S. had warned Rigg not to press for enlargement of his medical dispensary in T'ai-chou. Rigg ignored these warnings and collected materials to increase his facilities. Soon after, a Chinese mob gathered and destroyed his dispensary.[24] The violence spread and later that year other C.M.S. groups were driven from Chien-ning City and Ch'ing-ho in the same prefecture.[25] In all these riots the Chinese took care not to injure the missionaries, but their disdain for the missionaries was clearly registered. At Chien-ning City, for example, the Reverend Mr. Phillips first stood by while his residence was inundated with liquefied excrement, and then found himself victimized by a similar fate.[26]

Before these riots the missionaries had been warned by the Chinese authorities that native opposition to their presence could not be controlled. And the British consul, Hurst, while he sought full reparation for the outrages from the Chinese Government, felt that the missionaries had by their own overly aggressive conduct contributed to the outbreaks.[27] On Hurst's insistence Archdeacon Wolfe agreed to withdraw his missionaries from the turbulent area for a period of three or four months, while the consul pressed the Chinese to bring the sector under

---

[22] Minute by Salisbury in Angur to Salisbury, loc. cit.

[23] Latourette, A History of Christian Missions in China, pp. 417–418. Latourette contended that Britain took the attitude that the treaties did not give the missionaries the right of residence outside the treaty port. However, the British never formalized their attitude to that extent. Aside from this, Latourette stated the actual practice of missionary penetration with accuracy: "The governments of the United States and Great Britain, as we have seen, took the attitude that the treaties did not guarantee to Protestant missionaries the right of residence outside the 'open' ports, but if the missionary had acquired an entrance, and especially if he had obtained a house or land either by lease or purchase, he had by that act come into possession of quasi-legal rights in which he must be protected." P. 418.

[24] Phillips to Archdeacon Wolfe, Foochow, May 23, 1892. F.O. 17/1147.

[25] Hurst to Archdeacon Wolfe, Foochow, Oct. 20, 1892. F.O. 17/1149.

[26] Minute by Rosebery, Foreign Office, Feb. 10, 1892; and Hurst to Beauclerk, Foochow, Oct. 17, 1892. F.O. 17/1149.

[27] Hurst to Wolfe, Foochow, Oct. 20, 1892. F.O. 17/1149.

control. At the same time Wolfe denied that his missionaries were guilty of indiscretions, and insisted that the riots were the result of connivance by the local officials.[28] These incidents in Chien-ning led Hurst to conclude that increased control over the movements of the missionaries was a necessity.

Toward the end of 1892 Walsham was replaced as British minister in Peking by Sir Nicholas O'Conor, a rapidly rising, aggressive young man in the Foreign Service. His mission was to firm up Walsham's lax regime. One of the first decisions that he faced was a plea by Hurst for greater control over the issuance of passports to missionaries. O'Conor quickly grasped the essentials of the situation and allowed Hurst to withhold passports in those areas where the consul was convinced that the local authorities were truly unable to give protection. But this was a reluctant concession, and the hardheaded O'Conor warned Hurst not to implement this power except in case of real necessity; then, lest the Chinese be encouraged to extend their opposition to missionary penetration, he forbade Hurst to pass on any hint of these instructions to the Chinese.[29]

Whitehall had observed Hurst's difficulties, and had taken note of his plea that it urge the C.M.S. to discipline its missionaries who were straining to push their work forward in Fukien. Lord Rosebery, the new Liberal foreign secretary, had approved O'Conor's action, and appeared to be more willing than his Conservative predecessor to exert some form of pressure on the mission societies.[30] After consulting the Archbishop of Canterbury on the propriety of his procedure, in March 1893, he informed all the British mission societies of his new policy. Henceforth British consuls were to determine whether the missionaries were to reside in districts where Chinese officials were unable to control the population. This policy was necessary, Rosebery explained, since incidents which might lead to intervention with all its dangers must be avoided. To minimize these dangers of involvement passports might be withheld; but, in any case, the missionaries might always appeal beyond the decision of the consul to the minister in Peking and then on to Whitehall.[31]

The Archbishop of Canterbury approved Rosebery's new restrictions and observed that such limitations must seem "moderate even to the most fervid missionary."[32] But the Archbishop also reiterated Archdeacon Wolfe's warning that, if the Chinese officials were not compelled to do their part as well, the missionaries would feel a sense of duty to push on in spite of these restrictions. Most of the mission societies, however, fell into line and pledged their allegiance to the new policy. The C.M.S. was among the first of these and it noted that it would direct its missionaries "not to act contrary to the advice of Her Majesty's local representative in China." [33]

All this was to the good and it seemed that to a considerable extent missionary activities would be controlled. Rosebery's policy, however, was merely a general rule; it had to be applied by consuls in the field who had little time to keep abreast of the whereabouts and many activities of the ever multiplying missionary community. Then too, the missionaries had a genius for agreeing to such general rules, only to discover that their particular difficulties were exceptional and constituted a case outside the general directives.

Late in 1893 the British consul in Chungking, M. F. A. Fraser, passed on to O'Conor a lengthy critique of the new passport policy. Passports, he explained, were valid for one year, and during that time there was no telling where a missionary might feel the call to preach. Missionaries with passports from another consular area might suddenly appear in one's district; for example, a Miss Taylor of the C.I.M., who had obtained her passport in Shanghai, had crossed all of China into Tibet and on her return had suddenly appeared in Chungking. Equally dangerous, he explained, was the "unsparing criticism" which some few missionaries leveled at native prejudices. In Chungking after a recent fire had destroyed about 4000 native dwellings, the C.I.M. people spread placards ridiculing the impotent Chinese fire-god who was unable to prevent such catastrophes. For more effective protection, they urged the natives to turn to Christ. Fraser indicated that he soon scotched these placards, but that at uncontrolled inland stations passport-bearing missionaries might easily provoke a riot by such conduct.[34]

At the same time Fraser claimed that it was too late to confine the missionaries to the treaty ports. His solution lay in negotiating with the provincial authorities to establish the clear right of missionaries to re-

[28] Wolfe to Hurst, Foochow, Oct. 25, 1892. F.O. 17/1149.
[29] O'Conor to Hurst, Peking, Dec. 11, 1892. F.O. 17/1149.
[30] Rosebery to O'Conor, Foreign Office, Feb. 14, 1893. F.O. 17/1171.
[31] Circular to Mission Societies, Foreign Office, March 18, 1893. F.O. 17/1171.
[32] Archbishop of Canterbury to Rosebery, London, March 15, 1893. F.O. 17/1171.
[33] Collingwood to Rosebery, London, March 30, 1893. F.O. 17/1171.
[34] Fraser to O'Conor, Chungking, Nov. 8, 1893. F.O. 17/1172.

tain their presently held residencies outside treaty ports. These, if possible, should be so arranged as to be a few days' journey from each other. Female missionaries, presently scattered in isolated outposts, and children would be confined to these legally established stations, and from these the male missionaries could itinerate. Finally, as a *quid pro quo*, the societies would be forbidden to acquire homes in untouched cities unless permission was first granted by the Chinese authorities. This plan, Fraser suggested, might first be tried in Szechwan and, if successful, could be implemented in the other provinces.[35]

O'Conor, sensitive to the need of upholding British prestige in all ways, refused to approve Fraser's new recommendations. He pointed out that the Chinese authorities would obviously never approve any new extension of missionary work and, thus, could effectively ban the extension of Christianity in China. And to so limit English missionaries would simply give an unfair advantage to the missionaries of other countries. Consuls, he noted, were now authorized to withhold passports; each case should be judged on its own merit rather than by any drastic new rules. On any account, he remarked, such a sweeping new plan would require Foreign Office approval and thus would be reviewed again when this correspondence was forwarded through regular channels to Whitehall.[36]

Implied in O'Conor's reply was another consideration: it was especially inexpedient to put forward such proposals at that time, because the diplomatic corps, through its spokesman, the American minister, Colonel Denby, was just then fending off Chinese pressure to place added restrictions on the passports granted to missionaries by treaty. The Tsungli Yamen argued that itinerating missionaries should be required to present their passports to the local authorities through whose jurisdiction they passed; this, they contended, would ensure greater protection for them. The foreign representatives refused to consider this "useless obstruction" which went beyond the terms of the Treaties of Tientsin.[37] The Chinese had argued that unless these terms were met they could not guarantee the safety of the missionaries. Until this issue was settled O'Conor felt that he could not approve Fraser's new proposals.

When the Foreign Office finally studied Fraser's recommendations in February 1894, it supported O'Conor's negative view. But, strangely enough, while it evaded coming to grips with the central issue of missionary control that Fraser was concerned with, the Foreign Office took up with great vehemence his incidental comment concerning female missionaries who resided at isolated outposts and traversed the country-side on their own.[38] Perhaps this was done to enable Whitehall to put off the more fundamental issue of missionary status. Perhaps it was due to British concern for womanhood which bulked especially large in the Victorian's mind. But certainly the recent murder of two Swedish missionaries along with increasing reports concerning the reckless wander-ings of female missionaries was the immediate reason which led Rosebery himself to take up the issue as a special preoccupation.

The report of the brutal murder of the two Swedish missionaries, Wik-holm and Johanson, at Sung-p'u near Hankow, came in July 1893. They had pressed into the interior in spite of the warning of the Swedish con-sul who was informed by the Chinese authorities that the district was in a hostile state. In his report O'Conor pointed out that 200 more Swed-ish missionaries were on their way to China and that those who had al-ready arrived had inadequate language training, were without sufficient funds, and tended to itinerate from village to village singing hymns in the best Salvation Army fashion.[39] All this was of particular concern to the British, for Sweden soon asked their support in pressing for the dis-missal of the local Chinese authority within whose jurisdiction the mur-der took place. After some hesitation, and though aware of the fool-hardy conduct of the two victims, Rosebery agreed to support this attempt to degrade the local official. The joint effort met with suc-cess.[40]

Soon after the Foreign Office received a second report on the activi-ties of the newly arrived Swedish missionaries, a report which was de-scribed by one of the Foreign Office officials as "almost inconceiva-ble."[41] It was from Mr. St. George Littledale, who when traveling in Shansi had encountered twenty-five Swedish female missionaries of the

---

[35] *Ibid.*

[36] O'Conor to Fraser, Peking, Nov. 30, 1893. F.O. 17/1172.

[37] O'Conor to Rosebery, Peking, Jan. 6, 1894; and Denby to Tsungli Yamen, Peking, Dec. 30, 1893. F.O. 17/1192.

[38] Minute to draft of Rosebery to O'Conor, Foreign Office, Feb. 9, 1894. F.O. 17/1172.

[39] O'Conor to Rosebery, Peking, July 12, 1893. F.O. 17/1172.

[40] Minute of Sept. 24, 1893, attached to Swedish Minister of Foreign Affairs to Rosebery, Stockholm, Sept. 19, 1893. F.O. 17/1172. O'Conor to Rosebery, Peking, Jan. 9, 1893. F.O. 17/1192.

[41] Minute to O'Conor to Rosebery, Peking, Nov. 3, 1893. F.O. 17/1172.

C.I.M. at Kuei-hua-ch'eng, only one of whom could speak Chinese. Portions of his report are worthy of repetition:

It is hard to speak temperately of the individual or society that sends girls wholesale into the interior of such a country as China unprotected, practically uncared for, and with most inadequate means. There is an unmarried Swedish missionary living in the town who normally looks after them, but he is so carried away with religious fervour that were it not for the kindness of a solitary Missionary Doctor they would be entirely helpless. They told us how useless it was on their way up country to choose rooms in the inns with windows in good order, for the natives pushed holes through the paper and there would be twenty pairs of eyes watching their preparations for bed, and that the Chinese when asked to go away, only laughed and made insulting remarks. . . . These poor unfortunate women with the merest smattering of Chinese are being sent about the country — sometimes in pairs and sometimes alone — to pray, play the guitar, and sing hymns in the street, a life that none but an improper woman in China would lead, and which fosters the idea in the native mind that these girls were too bad to be allowed to remain in their own country: and they openly expressed their opinion that one girl must have been very bad indeed to have been sent out of the country so young. The day after we left one girl was going off alone in a cart for two or three days journey to a town where there was no European. . . .[42]

Littledale concluded his remarks by noting how short the step was between obscene remarks and actual violence, and that sooner or later some horrible outrage was bound to be committed on these ladies. He urged that something be done to change this distressing state of affairs.

Confronted with this perplexing picture, Rosebery dispatched a gentle admonition to the Swedish Government, advising it that the presence of its unprotected missionaries tended to weaken the position of all missionaries in China and was a cause of possible political complications.[43] Then he considered the possibility of drawing up a new circular for the English missionary societies, warning them not to allow female missionaries to proceed to their posts unaccompanied by men. But first the Foreign Office inquired of O'Conor if, in fact, there were any unaccompanied English female missionaries in the interior.[44] Before the necessary information could be gathered, British policy was to be absorbed in the larger issue of war in the Far East.

Control after the War

Growing apprehension concerning a Sino-Japanese clash over Korea and then the actuality of this war in the latter half of 1894 cut short any decisive action by Britain in regard to her missionaries. It also forestalled Chinese pressure to extend local control over the movement of missionaries which, according to the Swedish foreign minister, was to culminate in a proposal that missionaries be prohibited from entering China.[45]

Shamefully defeated in the war by her despised neighbor, China was shaken by a violent internal reaction in 1895. The missionaries, hated for themselves and now more than ever regarded as just another species of the foreign foe, suffered a reign of death and destruction which equaled or surpassed the violence of 1891. This meant that British officials were more concerned with beating down this violent upheaval than with extending a system of control over their missionaries. As a result this postwar period was even less productive of efforts to rationalize missionary penetration than the prewar period. There was, however, a lingering concern in regard to the position of female missionaries, and one or two plans came forth for the control of missionaries on the consular level.

Almost a year passed before O'Conor made a tentative reply to Rosebery's inquiry about the presence of unaccompanied female missionaries in the interior. Even then he explained that wartime pressures had not allowed a thorough investigation. But as a sort of interim report he suggested that the presence of unaccompanied female missionaries was objectionable to the Chinese and was liable to misinterpretation. However, he felt that their circumstances were no more dangerous than those of the male missionary.[46]

Before O'Conor was able to compile a detailed study of the female missionary problem a Conservative Government had replaced the Liberals and Salisbury, returning as Prime Minister in June 1895, again took up the reins at the Foreign Office. While the Liberals evidenced a slight,

---

[42] Report of Littledale enclosed in O'Conor to Rosebery, Peking, Nov. 3, 1893. F.O. 17/1172.

[43] Rosebery to St. John, Foreign Office, Jan. 8, 1894. F.O. 17/1227.

[44] Rosebery to O'Conor, Foreign Office, Feb. 21, 1894; and Minute of Feb. 9, 1894, to O'Conor-Fraser correspondence. F.O. 17/1172.

[45] Rosebery to O'Conor, Foreign Office, June 27, 1894. F.O. 17/1227. Later O'Conor replied that he had no information on the report that the Chinese would propose to exclude missionaries from China. O'Conor to Kimberley, Peking, Aug. 21, 1894. F.O. 17/1227.

[46] O'Conor to Kimberley, Peking, Feb. 27, 1895. F.O. 17/1227.

though ineffectual, concern to control the missionaries, the Conservatives generally preferred a hands-off attitude in regard both to the missionaries and to interference in China. It will be recalled that Rosebery had thrown his support behind a Swedish effort in 1893 to degrade a Chinese prefect. Now Salisbury declined to support the efforts of Swedish officials to rent a dwelling for their missionaries against strong Chinese resistance. In this instance Salisbury countermanded a decision to aid the Swedes made by a subordinate official at the Foreign Office and took the occasion to comment: "I should like to hear a little more before acting on this. If this missionary gets knocked on the head shall we be expected to interfere?" [47]

Under Salisbury the Foreign Office toned down the sort of concern that Rosebery had shown for the fate of female missionaries. The question was raised again by the British consul in Foochow, Clement F. R. Allen, who submitted a lengthy report on the conduct of the ladies of the Church of England Zenana Mission Society. It seemed that this society by its independence of action and overzealous conduct had stirred Allen's fears. He particularly objected to the rather haphazard adoption by its members of Chinese dress. "An English lady," he noted, "in Chinese jacket, shirt, and trousers with European shoes and stockings, and her hair smooth and braided in English fashion is neither one thing nor another." He suggested that the Chinese, seeing such a figure traveling alone in the interior, "says to himself that this is a man masquerading as a woman, in order to find his way into Chinese homes to seduce the women."[48]

As a solution to such difficulties Allen urged that the Zenana Society be compelled to submit to the discipline of the Church of England in the person of Archdeacon Wolfe of Fukien, that correct habits in dress and language be studied by the missionaries before they were set loose in the interior, and that the ladies' work be confined to those areas already opened by missionary penetration.[49] At the Foreign Office, Assistant Undersecretary of State Francis Villiers sought to kill further action on these proposals with the comment that it "seems rather questionable whether this [Allen's proposal] would do any good and may lead to a good deal of controversy." [50] Salisbury, however, decided that they should follow a safer but no more effective line; they would send Allen's proposals on to the Archbishop of Canterbury, the C.M.S., and the S.P.G. — but with no comment or advice attached.[51] These mission societies passed the criticisms on to the Zenana Society but its reply to the Foreign Office disputed Allen's charges.[52] Faced with this opposition the Foreign Office simply dropped the issue.

It was not long before Consul Allen's reports drew one more aspect of the missionary problem to the attention of the Foreign Office. This time he objected to the unwarranted interference by the younger missionaries in civil cases involving their converts. Allen claimed that every case against a Christian was described as persecutory by the junior missionaries and that then the consul's intervention was called for.[53] As a result, Allen informed Archdeacon Wolfe of the C.M.S., he would only intervene in certain cases; he specified these as "assault on missionaries, destruction of mission or church property, scurrilous placards, organized attacks on the native Christian community, and enforced contributions to idolatrous ceremonies."[54] The Foreign Office approved Allen's move as far as his particular district was concerned, and then sent his dispatch on to the Archbishop of Canterbury and the C.M.S. No attempt was made to establish Allen's criterion of judgment on intervention as a China-wide policy; and even though the Archbishop of Canterbury promised to take up the matter with the C.M.S. upon his return to England, there is no evidence of any concrete measures of reform being taken.[55]

The Foreign Office thus let pass one more opportunity to establish some sort of standard for missionary conduct. Nevertheless, the missionaries themselves were not unaware of the need to set up some norm for missionary and convert conduct; this was especially true with regard to interference in Chinese courts of justice.

In 1896 English and American missionaries of Fukien, eighty strong, gathered at their summer retreat and drew up a pastoral letter addressed to their Chinese converts. The pastoral outlined a twelve-point program

---

[47] Minute attached to Lewenhampt to Salisbury, Swedish Legation, Oct. 30, 1895. F.O. 17/1263.

[48] Allen to Beauclerk, Foochow, Feb. 1, 1896. F.O. 17/1260.

[49] Ibid.

[50] Villiers' Minute to this dispatch. Allen to Beauclerk, Foochow, Feb. 1, 1896. F.O. 17/1260.

[51] Salisbury's Minute of May 9, 1896. F.O. 17/1291.

[52] Tonge to Salisbury, London, June 29, 1896. F.O. 17/1291.

[53] Allen's Intelligence Report, Foochow, June 30, 1896. F.O. 17/1291.

[54] Ibid.

[55] Archbishop of Canterbury to Salisbury, Ireland, Sept. 30, 1896. F.O. 17/1291.

to be followed by their converts so as to foster better relations with Chinese officials. Chief emphasis was placed on the fact that in ordinary legal action the Chinese convert might expect no aid from the missionaries. In cases where religious liberty was threatened the convert was advised to turn first to the Chinese authorities for redress; and even if certain properties were extorted from the convert because of his religion, he should not turn to the missionary or consul for aid. Finally, only in cases of "severe persecution" might the consul be appealed to for assistance.[56]

Without a doubt the pastoral constituted a worthy statement of principles for the conduct of the missionaries and their fold. It was, however, merely advisory in nature and represented the views of one particular group of missionaries in one province of China. Then too, the thin line between "severe persecution" and those forms of harassment which were to be readily endured would be difficult to establish in practice. Still, it was a good instrument and it gave the Foreign Office a renewed opportunity to take up the question of missionary conduct.

True to form the Foreign Office chose to remain passive. No attempt was made to use this pastoral as a guide for missionary conduct throughout China. Yet Whitehall did act upon the pastoral in a negative manner. It was suggested that certain objectionable portions of the pastoral be toned down. In itself this suggestion was wise, for the missionaries had rather crudely referred to "the superstitious belief and practices of the heathen." And, worse, by implication they were advising their converts to accept the persecutions of the Chinese regime as a passing phenomenon. For, as the pastoral put it, "As the people become Christianized then gradually Christian law and methods will become possible and can prevail." [57]

Chinese officials could hardly be expected to regard this as anything but a thinly veiled declaration of war upon their centuries-old system of government. But even here the Foreign Office was easily put off in its effort to correct the pastoral. The lay secretary of the C.M.S., who was asked to eliminate the objectionable portions of the pastoral, replied that while he would endeavor to obtain the required modifications the pastoral had its origin in China and the society's control over these far-off missionaries was limited.[58] Even this minor gesture of control by the Foreign Office was frustrated.

On at least one occasion, however, the pastoral did prove to be helpful to a British consul in smoothing over relations with the Chinese. In March 1897, a Chinese prefect complained to Consul Allen that the missionaries were attracting converts who relied on their status as Christians to undertake "arrogant and violent actions." [59] Allen passed on to the prefect a copy of the pastoral letter. The Chinese was so delighted by the restraints which were urged upon the converts that he circulated notice of it to all his underlings and issued a proclamation specifying the duties of the local officials toward the converts. [60] But again Allen's use of the pastoral merely constituted his individual approach to the missionary problem. In no sense was it an indication that the Foreign Office had adopted it as a norm for regulating missionary activity.

After 1896 one no longer comes across the detailed plans for greater missionary control which had previously cropped up with regularity in the letters of the consuls and in reports to the Admiralty. No doubt the increasing tempo of the battle for concessions and fear of an imminent partition of China did much to shift the attention of British officialdom away from the missionary problem. And undoubtedly the word had passed among the consular force that Lord Salisbury was not receptive to any suggestion which might extend responsibility and control over the missionaries. Lastly, one cannot help suspecting that, as the impression spread that the partition of China was about to take place, the British had no desire to limit their stake in China, whether it was based on commercial or missionary presence. There is no direct evidence to support this point; indeed, it is only suggested here that it was likely that such a psychological attitude was operative. But since Salisbury was determined to keep as much of China as possible open to British influence, it would have been strange indeed if he sought to limit the expansion of British influence in the case of the missionaries. Yet this was no more than a negative policy; that is, missionary penetration was in no way encouraged but plans to subdue this activity were no longer entertained.

---

[56] "Memorandum of the Fukien Missionaries to Their Respective Boards, and Pastoral Letter to the Native Christians of the Province," August 1896. F.O. 17/1225.

[57] Ibid.

[58] Minute by Francis Bertie, Nov. 13, 1896; and C.M.S. to Foreign Office, London, Nov. 3, 1896. F.O. 17/1291.

[59] Allen to MacDonald, Foochow, March 25, 1897. F.O. 17/1368.

[60] Ibid.

To sum up, Foreign Office efforts to control British missionaries in China in the 1890's were fitful, tentative, and feeble. The Liberal Government, under Rosebery, gave evidence of a certain concern to rationalize missionary procedures. But in attempting to implement its designs it was no more effective than the Conservatives who stood aloof from any concerted plan of missionary control. Both governments accepted the necessity of some form of passport control over the missionaries, but this really rested on the local decision of the consul. Both governments would on occasion transmit admonitions to the various mission headquarters in London, but these carried no note of compulsion. Any effort to extend control was, in part, politically inexpedient; neither government could afford to offend the church groups, especially the nonconformists, who had the organization to exert considerable pressure at election time.

Finally, the primary factor in this hands-off attitude toward the missionaries lay deep within the whole concept of British empire; in fact, it was an essential element in the whole liberal concept of government. The free play of individual effort had raised Britain to greatness on the domestic scene; free trade and the enterprise of uncontrolled agents had helped to raise a new and greater empire overseas. To limit or control missionary activity, then, went against this system as a whole and British officials naturally tended to reject such restrictions.

CHAPTER IV

British Efforts to Control the Chinese

IT BECAME part of the nebulous give-and-take relationship between Britain and China that the Western nation would only
support her missionaries in an indirect and limited manner. Indirect because interference by British arms to suppress the antimissionary outbreaks would diminish the sovereign status which Britain desired China
to maintain; limited because the unstable Manchu dynasty could only
withstand so much outside pressure, and the demise of that regime seemed to promise only chaos for China.

When instances involving the loss of mission property or the murder
of a missionary arose, the British relied on an accepted formula of reparation. Monetary compensation would be demanded for the missionary society involved, and punishment was to be inflicted by the Chinese authorities on the culprits. Compensation was paid with relative
dispatch but the missionaries frequently complained that the actual
rioters escaped. Any effort to secure the punishment of the officials or
gentry who were often believed to be behind the riots would expand a
missionary case into a major diplomatic incident. As more serious missionary outbreaks confronted the British, they saw the need to force the
Chinese to reprimand their own officials. This, however, could only be
achieved by threatening the already weakened Manchu regime.

[65]

Gardner's Forward Efforts

In the wake of each large-scale antimissionary rising there came increased efforts to root out the cause of the perplexing outbreaks. After the riots of 1891 Christopher Gardner, the British consul in Hankow, was convinced that acceptance of the usual compensation constituted an inadequate preventive. This expansionist-minded consul led the way first in a campaign to stamp out the provocative antimissionary literature and then in efforts to quell the unrest in the turbulent province of Hunan.

Appropriately enough it was a missionary who gave impetus and direction to Gardner's fight to suppress the propaganda literature. This commanding personage was Rev. Griffith John, a patriarchal figure of mountainous energy who from his headquarters in Hankow directed the work of the London Missionary Society in Central China.[1] The missionary and the consul came to constitute an alliance dedicated to forwarding what Gardner liked to call the work of "Christendom."

In 1891, after supplying Gardner with information on the location of some distributors of the antimissionary literature, Dr. John suddenly unearthed evidence about the source of the material.[2] It was in the form of a letter from a certain Chou Han to the governor of Hupeh. The letter urged the release of one of Chou's followers, imprisoned for distributing the vile literature. Chou announced that he was responsible for printing and distributing the pamphlets, the purpose of which was to stamp out false doctrine. If anyone were to be punished for this Chou claimed that he should be the first.[3] Dr. John noted that Chou had thus obtained his agent's release and he urged Gardner to apprehend Chou, the real cause of the riots.[4]

While Gardner pressed for the arrest of Chou Han, Dr. John gathered more evidence. This led to a pawnshop in Ch'ang-sha, the capital of Hunan; here was the center for the distribution of the literature.[5] On the basis of these discoveries the foreign representatives in Peking jointly demanded action against the Ch'ang-sha pawnshop.[6] Early in December the governor-general of Hunan and Hupeh had the pawnshop owners arrested. But before the month was out Chou Han's influence was sufficient to obtain their release.[7]

By this time, however, Whitehall was determined that the instigators of the riots should be sought out. This was in part due to Gardner's relentless insistence that the riots must be throttled. And his word was strengthened by Sir Halliday Macartney, British secretary at the Chinese legation in London, who warned that only a strong stand would halt the riots. He told Sir Thomas Sanderson in a private conversation that the whole antiforeign movement was an attempt by the *literati* and mandarins to force a treaty revision. He insisted that the native converts would be their first target and that the missionaries and merchants would be next.[8] As a result Sanderson sent a memorandum to Salisbury urging that the Chinese be made to realize that the British Government was in earnest. Salisbury agreed that Walsham should be instructed to push for the punishment of the pawnshop owners and guilty officials. But knowing the limits imposed by Britain's loose dominion in China he inquired cryptically of Sanderson: "What do you mean by making the Chinese understand we are in earnest?"[9] There was no answer since Sanderson knew that Britain's position in China allowed no full-fledged implementations of power.

In any case Walsham was ordered to press his case against the pawnshops. And when Dr. John's evidence against Chou Han reached the Foreign Office his arrest was also demanded.[10]

But this determination slowly ebbed away. In January 1892, the Tsungli Yamen promised Walsham that it would address a special memorial to the throne — if it was necessary — to ensure the prosecution of Chou Han.[11] In February the Tsungli Yamen pleaded that it required more time to move against the Hunan propagandists.[12] In March, Salisbury agreed to make allowances for the "difficulties" encountered by the Chinese Government in bringing Hunan to order.[13] By June, Gardner was able to report that Chou Han had been degraded and that he would be placed under supervision; that the society in Ch'ang-sha

---

[1] R. Wardlaw Thompson, *Griffith John: The Story of Fifty Years in China* (New York: A. C. Armstrong and Son, 1906), p. vii.
[2] Gardner to Salisbury, Hankow, Oct. 22, 1891. F.O. 17/1128.
[3] Gardner to Salisbury, Hankow, Oct. 20, 1891. F.O. 17/1128.
[4] John to *North China Daily News*, Hankow, Oct. 22, 1891. *A.F.R.*, p. 201.
[5] John to *North China Daily News*, Hankow, Nov. 6, 1891. *A.F.R.*, p. 205.
[6] *A.F.R.*, p. 263.
[7] John to *North China Daily News*, Hankow, Dec. 28, 1891. *A.F.R.*, p. 213.
[8] Minute by Sanderson, Foreign Office, Dec. 7, 1891. F.O. 17/1129.
[9] Minute by Salisbury, Foreign Office, Dec. 7, 1891. F.O. 17/1129.
[10] Salisbury to Walsham, Foreign Office, Dec. 10 and 13, 1891. F.O. 17/1129.
[11] Walsham to Salisbury, Peking, Jan. 27, 1892. F.O. 17/1129.
[12] Walsham to Salisbury, Peking, Feb. 29, 1892. F.O. 17/1129.
[13] Salisbury to Walsham, Foreign Office, March 2, 1892. F.O. 17/1147.

which distributed the vile literature had been disbanded; and that several of the blocks used in printing the antimissionary literature were to be burned publicly.[14] But the next couple of months proved this settlement to be illusory.

Indeed the British had accepted a good deal less than half a loaf. Chou Han had been degraded but his supervision was a farce, for his name continued to be connected with the distribution of antiforeign literature through the decade. One distribution point may have been closed, but before the summer was over antimissionary posters were up in Ch'angsha by the thousands.[15] And so few of the printing blocks were confiscated in Hankow that Gardner refused to witness their public burning.[16] All the British had done was to decrease momentarily the intensity of the distribution of antiforeign literature. But since the riots which racked the Yangtze Valley had subsided the British reduced their pressure on the Tsungli Yamen. The balance necessary for informal empire was, for the moment, preserved.

A dogged attempt to pursue the riots to their cause might have permanently ruptured the delicate relationship between England and China. This danger, however, was ignored by Gardner as he laid out fresh plans to flush the rioters from their lair in Hunan. Again Gardner and Rev. Griffith John were working along similar lines. At almost the same moment that Gardner presented his new proposal to the Foreign Office, Dr. John wrote his London headquarters urging radical action by the foreign Powers.[17]

Gardner's program, submitted in October 1891, called for the elimination of antimissionary outbursts by proving that the "force of Christendom is irresistible."[18] As a first step he would have the treaty rights of missionaries cut upon stone tablets and set up around the Empire, especially in Hunan. He would have the foreign consuls make calls upon the provincial officials and require that these visits be returned with the proper courtesy. And he would establish a British consulate in Ch'angsha until the instigators of the outbreaks were captured and punished. At the same time he tried to convince the Foreign Office that the laxity of the Tsungli Yamen had contributed to the spread of antimissionary literature. But Salisbury agreed with Sanderson that Gardner's condemnation of the Yamen was "too severe"; no move was to be contemplated until more substantial evidence was available.[19]

Gardner was persistent. In November he urged a peaceful demonstration of the power of "Christendom" in Ch'ang-sha; and in January 1892, he again detailed his whole program, including the temporary residence of a consul in Ch'ang-sha to see that treaty (missionary) obligations were observed.[20] In February he went so far as to warn the governor-general in Wu-sung that "serious action" by Britain might follow if the agitators were not dealt with. At virtually the same moment Salisbury was rejecting Gardner's call for strong pressure on the Chinese with the comment that joint action was not desirable at that time.[21] In March, and again in June, Gardner plagued the Foreign Office with his plans for more active measures in Hunan.[22]

Having received no backing in Whitehall, Gardner proceeded on his own initiative with his scheme to bring order to Hunan. He was driven on by the belief that once Hunan was open to Western influence its fierce opposition to the missionary either would cease or could be controlled. He was equally convinced that Hunan would offer an inviting market for British manufacturers.[23]

In August 1892, Gardner decided that he could best forward his cause by personally visiting Ch'ang-sha. Immediately the Chinese Government raised objections in London to this proposed visit. It complained that Gardner had announced that he would proceed to Ch'ang-sha with two gunboats by way of Tung-t'ing Lake and that he proposed to suppress the antimissionary literature himself.[24] Lord Rosebery, the new

[14] Gardner to Salisbury, Hankow, June 11, 1892. F.O. 17/1147.

[15] Gardner to Salisbury, Hankow, Sept. 19, 1892. F.O. 17/1148.

[16] Gardner to Salisbury, Hankow, June 11, 1892. F.O. 17/1147.

[17] John to Thompson, Hankow, Sept. 28, 1892. L.M.S./CC/1891, No. 6.

[18] Gardner to Gervoise, Hankow, Oct. 26, 1891. F.O. 17/1128.

[19] Minute by Sanderson to Gardner to Salisbury, Hankow, Oct. 31, 1891. F.O. 17/1128.

[20] Gardner to Salisbury, Hankow, Nov. 17, 1891. F.O. 17/1129. Gardner to Salisbury, Hankow, Jan. 27, 1892. F.O. 17/1146. Rev. Griffith John was working along parallel lines. In January 1892, he informed the L.M.S. of the need for Britain to push China to suppress the antiforeign propaganda in such a way that "the Chinese Government would feel bound to obey." On receipt of this the L.M.S. called a meeting (April 1892) to unite the English mission societies in an appeal to Lord Salisbury to bring pressure on the Chinese Government. While evidence is incomplete it would seem that the mission societies failed to come together in backing this measure. Thompson to S.P.G., London, April 14, 1892. S.P.G. Letters, 1892, No. 20.

[21] Gardner to Viceroy, Hankow, Feb. 6, 1892; and Minute by Salisbury, Foreign Office, Feb. 22, 1892. F.O. 17/1146.

[22] Gardner to Salisbury, Hankow, March 18 and June 11, 1892. F.O. 17/1147.

[23] Gardner to Gervoise, Hankow, June 13, 1892. F.O. 17/1147.

[24] Minute by Sanderson, Foreign Office, Aug. 19, 1892. F.O. 17/1148.

Liberal foreign secretary, telegraphed Gardner to halt this move. In reply Gardner claimed that he had merely proposed a friendly visit to the governor of Hunan and that this was quite in accord with regulations; he had intended to proceed in a single vessel and had now postponed his trip pending the approval of the new governor.[25]

However much Gardner might protest, his plan hardly constituted a friendly move. His correspondence with the Hunan governor in preparation for the visit gave ample proof that the consul was forcing the trip in spite of all Chinese objections. As Lord Rosebery observed, he could not, even on Gardner's own evidence, approve his conduct.[26]

There were limits beyond which the Foreign Office would not step in pressuring the Chinese. It would not permit Gardner to precipitate a major crisis by bursting into Hunan. It rather chose to bow to Chinese protests. The Chinese then attempted to push home their objections: they asked that Gardner be removed from Hankow for his threatening attitude toward Hunan and his "exaggerated" reports on the 1891 riots.[27] By mid-October the Foreign Office had gathered together the various correspondence bearing on this incident. Sanderson concluded that, while Gardner's actions were injudicious and even unfriendly, he had not threatened to go to Ch'ang-sha with two gunboats. He suggested that the Chinese might be persuaded to withdraw the demand for Gardner's removal. Later the consul might be transferred to another post where the strain would be less, and a man of "more solid judgment" could be sent to Hankow.[28]

In November, Rosebery set down his final word on the affair. He informed Gardner that the legality of his visit to Ch'ang-sha was not denied, but that he "doubted the expediency of exercising it in the manner proposed." [29] As expected, the Chinese withdrew their demand for Gardner's removal.[30] He was forthwith transferred from Hankow to Seoul, Korea, which, ironically enough, soon became a post of greater strain than Hankow.

In retrospect this incident demonstrated that the Foreign Office was determined to occupy a middle position with regard to intervention in Chinese affairs. It would not relinquish the theoretical right to move its gunboats where it pleased in China, nor would it consent to humble its consul under Chinese pressure. On the other hand, it would not permit the machinations of an aggressive-minded consul to raise the struggle for missionary rights to a new height of intensity.

Compensation and Retribution

The Foreign Office sought to avoid such extravagant modes of action as Consul Gardner had proposed. In the wake of a given antimissionary riot the British consul in the area affected was usually satisfied if compensation for property loss was forthcoming and if steps were taken to capture and punish the rioters. While the seriousness of the offense and the ability of the missionary group to bring pressure on the Foreign Office influenced the vigor of demands for reparation, most incidents were considered closed after proper compensation had been paid.

The procedure in these cases had become somewhat uniform. The consul obtained from the missionaries an estimate of the damage they had sustained both in property and in personal effects; and, if physical injury was involved, this, too, was added to the total. In minor cases, an adjustment of conflicting demands might be worked out between the British consul and the local authorities. In the more serious disturbances, settlement on the local level was impossible and the issue had to be worked out between the British minister and the Tsungli Yamen. After some haggling a payment of approximately the sum demanded was agreed to, the actual payment being extracted from the foreign-controlled Chinese customs revenues.[31] This amount was then passed on to the missionaries.

Certain missionary groups declined to claim compensation; in fact, this was the regular policy of the China Inland Mission.[32] But most missionaries considered that it was only just that they receive equitable compensation for their property losses. Some few tended to push their demand for compensation beyond reasonable limits. Such instances

---

[25] Gardner to Rosebery, Hankow, Aug. 20, 1892. F.O. 17/1148.

[26] Minute by Rosebery, Foreign Office, Oct. 3, 1892. F.O. 17/1148.

[27] Rosebery to Walsham, Foreign Office, Aug. 29, 1892. F.O. 17/1148.

[28] Minute by Sanderson, Foreign Office, Oct. 15, 1892. F.O. 17/1149.

[29] Minute by Rosebery, Foreign Office, Nov. 25, 1892. F.O. 17/1149.

[30] Chinese Legation to Foreign Office, London, Dec. 21, 1892. F.O. 17/1149. The Chinese Government was quite justified in its fears of Gardner. While the Foreign Office was considering his transfer he continued to urge a "bold course" in China; he insisted that Asiatics do not understand philanthropy in politics and would attribute magnanimity to fear. If Britain did not act some other nation (France) would, and such a war, he warned, would have a disastrous effect on the commerce of Lancashire. Gardner to Gervoise, Hankow, Sept. 19, 1892. F.O. 17/1148.

[31] O'Conor to Salisbury, Peking, Aug. 29, 1895. F.O. 17/1262.

[32] C.I.M. to Foreign Office, London, March 2, 1892. F.O. 17/1147.

led the Chinese to regard all missionary claims with suspicion; and one more irritant was added to Anglo-Chinese relations.[33]

The case of medical missionary Dr. James Grieg, of the Presbyterian Church of Ireland, testified to the abuse which could develop. In August 1891, soldiers of the Tartar general of Manchuria attacked and brutally beat Grieg. For a time Grieg hovered near death, and the British minister demanded a considerable amount in compensation. But once Grieg had recovered and consulted with his society in Ireland, he requested a compensation far exceeding that which the minister had demanded of the Tsungli Yamen.[34] Grieg included in his estimate the salary he would have received had he still been on duty as a medical missionary, and he demanded a grant of land in Manchuria for his new hospital.[35] His claim was supported in London by a delegation of Liberal Unionists from Ireland who sought unsuccessfully to gain an interview with Lord Salisbury.[36] In mid-1892, when a Liberal victory placed Lord Rosebery in the Foreign Office, he too faced steady pressure in favor of Grieg. In Parliament, Mr. T. W. Russell called for the settlement of Grieg's claims.[37] Finally, Rosebery was provoked to comment in a confidential minute: "I must confess it is something of a comedown from St. Francis Xavier and one's early missionary ideals to this good man's schedule and to the perhaps more amazing claim of his Church for the temporary loss of his service."[38]

Not until late 1893 was the Grieg case finally settled. Sir Nicholas O'Conor, who was then minister in Peking, forced through a settlement with Foreign Office backing which satisfied neither the Tsungli Yamen nor Grieg. O'Conor replied sharply to Grieg's objections that while he was aware of his parliamentary support both the public interest and the interests of missionaries in general required this compromise settlement.[39]

The Chinese Government would, for the most part, readily grant reasonable claims for compensation. But British demands for the punishment of the rioters met with evasive and, at times, unyielding opposition. The Tsungli Yamen faced such demands with a litany of excuses: that lengthy investigations were necessary, that most of the rioters were merely ignorant and foolish, that the ringleaders had fled, and that punishment would simply encourage rebellious elements. When the Chinese did reply that a certain number had been degraded, banished, or executed there was no way of checking the reliability of the statement.

Indeed the missionaries often claimed that those executed were criminals already condemned for other offenses, but they could offer no evidence to support these charges.

There was every reason for the Chinese to avoid punishing their subjects. To assume the role of executioner for the West could only degrade the regime in the eyes of its countrymen, and to punish the ignorant who took to violence in defense of the ancient values of China seemed unjust. But most of all the Manchu Government could not afford to chastise those *literati* and officials, high and low, who encouraged or fomented the riots; to do so would alienate their own supporters and tend to unite the *literati* with the anti-Manchu secret societies.

The British were not completely insensitive to these difficulties. Normally they would accept the word of the Chinese concerning those executed and punished. At least that had been the case in the riots of 1891. Then, too, there was a tendency on the part of both the British and Chinese to drop a missionary case once compensation was forthcoming. In those more serious cases where the death of a British subject was involved there was a more substantial effort by the British to force the capture of the culprits. This practice was encouraged by the missionaries who came to insist that compensation be accepted only after proper punishments were imposed.

The murder of the two Swedish missionaries at Sung-p'u in Central China in 1893 brought all these unresolved approaches to the problem to the forefront. Speaking for the English population, the Shanghai *Mercury* blamed the murders on the "flabby consular officials" who let the riots of 1891 go unpunished.[40]

A series of "indignation meetings" were held at the various treaty

---

[33] Minute by Sanderson, Foreign Office, Feb. 11, 1893. F.O. 17/1171.

[34] Walsham to Salisbury, Peking, Aug. 8, 1892. F.O. 17/1128.

[35] *Ibid.*

[36] Liberal Unionist Association to Barrington, London, Aug. 5, 1892. F.O. 17/1148.

[37] Foreign Office Minute of Aug. 11, 1892. F.O. 17/1148. For later questions in Parliament on Grieg see Minutes of Feb. 9 and June 8, 1893 (F.O. 17/1171); and Sept. 4, 1893 (F.O. 17/1172).

[38] Minute by Rosebery, Foreign Office, Sept. 3, 1892. F.O. 17/1148.

[39] O'Conor to Grieg, Peking, Aug. 30, 1893. F.O. 17/1172. For an equally difficult case of missionary compensation consult the claims of the Reverend Mr. Cockburn arising from the I-ch'ang riot of 1891. O'Conor to Rosebery, Peking, Jan. 13, 1893. F.O. 17/1171.

[40] *Shanghai Mercury*, July 8, 1893. Clipping in F.O. 17/1172.

ports, culminating in a giant conclave of the merchants and missionaries in Shanghai on July 18. This meeting with its Biblical indignation, coarse jeers, and ready invective demonstrated the worst aspect of the missionary movement.[41] Each speaker who rose seemed determined to outdo the wrathful cry raised by the chairman who recalled Milton's exhortation: "Avenge, oh Lord, Thy slaughtered Saints!" When the chairman mentioned the name of the Swedish consul-general, Bock, who had recommended a compromise solution to reparation for the Swedes' murder, wild hisses and groans filled the hall. Then R. C. Campbell, representing the merchant community, called for Bock's dismissal. This was greeted by cheers of approval. Campbell went on to demand the punishment of the real offenders — those Chinese officials who allowed the atrocity to take place.

Next the missionary community spoke forth. Rev. J. N. B. Smith denied that their object was revenge. But he observed that if the atrocities were not stopped war itself might follow. He conjectured that the lost Swedes might still be alive had they had Gatling guns to defend themselves. Still, he cautioned, missionary societies did not deal in such weapons — they were too expensive. This was greeted by a burst of laughter, but Rev. John Stevens immediately demanded recognition. His quiet demeanor clashed with the raucous scene which surrounded him. He submitted that the last thing he would desire was a Gatling gun and that he did not share the feeling of those who were demanding vengeance. Before Smith could conclude he was greeted by a shout that he should try to take up residence at Sung-p'u.

Both merchant and missionary agreed with a motion put by Rev. C. F. Reid. He proposed that the guilty officials must be punished before monetary compensation could be considered.

Sir Nicholas O'Conor was not impressed by these demands or by the ravings of the English-language press which, he noted, had "exhausted the resources of its slang dictionary." [42] When the British decided to join the rest of the diplomatic corps in extracting a settlement from the Chinese, its terms could not be called excessive. The two chief criminals were to suffer death by strangulation and the magistrate at Ma-ch'ang, where the crime took place, was removed from office. This appeared to be a victory for the missionaries who had demanded that the officials share in the punishment. But, in fact, the magistrate's term of office had just expired and his removal took place under circumstances which were certainly ambiguous.[43]

War and the Dangers in Peking

We have just seen that before the outbreak of the Sino-Japanese War (1894–1895) the British Government had no desire to involve itself in any prolonged dispute with China to gain compensation and punishment for attacks on missionaries. But the war heightened the danger for missionaries and brought with it the need for special measures of precaution. It also increased the possibility that when offenses occurred the British would no longer be satisfied with mere payment of compensation. Most essentially, the war opened the possibility that China would be thrown into turmoil and that such resentment against all foreigners would arise that the missionaries would have to be withdrawn to prevent a mass slaughter. Immediately after the attack by Japan the Tsungli Yamen assured O'Conor that instructions had been sent forth to the provinces especially providing for the protection of foreigners.[44] More than ever before the Chinese had reason to protect the missionaries, for the good will of the Western nations was being courted in hopes that they would press the Japanese into an equitable settlement of the conflict.

But all this did not remove the increased danger of antiforeign assaults. The Foreign Office through its consuls urged missionaries who were dwelling in the interior to return to the treaty ports.[45] Yet even after a band of Chinese soldiers on their way through Manchuria to the front had murdered a British missionary, Rev. James A. Wylie, the British shrank from making this suggestion mandatory.[46] British reluctance to enforce directives was based, in part, on the real fear that the first step toward withdrawal would encourage attacks on the native

---

[41] This account of the indignation meeting is taken from the *North China Daily News*, Shanghai, July 18, 1893. F.O. 17/1172.

[42] O'Conor to Rosebery, Peking, Aug. 16, 1893. F.O. 17/1172. The type of comment to which O'Conor referred is found in the *Shanghai Mercury* of July 8, 1893. It announced that those really responsible for the Swedes' murder were the Chinese officials and *literati* who had the foreign diplomats "by the nose." *Ibid.*

[43] O'Conor to Rosebery, Peking, Jan. 9, 1894. F.O. 17/1192.

[44] Tsungli Yamen to O'Conor, Peking, Aug. 3, 1894. F.O. 17/1227.

[45] O'Conor to Kimberley, Peking, Aug. 19, 1894. F.O. 17/1227.

[46] Bertie to Homer, London, Oct. 20, 1894. F.O. 17/1214.

Christians and the destruction of mission property. Then too, the danger seemed limited to certain areas in northeastern China.

As it turned out, the British and their missionaries simply held tight during the Japanese war and hoped for the best. Near Chefoo, where a Japanese invasion was feared imminent, the British consul relied on persuasion to bring his missionaries to the safety of the port — and such a light-handed policy was none too successful.[47] At Wenchow City the British consul pleaded with the Foreign Office to ban the travel of female missionaries in the interior, citing the case of two C.I.M. ladies who had recently been robbed in the interior while traveling without passports. Still the Foreign Office was not moved. It simply referred to the incident as "an old story" and sent a warning to the C.I.M. in London.[48] Fortunately, there was no marked increase in violence directed against the missionaries during the war; such good luck may have helped create a false illusion of safety with respect to the missionaries scattered deep in the provinces of China. In the tense period just before and during the Boxer rising in 1900, there was even less concern with the need to withdraw the missionaries to the safety of the treaty ports until Peking itself came under siege.

In 1895, in contrast to its rather lax attitude toward the missionaries in the provinces, the British Government did evince considerable concern about the safety of Peking. Here was the prime target for advancing Japanese armies and here massive hatred for all things foreign reached fever pitch. All this constituted a situation strikingly similar to that which arose on the eve of the siege of the legations during the Boxer rising of 1900. So parallel were the two crises in Peking, those of 1894–1895 and of 1900, that to contrast Manchu and European policy on these two occasions may throw some light on the relative tranquillity of 1894–1895 and the tragedy of 1900.

That during both periods there was fear of a rising in Peking is clear. In fact, it was regarded as a specific danger that, as troops were shifted from Tientsin to the front, riotous elements and antidynastic groups might turn against the foreigners.[49] As a missionary's wife put it, she and her husband feared neither the Chinese Government nor the oncoming Japanese but rather the "unbridled license of the mob" in Peking.[50] Once the rabble was without the restraining hand of the government she felt that the only chance the missionaries had was to make a last stand at the foreign legations. A sober report by British intelligence confirmed these fears. It estimated that while the distant missionary outposts were comparatively safe, Peking was the real danger spot. There the antiforeign party at court was growing in power. There the government would have increasing difficulty controlling the troops pouring in from the south. At any time the troops and the Peking mobs might join in an antiforeign outbreak. It was urged that women and children be withdrawn to Tientsin which, since it was near the coast, could be more easily defended.[51]

Britain's vigilant minister, O'Conor, was alert to the needs of the moment. Early in 1895 he brought in a legation guard of fifty men as did some of the other Powers. This was an act which could have turned both the Chinese Government and the mob against the foreigners; but it was carried out in agreement with the Tsungli Yamen, and caution was observed in determining the size and method of transporting the guard so as not to cause "public excitement."[52]

It may well have been the case that it was the Manchus themselves who had pushed the Europeans to develop their plans for safeguarding European nationals. As early as October 1894, the Chinese chargé d'affaires in Paris inquired of the French Government what protective measures the French, Russian, and British governments might undertake if the Imperial family were forced to flee Peking and leave the Europeans there to their fate. Taking the hint, Britain instigated a plan among the Powers for joint naval protection. That October, she called on France, Germany, Russia, Italy, and the United States to be prepared to block a possible "massacre of Europeans" in Peking by "prompt collective action."[53] Germany agreed and suggested that their naval commanders in the Far East pool their ships.[54] Italy and the United States fell into

---

[47] Allen to O'Conor, Chefoo, Jan. 22, 1895. F.O. 17/1260.

[48] Fraser to Kimberley, Wenchow, Jan. 18, 1895, and the Foreign Office Minute attached to this dispatch. F.O. 17/1260.

[49] Bristow to O'Conor, Tientsin, July 26, 1894. F.O. 17/1195.

[50] Letter of Mrs. Mary Simcox quoted in Isaac C. Ketler, *The Tragedy of Paotingfu* (New York: Fleming H. Revell, 1902), p. 75.

[51] Memorandum of General Chapman, Intelligence Division, War Office, "Safety of Europeans in China," Oct. 6, 1894. F.O. 17/1214.

[52] Sanderson to Macartney, Foreign Office, Dec. 31, 1894. F.O. 17/1210.

[53] Kimberley to Representatives in Paris, Berlin, St. Petersburg, Rome, and Washington, Oct. 4, 1894; and Lascelles to Kimberley, St. Petersburg, Oct. 4, 1894. F.O. 17/1214.

[54] Malet to Kimberley, Berlin, Oct. 5, 1894. F.O. 17/1214.

line.[55] And by October 8, France agreed to cooperate, but noted that she did not want to take any initiative in the scheme.[56] This reluctance was undoubtedly due to fear of offending her new ally, Russia, who did not agree to cooperate until October 14.[57]

But once the Powers came to devise detailed plans for the defense of Europeans in Peking, it was apparent that changes were required in their basic thinking. It was concluded that if serious rioting broke out in Peking the Europeans must be evacuated from the capital.[58] The combined naval Powers, it was estimated, could not detach a sufficient force from their ships to defend the legations adequately. In addition, probable Chinese reaction was taken into consideration, and it was decided that the Manchu regime would certainly not countenance the presence of such a large foreign military force in Peking. It was adjudged best, on all accounts, to evacuate the legation personnel to Tientsin if acute danger arose.

No massacre occurred in Peking during the Japanese War, but five years later in the midst of the Boxer rising the so-called rabble of the capital did join with the Imperial Army in attacking the foreign legations. Much had changed in those five years. Most significantly, not until 1900 had internal discontent reached revolutionary proportions. But there were other crucial differences. The ready cooperation between Manchu and European, evident in 1895, had been replaced by 1900 with a mutual distrust; in reality, the Manchus were fearful that the Europeans were poised to destroy their Empire. In addition, a certain concern for Chinese sensibilities, such as the caution exercised by O'Conor in his transfer of guards to Peking, was noticeably lacking.

In the uneasy sphere of international politics, cooperation between the Powers had been successful in 1895; five years later increased animosity made this impossible. In 1900, an attempt at European naval cooperation in the face of Chinese disturbances was to fail because of the mutual suspicion it created among the Powers. And the same fear prevented the Powers from undertaking an evacuation of Peking which, in 1895, had been thought necessary for the safety of European lives should the capital be overrun by mobs. In the earlier period, mutual suspicions had not yet solidified. There was still a flexibility, a willingness to cooperate which abated soon after the Sino-Japanese War.

Perhaps it was because of the thorough preventive measures taken during the war that no extensive antimissionary riots occurred at that time. The incidents which did arise were settled with dispatch on either side. For example, the murder of Mr. Wylie in 1894 by Chinese troops on their way to Korea could have led to a major diplomatic dispute. But O'Conor, though he showed some dissatisfaction with the first Chinese offer of settlement, played down the incident. And the Chinese executed Wylie's two murderers, degraded three of their officers who were involved, and offered adequate compensation.[59]

This era of relative good feeling was not to last. The tensions of the wartime period were aggravated by the impact of defeat and the immediate postwar period brought with it the most shocking missionary massacre ever endured by the English in China.

Missionaries as Officials

Before we move on to a description of the violent summer of 1895, it might be well to look beyond that date in order to discuss one final episode in which the British came close to accepting participation in an extensive system to control antiforeign agitation. On March 15, 1899, an Imperial decree was issued which granted a certain official status to the Catholic missionaries in China. It was the product of negotiations between the Catholic vicar-apostolic, Mgr. Favier, working through the French minister and the Tsungli Yamen. In this chapter we must confine ourselves to a consideration of the new procedures it set forth for the settlement of missionary disputes and how they were to affect British policy. Article Four of the edict clearly explained these new procedures: "When a grave or important missionary affair arises in any of the provinces, the Bishop and the missionaries in the place should request the intervention of the Minister or the Consuls of the Power [France] to which the Pope had confided the protection of religion . . . to avoid numerous diplomatic proceedings, however, the Bishop and the missionaries may equally address themselves at once to the local authorities with whom they may negotiate and conclude the affair." [60] Before

[55] Edwards to Kimberley, Rome, Oct. 6, 1894; and Goschen to Kimberley, Washington, Oct. 6, 1894. F.O. 17/1214.
[56] Phipps to Kimberley, Paris, Oct. 8, 1894. F.O. 17/1214.
[57] Lascelles to Kimberley, St. Petersburg, Oct. 14, 1894. F.O. 17/1214.
[58] Kimberley to Lascelles, Foreign Office, Oct. 5, 1894. F.O. 17/1214.
[59] O'Conor to Salisbury, Peking, Aug. 12, 1895. F.O. 17/1261.
[60] Henri Cordier, *Histoire des Relations de la Chine avec Les Puissances Occidentales, 1860–1902* (Paris: Ancienne Librairie Germer Balliere et C', 1902), III, 471.

the year was out it was clear the Chinese were offering similar rights to the English Protestant missionaries, and immediately the question of the status of British missionaries was thrown open.[61]

The British minister to China, Sir Claude MacDonald, pushed the Foreign Office to take up these new rights and he added that the missionaries would follow his lead in welcoming the new system.[62] The Foreign Office yielded to MacDonald's suggestion, and it seemed that at last the British were to involve themselves and their missionaries in a formalized system of control in China. The hope was that this new procedure might check antimissionary agitation, but considerations of prestige no doubt played an equally large part in this decision. Britain could not allow the French missionaries to assume virtually official status in China without losing face, and that at a time when it was supposed that the partition of China was drawing near.

Politics may have led the Foreign Office to move toward formalizing the rights of its missionaries, but this did not make the situation acceptable to the missionaries. In their own way they shared in a certain liberal repugnance for controls usually found at the Foreign Office, in this case a repugnance which was reinforced by the traditional Protestant distaste for formal governmental status. Bax-Ironside, chargé d'affaires in Peking, reported that the problem was not one of winning Chinese extension of these rights, but that the chief obstacle actually lay in the divided opinion among the mission societies about accepting them.[63]

Consular surveys of Protestant opinion indicated that the majority declined to acquire the rights of the new edict. Rev. Arnold Foster of the London Missionary Society was perhaps the most outspoken opponent of participation in the edict; he rejected the whole business as a play by Rome for political power and insisted on the moral superiority of Protestant ecclesiastical policy.[64] Rev. Griffith John of the same society thought, however, that it was necessary to partake in the edict because the Protestants could not afford to place themselves below the Catholics in the eyes of the Chinese.[65] And the Shanghai Missionary Association, 100 strong, voted with only two opposed to accept the edict.[66]

Confronted with these divergent opinions, the Foreign Office compromised. MacDonald was ordered to secure the rights of the edict for the Church of England missionaries whose hierarchical framework could more easily be adapted to Chinese official ranks. But no status would be sought for the nonconformist societies.[67] In December 1899, even these instructions were suspended when a resolution by the Anglican Communion in China reached Whitehall. It stated that the Anglican bishops had no wish "to complicate our spiritual responsibilities by the assumption of political rights. . . ." [68]

At this point Lord Salisbury sent the entire correspondence on the subject to the Archbishop of Canterbury, hoping for a conclusive decision from him. In his reply the Archbishop aligned himself with the Anglican bishops, explaining that "Even as a matter of policy it is not well to bring on ourselves a share of the resentment so many of the Chinese feel at the interference in their concerns. But, it is on grounds of principle and not merely of policy that our Bishops in China, it seems to me, have given the advice contained in the resolution." [69]

At this Salisbury terminated all efforts to place the British missionaries within the new framework of control proffered by the Chinese. Thus, on the one occasion when the Foreign Office had put aside its reluctance to formalize, even partially, the standing of their missionaries and agree on certain joint responsibilities with China with respect to curbing antimissionary agitation, the missionaries themselves spoke out to negate the move. For reasons of principle and for reasons of practical advantage the missionaries preferred to leave the settlement of missionary and convert cases, large and small, to the British consul. The situation was not without an element of paradox. The missionaries by rejecting the odium of involvement in political affairs sought to demonstrate the nonpolitical nature of their cause; however, by assuming this attitude, they may well have increased the occasions for direct intervention by British officials in the political affairs of China.

---

[61] Bax-Ironside to Salisbury, Peking, Oct. 20, 1899. F.O. 17/1379.

[62] Minute by Francis Bertie attached to Bax-Ironside to Salisbury, Peking, June 19, 1899. F.O. 17/1375.

[63] Bax-Ironside to Salisbury, Peking, Oct. 20, 1899. F.O. 17/1379.

[64] Foster to *North China News*, Wu-ch'ang, Aug. 21, 1899. F.O. 17/1379.

[65] John to Giles, Ku-ling, Aug. 5, 1899. F.O. 17/1379.

[66] Howard to MacDonald, Shanghai, Feb. 9, 1900. F.O. 17/1411.

[67] Minute by F. A. Campbell, Foreign Office, Dec. 11, 1899. F.O. 17/1379.

[68] Bishops to Bax-Ironside, Shanghai, Oct. 21, 1899. F.O. 17/1379.

[69] Archbishop of Canterbury to Salisbury, London, Feb. 16, 1900. F.O. 17/1437.

CHAPTER V

The High Tide of
Missionary Diplomacy

UNTIL 1895, it remained a moot point as to just what policy Britain might follow were a widespread and deadly antimissionary uprising to take place. It would call for skilled diplomacy to force the Manchu regime to action against the rioters without at the same time publicly humiliating the government and thereby diminishing its authority to act. Such an occasion, by embarrassing the Chinese claim to independence of decision, would do much to damage the tenuous relationship existing between Britain and China. It would also have repercussions in international politics. Once Britain brought pressure to bear on the Chinese for the sake of her missionaries, her rivals in China would undoubtedly seize the opportunity to play up their support and friendship for the Manchu. Britain was soon confronted by these very problems.

The Outbreaks of 1895

The summer of 1895 brought destruction and death to widespread groups of English missionaries. In May riots swept Szechwan, deep in the interior of China, and virtually routed the missionaries from their outposts in that province. In August, eleven missionaries, mostly women, were killed in the coastal province of Fukien, apparently by secret society members. No longer could the British content themselves with demands for monetary compensation. No longer would a weak gesture toward punishing the offenders be sufficient.

Sir Nicholas O'Conor was by his very nature the last to shirk such a challenge to British authority. This blunt Irishman had been in the diplomatic service since the age of twenty-three.[1] He was little given to the oily niceties associated with his profession. He was confident of the power he represented and he never hesitated to express clearly to his adversary just what that power implied. With the outbreaks of 1895 O'Conor faced for the first time a full-scale and unabashed challenge to the missionary movement. He threw all his energy into extracting a meaningful settlement from the Chinese. His aim was to drive home to the Chinese Britain's determination to defend her missionaries. He sought, therefore, to fasten blame for the outrage on the responsible Chinese authorities.

There was ample justification for singling out the Chinese officials in the Szechwan riots. These outbreaks originated at Ch'eng-tu, the capital of the province. There the presence of perhaps 12,000 government troops would normally have precluded any chance of riot.[2] But on May 28, as the outbreak gained momentum, the local *taotai* ignored an appeal for help from the Methodist mission. Then the governor-general himself chose to overlook the destruction of the Jesuit mission which lay adjacent to his residence.[3] The crowning offense came when a telegram was sent out on the government line declaring that the riot was caused by the abduction of a young boy by the missionaries and that the remains of other kidnapped children had been dug up within the mission. The message carried the authorization of Chou, the police superintendent of Ch'eng-tu.[4] The dispatch of such an inflammatory telegram might have unleashed a chain of riots throughout China had the officials who received the wire been inclined either to accept its accusations or cooperate in the scheme.

That no such extensive antimissionary rising took place must be cred-

---

[1] "O'Conor, N. R.," *Dictionary of National Biography*, Supplement, January 1901–December 1911, Vol. III, pp. 37–40.
[2] O'Conor to Salisbury, Peking, July 3, 1895. F.O. 17/1260.
[3] Tratman to O'Conor, Chungking, June 8, 1895. F.O. 17/1260.
[4] Tratman to O'Conor, Chungking, June 23, 1895. F.O. 17/1260.

ited to the basic good sense of the average Chinese official. But in Szechwan the riots did spread. To substantiate their charges the rioters in
Ch'eng-tu had seized a supply of tinned meats which they displayed as
the boiled remains of children; in addition, they spread the blood of
fowl and scattered a supply of bones through the mission houses.[5] This
was sufficient to stir up the smoldering anger of the people, and enraged
mobs carried destruction through the province. The missionaries fled
toward the Yangtze River where lay the supposed safety of Chungking.
But Chungking, too, was fearful of attack and the British consul was beg-
ging the aid of Chinese troops.[6]

O'Conor's first duty was to check the spread of the riots. Early in June
there was fear that the riots would be carried down the Yangtze Valley
to the coast where newly disbanded Chinese troops, released after the
Japanese war, might join in the outbreak. Without apparent qualm,
O'Conor had sent two British gunboats up the Yangtze River. He was
quite ready to threaten the bombardment of Wu-ch'ang or Nanking if
necessary to ensure the safety of British lives. This did not prove to be
necessary. His pressure on the Tsungli Yamen resulted in the proclamation of two Imperial edicts on June 5 and 11, ordering the quick re-
pression of the riots.[7]

The violence of these attacks should not be exaggerated. No British
lives were lost and no serious injuries were sustained. In Chungking, the
taotai worked closely with Consul Tratman to calm the situation. Apparently the missionaries were not totally innocent in aggravating the
riots. Indeed, one interpretation held that the riots grew from an exchange of insults between a missionary and certain Chinese during the
Dragon Boat Festival. This led to plum throwing, then stone throwing,
and finally a mob gathered outside the Canadian Methodist Mission.
The frightened missionaries used their guns and fired several shots over
the heads of the Chinese. This was to no avail and the mob swept in and
destroyed the mission. With these facts in hand, Rev. J. Haywood Horsburgh of the Church Missionary Society deplored the attitude of the
Canadians which countenanced the keeping of loaded guns on their mission premises. He contended that their use had made the mob far more
desperate in their dreadful work and seriously endangered the lives
of the missionaries and of all foreigners who might be apprehended.[8]

But the facts on which O'Conor had to act came down to these: the
authorities had, for the most part, stood by while Ch'eng-tu was rocked

by riot and in the following two weeks they had done little to prevent the spread of destruction to the countryside. The minister was convinced that exemplary punishment must be imposed upon these negligent authorities. His steady purpose was first revealed in a telegram of June 15 to the Foreign Office; he predicted that no lasting impression would be made upon the Chinese until a governor-general or mandarin was hung.[9]

O'Conor's determination to see the guilty punished was almost dissipated, however, amid Chinese administrative entanglements. On June 28, he had asked the Tsungli Yamen to cooperate in the appointment of an inquiry commission for Ch'eng-tu.[10] But with the inability of Consul Tratman to leave riot-threatened Chungking and Chinese evasions about the composition of the commission, this proposal was never carried out.[11] Soon control seemed to escape from O'Conor's hands. Chou, who had sent the antimissionary telegram from Ch'eng-tu, was promoted to acting *taotai* in Ya-an.[12] This affront was compounded toward the end of July when fresh antiforeign placards appeared in Ch'eng-tu.[13] But O'Conor had only been temporarily put off. On July 10, he had impressed upon Prince Ch'ing of the Tsungli Yamen that any high officials implicated in the rising must be punished.[14] At the same time he warned that if British lives were lost in such risings reprisals might be expected. Perhaps, however, a major catastrophe was required to bring

---

[5] *Ibid.*

[6] O'Conor to Kimberley, Peking, June 13, 1895. F.O. 17/1260.

[7] O'Conor to Kimberley, Peking, June 19, 1895. F.O. 17/1260.

[8] Horsburgh to Stock, Chungking, June 19, 1895. C.M.S./G1/CH2/P2, 1895, No. 234. There is little doubt, however, that once the attacks were underway the officials did virtually nothing to stop them. The governor-general's antiforeign attitude was well known. Then too, there was some hint of secret society involvement. One of the ringleaders in the riot, Yin Wan-shan, was head of the Pao-ko secret society. Enclosure No. 7 in Tratman to O'Conor, Chungking, June 23, 1895. F.O. 17/1260.

[9] O'Conor to Kimberley, Peking, June 15, 1895. F.O. 17/1260.

[10] O'Conor to Salisbury, Peking, July 3, 1895. F.O. 17/1260.

[11] O'Conor to Tratman, Peking, July 11, 1895. F.O. 17/1260. In 1895, however, a French inquiry was held at Ch'eng-tu which the British considered to be excessively mild in its findings. At about the same time the Americans sent an extensive mission of inquiry overland from Peking to Ch'eng-tu. Denby to Olney, Peking, Sept. 30, 1895. *F.R.U.S., 1895*, No. 2371, p. 147.

[12] O'Conor to Tsungli Yamen, Peking, July 24, 1895. F.O. 17/1260.

[13] O'Conor to Tsungli Yamen, Peking, July 30, 1895. F.O. 17/1260.

[14] O'Conor to Salisbury, Peking, July 17, 1895. F.O. 17/1260.

the Foreign Office to support O'Conor's fulminations. If so, it was not long in coming.

The Ku-t'ien Massacre

It was customary for the missionaries to seek refuge from the heat of July and August. Usually they retreated to somewhat isolated dwellings in the highlands. Mr. and Mrs. Robert Stewart of the Church Missionary Society and their family of five, all under thirteen years of age, retired to the hills near Ku-t'ien in Fukien Province during the summer of 1895. Two lady missionaries and a nurse lived with the Stewarts, and five ladies of the Zenana Society had their own cottage nearby. This innocent group became the target for what appears to have been a calculated attack by the Vegetarian secret society.[15]

There was virtually no warning. Two of the Stewart children had risen for a stroll as dawn broke. They encountered the advance runners of a party of perhaps a hundred Vegetarians moving in around the cottages. Without hesitation the Vegetarians slashed at the girls with their swords and tridents. The girls ran screaming into their house. But the Vegetarians were quick upon their heels. Neither woman nor child was spared the nip and slash of sword. The elder Stewarts were killed but one of the daughters was able to pull her brothers and sisters from the house before it was consumed by fire set by the attackers.

At the adjacent cottage the five Zenana women were ousted from bed and lined up on a slope outside. Their lives were almost saved when a friendly villager interceded for them; but, at the shout of a leader that orders were to kill them all, they were struck down. Only Miss Codrington, though terribly wounded, was able to feign death and escape alive. In all, nine of the group were killed on the spot and two of the young Stewarts died soon after. Three of the Stewart children and Miss Codrington survived with the aid of two other missionaries who lived nearby.

News of the massacre reached British officials on August 3, and instantly protection for the missionaries in the area was demanded. There could be no doubt that the Szechwan affair now compounded by the Ku-t'ien massacre would bring a period of intense strain in Anglo-Chinese relations. No longer could prompt compensation and scattered punishments smooth over a missionary outrage.

O'Conor set out to make the occurrence of such outbreaks as painful

to the Chinese authorities as to the British. At first there was some reluctance at Whitehall to follow his lead. This was especially true when
he reminded the Foreign Office that he had warned the Chinese that
reprisals would be taken. Sanderson commented that they should take
decisive action only if China delayed in moving against the outlaws
and, in any case, they must first carefully plan what action would be
taken.[16] Salisbury agreed and went on to criticize O'Conor's loose rhetoric: "What does he mean by reprisals: we can't carry off eight Chinese ladies: and we should not know what to do with them." [17]

But by the following day the tone had changed at Whitehall. A Reu-
ter's dispatch had drawn an ugly picture of the decaying situation in
China and demands for action began to pour in from missionary
groups.[18] Now O'Conor was instructed to insist that any *literati* or official who could have prevented the riots be given exemplary punishment.[19] And on the following day O'Conor was telegraphed that he
might warn the Chinese, whenever he thought necessary, that the admiral commanding British forces at the China Station would be authorized to take any measures necessary to prevent or punish such outbreaks. As further evidence that Whitehall stood ready to move against
the Chinese, O'Conor was asked to forward his views on what measures he and the admiral thought would be most expedient.[20]

O'Conor was encouraged by this attitude. He replied that warnings
could move the Chinese to action; but, if they failed, a strike at the
center of the antiforeign movement at Ch'ang-sha or Wu-ch'ang might

---

[15] The details of the description of the Ku-t'ien attack are taken from the report
of Commander J. S. Newell of the United States Navy. Denby to Olney, Peking,
Dec. 18, 1895. *F.R.U.S., 1895*, No. 2451, pp. 174–189.

[16] Minute by Sanderson to O'Conor's telegram, Aug. 5, 1895. F.O. 17/1261.

[17] Minute by Salisbury to O'Conor's telegram. F.O. 17/1261.

[18] Minute by Sanderson, Foreign Office, Aug. 6, 1895. F.O. 17/1260. A list of
the church leaders, mission groups, and similar organizations that called on the
Foreign Office to take strong measures after the Ku-t'ien massacre would include
the following: the Church Missionary Society, the Evangelical Alliance, the Free
Church of Scotland, the Presbytery of Glasgow, the Armaga Diocesan Council, the
British and Foreign Arbitration Association, the Anglican bishop of Hong Kong (a
protest to the Colonial Office), and the Wesleyan Missionary Society. Public protest meetings urging strong measures were held by the residents of the following
treaty ports: Shanghai, Foochow, Amoy, Swatow, Canton, Tientsin, and the Crown
Colony of Hong Kong. This list should by no means be considered complete. F.O.
17/1261, 1262, and 1263 *passim*.

[19] Salisbury to O'Conor, Foreign Office, Aug. 6, 1895. F.O. 17/1260.

[20] Salisbury to O'Conor, Foreign Office, Aug. 7, 1895. F.O. 17/1260.

be necessary.[21] His stand was strengthened by a cabinet decision that the mandarins whose duty it was to keep order at Ku-t'ien should be punished. And at the same time he was alerted that his government "may" take "material measures" against China if she refused his demands.[22]

In reply to Whitehall's request for advice, O'Conor suggested that the most effective move against the mandarins would be to demand the degradation and banishment of Liu Ping-ch'ang, the ex-governor-general of Szechwan.[23] He explained his motive in a private note to Sanderson: "I hope the degradation of the ex-Viceroy [governor-general] of Szechuan [Szechwan] will be effective as a few cannon balls in bringing the Chinese to their senses. We must at any price stop these horrible anti-missionary outrages." [24] Salisbury gave his immediate approval.[25] And so the settlement of the outrages at Szechwan and Ku-t'ien came to rest on O'Conor's ability to secure the degradation of the ex-governor-general.

But in spite of O'Conor's heated demands and even his threat of independent British action the Tsungli Yamen refused to punish the ex-governor-general.[26] O'Conor became convinced that a naval demonstration was essential; otherwise proper reparation for the Ku-t'ien massacre might never be forthcoming. There was a certain risk involved, but the minister was convinced that the Chinese would yield in the face of direct force. He proposed that elements of the fleet be sent up the Yangtze River to an anchorage off Wu-ch'ang. When the fleet was in position a final warning would be given.[27]

But the Foreign Office, especially under Salisbury, was not inclined to assume nonessential risks. "What do you propose," Salisbury hastily telegraphed O'Conor, "the ships should do when they get off Wuch'ang [Wu-ch'ang]?" He pointed out that it would be thought barbarous to burn an open town to procure the exile of a mandarin who lived elsewhere. He inquired if there were not a less questionable mode of expressing indignation.[28] O'Conor, however, was not to be put down. The attack, he replied, would involve no danger to Wu-ch'ang City, since it would be limited to certain forts in and near the city. He insisted that other measures would be more warlike and less effective.[29]

Next, the Admiralty raised a series of objections. To pass the Chinese forts downriver under the guise of friendship was a questionable method. To escape the guns of the same forts after bombarding Wu-ch'ang involved certain risks. To stage such an attack in peacetime might have grave consequences for the legations at Peking and for their consuls and nationals throughout China. And to enable the larger vessels to mount the river before the change in tides, action must be taken within three weeks.[30]

The cogency of these objections appealed to Salisbury. In irritation he noted that "O'Conor seems to have taken no trouble to inquire into the practicability of executing his threats."[31] Then Salisbury gave tentative approval to Sanderson's suggestion that if the Tsungli Yamen agreed to prepare a decree degrading the ex-governor-general it be allowed a certain time before being required to publish it.[32]

O'Conor would not bend. He admitted that there were risks but he was confident that the Chinese would yield. His plan was not underhanded, he argued, for the Chinese had been given warning of British intentions. He insisted that if delays were permitted the Tsungli Yamen would seek new ways to evade British demands and this would merely prolong their strained relations.[33] Salisbury could not reject such a plea from his representative in the field. He instructed the Admiralty to carry out O'Conor's directives.[34]

---

[21] O'Conor to Salisbury, Peking, Aug. 10, 1895. F.O. 17/1260.

[22] Salisbury to O'Conor, Foreign Office, Aug. 14, 1895. F.O. 17/1260. The ever cautious Salisbury had personally changed the draft dispatch from "shall" take material measures to "may" take material measures.

[23] O'Conor to Salisbury, Peking, Aug. 15, 1895. F.O. 17/1260.

[24] O'Conor to Sanderson, Peking, Aug. 15, 1895. F.O. 17/1260.

[25] Salisbury to O'Conor, Foreign Office, Aug. 15, 1895. F.O. 17/1260. This move was taken before it was possible to investigate the actual conduct of the governor-general of Szechwan. But O'Conor was convinced that he was guilty.

[26] O'Conor to Salisbury, Peking, Aug. 27, 1895. F.O. 17/1262. Weng T'ung-ho, a newly appointed minister to the Tsungli Yamen, presented this tough stand. He admitted that the governor-general was guilty of misconduct but insisted that the Yamen would act on the matter in its own good time. *Ibid.*

[27] O'Conor to Salisbury, Private, Peking, Aug. 28, 1895; O'Conor to Salisbury, Tel., Peking, Aug. 29, 1895; and O'Conor to Salisbury, Peking, Aug. 31, 1895. F.O. 17/1262.

[28] Minute by Salisbury, Foreign Office, Aug. 31, 1895. F.O. 17/1262.

[29] O'Conor to Salisbury, Peking, Sept. 3, 1895. F.O. 17/1262.

[30] Richards to Admiralty, Confidential, Admiralty, Sept. 2, 1895. F.O. 17/1262.

[31] Minute by Salisbury, Foreign Office, Sept. 5, 1895. F.O. 17/1262.

[32] Sanderson to Salisbury, Foreign Office, Sept. 5, 1895. F.O. 17/1262.

[33] O'Conor to Salisbury, Peking, Sept. 11, 1895. F.O. 17/1262. O'Conor also noted in this dispatch that the Tsungli Yamen had just gone back on its promise to publish notice of the suspension of the police superintendent of Ch'eng-tu in the *Official Gazette.*

[34] Minute by Salisbury, Foreign Office, Sept. 11, 1895. F.O. 17/1262.

Strengthened by Salisbury's backing, O'Conor engaged in a stormy interview of three hours with the Tsungli Yamen. He threatened the establishment of foreign courts of justice to handle all missionary cases. He argued that the next step would be the institution of foreign financial courts. China's independence, he warned, would be taken away piecemeal. Finally he stated that the British admiral would be on the coast of China in two days and would take action unless an edict was issued announcing the ex-governor-general's degradation by September 29.[35] Four days later, on the evening of September 29, the required edict was delivered to O'Conor.[36] Missionary diplomacy had won its greatest victory.

Success inspired O'Conor to apply the same tough policy elsewhere. He asked the admiral to move his heavy ships toward Foochow. This, he noted, would have a "wholesome effect" on the trials at Ku-t'ien where the Chinese officials were dragging their feet.[37] Within two days after the admiral's arrival off Foochow, the governor-general there asked the British consul to set his own terms concerning the fate of thirty-seven Vegetarians yet to be sentenced.[38] Next O'Conor requested that the admiral divert his ships once more, this time to forward demands for the dismissal of Chou, the police official involved in the Ch'eng-tu rising.[39] The admiral could not spare his ships from Foochow, but the Chinese took the hint. On November 1, a decree was issued dismissing Chou and written assurances were given O'Conor that he would never be employed again.[40]

In sum, O'Conor's success at obtaining punishment for Ch'eng-tu and Ku-t'ien was considerable. For the first time a high Chinese official, an ex-governor-general, had been punished for an antimissionary outbreak. Six other officials, including Taotai Chou, had been degraded because of their negligence in the Szechwan risings; as for the rioters themselves, six were executed and seventeen banished or imprisoned. By October 30, 1895, twenty-five who had participated in the massacre at Ku-t'ien had been executed and twenty-one banished or imprisoned.[41]

General Policy

O'Conor's forward approach was not confined to the manipulation of gunboats. He was aware of the need to confront the missionary problem in its broader aspects. In August 1895, he urged the Foreign Office to impose upon the Chinese new provisions for dealing with antimissionary outbreaks. These were to be directed against the literary class. They were the chief instigators of the riots but because of their official connections they had avoided punishment. Thus O'Conor proposed:

1. That officials who neglected their duties be promptly punished and that their punishment be announced in the *Official Gazette*.

2. That compensation payments be levied on the district (officials and people) and not taken from the customs revenue.

3. That no examinations for degree be held for three years in areas where serious riots occurred, and that no candidate for higher degree be accepted from these areas for three years.

4. That a town in Hunan Province be opened to trade so as to defeat the boast of Hunan men that they knew how to keep out the foreigner.[42]

O'Conor especially urged the Foreign Office to adopt the provision concerning examinations for degrees. This, he allowed, would meet the strongest resistance but it would bind the *literati* to keep order in their districts. However, as we shall see, O'Conor was transferred from Peking before he had the opportunity to press forward with this program.

Nevertheless, when the Manchus were forced to dismiss their ex-governor-general, it was a public acknowledgment of impotence. By forcing the regime to humble itself publicly O'Conor may have played into the hands of those who sought to overthrow the dynasty — those

---

[35] O'Conor to Salisbury, Tel., Peking, Sept. 30, 1895. F.O. 17/1263. The admiral in China waters had informed the Admiralty on September 28 that he had arrived off Wu-ch'ang and was awaiting O'Conor's orders. Commander in Chief, China Station, to Admiralty, Wusung (Wu-ch'ang), Sept. 28, 1895. F.O. 17/1263.

[36] *Ibid.*

[37] O'Conor to Salisbury, Tel., Peking, Oct. 2, 1895; and O'Conor to Salisbury, Peking, Sept. 26, 1895. F.O. 17/1263.

[38] Mansfield to O'Conor, Ku-t'ien, Oct. 21, 1895. F.O. 17/1264. The British asked that all these criminals be condemned to death. This was done with the understanding that clemency would be offered later but only through the British.

[39] O'Conor to Salisbury, Tel., Peking, Oct. 15, 1895. F.O. 17/1264.

[40] O'Conor to Salisbury, Tel., Peking, Oct. 24, 1895; O'Conor to Salisbury, Tel., Peking, Nov. 1, 1895. F.O. 17/1264. Full punishment was inflicted on Chou at O'Conor's insistence. The Foreign Office had, at first, been inclined to bow to the personal pleas of the Chinese minister in London for a lighter sentence. O'Conor to Salisbury, Tel., Peking, Oct. 29, 1895. F.O. 17/1263.

[41] Mansfield to O'Conor, Ku-t'ien, Oct. 30, 1895. F.O. 17/1264. The figures for the Szechwan riots record the punishments as of October 24, 1895. O'Conor to Salisbury, Tel., Peking, Oct. 24, 1895. F.O. 17/1263.

[42] O'Conor to Salisbury, Peking, Aug. 29, 1895. F.O. 17/1262.

very groups who may have unleashed the riots. To understand this possibility we must glance again at the riots.

The massacre at Ku-t'ien was, according to most European observers, the work of the Vegetarian secret society who for the previous two years had been spreading antidynastic propaganda through Fukien. The relations of the Vegetarians with the missionaries had been relatively cordial. But it seems that word was passed from the inner circle of the society that the missionaries at Ku-t'ien were to be attacked. Their mysterious leader, known as Long Finger Nails, came to the Ku-t'ien area to organize the attack. He made sure that the Stewarts were to be the victims of the onslaught and gave strict orders that all the missionaries in their compound were to be killed.[43]

Why should this antidynastic society suddenly turn on the missionaries? The motivation may not have been dissimilar to that which some claimed inspired the 1891 riots. It was evident that no rising against the Manchus could succeed as long as Britain was willing to support the regime; the failure of the Taiping Rebellion testified to that. However, if Anglo-Chinese friendship was shattered by the inability of the Manchus to prevent the slaughter of missionaries, a rising of the secret societies might successfully topple the government. The Foreign Office was not totally unaware of the possible strategy of the antidynastic groups. A missionary, Rev. John Ross, had written to Sanderson pointing out that no such movement could succeed if the Western Powers supported the Manchus, but that a revolt was possible if the Manchus were at war with the West. Sanderson thought that it was an interesting letter and asked that it be typed up for Lord Salisbury.[44]

By 1895, events seemed to be running in favor of the secret societies. Defeat by Japan had weakened the regime. Britain had failed to support China in the face of Japan's harsh peace terms. And the rising in Szechwan had increasingly strained Anglo-Chinese relations.[45] One more strike at the missionaries — especially female missionaries — might rouse the British to take active measures against the Manchus. In such a context the British were less likely to support the regime against a secret society rising.[46]

In another sphere O'Conor's forthright policy skirted dangerous grounds. There was a clear possibility that his bold tactics would push China toward friendlier relations with England's potential foes. O'Conor carried out his plans without consultation with or concern for the reaction of the other European Powers. And this took place at a time when Russia, France, and Germany had assumed a new prominence in the affairs of the Far East.

It was the Franco-Russian bloc in particular which, after forcing a modification in Japan's vindictive peace terms, sought to play the role of China's friend. France hastily accepted China's offer of compensation for the devastated Catholic missions in Szechwan.[47] They sloughed off a British proposal that they form a joint commission to investigate the Szechwan rising.[48] And they were slow to pass on to O'Conor evidence regarding the misconduct of Chinese officials in that province.[49]

Even more obstructive to British policy were the efforts of the agile and resourceful French minister, M. Gerard. He sought to confound O'Conor's efforts to degrade the ex-governor-general of Szechwan by voicing it about that his government doubted Britain's right to prescribe punishment for a Chinese official.[50] Later he suggested to the Tsungli Yamen that they should issue an edict punishing the ex-governor-general but without stating the reason.[51] This would avoid bowing di-

---

[43] *F.R.U.S., 1896*, pp. 183–185. A recent essay by Mary Backus Rankin contains the best analysis of the nature of the Vegetarian operation at Ku-t'ien. "The Ku-t'ien Incident (1895): Christians versus the Ts'ai-Hui," *Papers on China* (East Asia Regional Studies Seminar, Harvard University; henceforth referred to as *Papers on China*), XV (1961), 30–61.

[44] Ross to Sanderson, Glasgow, Aug. 13, 1895; and Sanderson's Minute to the letter. F.O. 17/1261. Denby, the American minister, was also convinced that the murders at Ku-t'ien were part of a revolutionary plot. He had warned the Tsungli Yamen that riot leaders had connections in other provinces and that their intention was to foster revolution. Tsungli Yamen to O'Conor, Peking, Oct. 3, 1895. F.O. 17/1263.

[45] The risings in Szechwan may also have been the work of secret society agitators. But while a member of the Pao-ko secret society was involved in the rising, there is insufficient evidence to establish that the risings were caused by the societies. Enclosure No. 7 in Tratman to O'Conor, Chungking, June 23, 1895. F.O. 17/1260.

[46] Reports were current that the Vegetarians in Fukien had encouraged simultaneous risings elsewhere. Tsungli Yamen to O'Conor, Peking, Oct. 3, 1895. F.O. 17/1263.

[47] O'Conor to Salisbury, Peking, Sept. 25, 1895; and O'Conor to Salisbury, Peking, Oct. 9, 1895. F.O. 17/1263.

[48] O'Conor to Salisbury, Peking, Oct. 25, 1895. F.O. 17/1263. Gerard had told the American minister that France would cooperate on a commission with the United States but not with Britain. Denby, the American minister, immediately reported this information to O'Conor. *Ibid.*

[49] O'Conor to Salisbury, Peking, Sept. 25, 1895. F.O. 17/1263.

[50] O'Conor to Salisbury, Peking, Oct. 9, 1895. F.O. 17/1263.

[51] *Ibid.*

rectly to British pressure. When O'Conor made known his plan to insist on compensation from the officials and people of a riotous district rather than accept payment from customs revenues, Gerard declared that this amounted to interference with the sovereign power of China.[52]

In fact, the artful Gerard had placed France — and indirectly Russia — in such a position that they could only profit from O'Conor's increasingly forceful missionary policy. By the summer of 1895 the Franco-Russian bloc had already received partial repayment for their assistance to China against Japan, when China contracted a loan from a Franco-Russian syndicate for partial payment of her war indemnity to Japan. It seems unlikely that missionary disputes between Britain and China were the decisive factor in China's agreement to the loan on July 6, but both events combined to bring about an estrangement in Anglo-Chinese relations.[53]

Nor should it be assumed that O'Conor's dogged determination to extract reprisals for the antimissionary outbursts was due to China's acceptance of the Franco-Russian loan. By mid-August O'Conor was fully determined to have the ex-governor-general degraded and, at that time, he still believed he could win the loan for England.[54] But discovery that the loan had already been settled could hardly have diminished his determination to get the ex-governor-general. The Tsungli Yamen had assured O'Conor that no loan would be contracted with the Russians. On this promise O'Conor left for a journey to the hills. When he learned of the loan he returned in anger to Peking. He confronted the Tsungli Yamen and denounced its duplicity in his usual frank terms. His relations with the Chinese Government were henceforth strained, and this undoubtedly increased his willingness to use force in the missionary cases. The Tsungli Yamen was so disturbed that it requested that O'Conor be removed as minister to China.[55] In November, O'Conor was moved to St. Petersburg where he took up the duties of ambassador. Only in a limited sense had O'Conor failed, for such checks to British ambitions were almost inevitable as the other great Powers pushed into China. And, apparently, the Foreign Office felt no sense of defeat in removing O'Conor to a more distinguished assignment.

O'Conor matched his forceful demands with a flexible approach to the whole missionary problem. In August 1895, he had alerted the Foreign Office to the necessity of re-examining the whole missionary problem once the current disputes were settled. Later, when the Tsungli

Yamen pointed to the necessity of readjusting the status of missionaries, O'Conor agreed to take up this problem after their present difficulties were settled.[56] His conduct was blunt and aggressive, but he recognized that the missionary problem could only be solved by negotiation. Unfortunately, before he could carry out the constructive side of his program he was transferred from Peking. This reassignment was particularly ill-timed, for his opening maneuvers had menaced the stability of the Manchu regime and had pushed the Chinese closer to Britain's foes in China. Now he was departing without having implemented his conciliatory scheme. This ended the hope that a general solution of the missionary problem would be worked out with the Tsungli Yamen. The mutual grievance caused by missionary activity was left to work itself out. And worse, efforts to eliminate or seek redress for antimissionary outbreaks would become entangled with the battle for concessions which was soon to develop among the Powers in China.

---

[52] *Ibid.* Once the governor-general was deposed, however, the French press credited Gerard and French diplomacy with the victory. Colonel Denby, the American minister, was even more vehement in claiming credit for the deposition. In a dispatch to the State Department he gave some credit to the French and British ministers, but declared that it was American efforts to send an Investigation Commission to Ch'eng-tu that forced the Chinese to issue the edict against their governor-general. Denby to Olney, Peking, Sept. 30, 1895. *F.R.U.S., 1896*, p. 150. A remark by O'Conor throws light on Denby's special zeal to claim credit for acting against the governor-general: "The missionaries have frightened my American colleague out of his senses and he wants to change and do something else with every breeze from the Ports. He avows frankly that he owes his last appointment to the missionary interest (he has been here ten years) and is bound to play up to them as much as possible." O'Conor to Foreign Office, Private, Peking, Aug. 28, 1895. F.O. 17/1262.

[53] Stanley F. Wright, *Hart and the Chinese Customs* (Belfast: William Mullan and Son, 1950), p. 659.

[54] O'Conor to Foreign Office, Private, Peking, Aug. 28, 1895. F.O. 17/1262.

[55] Wright, *Hart and the Chinese Customs*, p. 660.

[56] O'Conor to Sanderson, Private, Peking, Aug. 14, 1895. F.O. 17/1261. O'Conor to Salisbury, Peking, Aug. 27, 1895. F.O. 17/1262.

CHAPTER VI

Missionary Involvement in the Battle for Concessions

IN THE years following China's humiliating defeat at the hands of Japan in 1895, it was evident that the European Powers would soon levy their various claims upon the decaying Manchu regime. This was particularly true of the triumvirate of Russia, France, and Germany, who had forced from Japan the retrocession of the Liaotung Peninsula. Such aid was altruism at a price and, once China began to pay, the debt seemed to be boundless. Britain did not absent herself from this stark and brutal race for power and position in China, but her peculiar interests dictated a somewhat different approach. E. M. Detring, a German member of the Imperial Chinese Customs Service, set forth an apt characterization of the situation. China, he mused, might be likened to a cow. The English and Germans were milkmen whose interest lay in keeping the cow alive; the French and Russians, however, were the butchers who would seek to carve up the cow.[1]

It has been shown that Lord Salisbury rejected overly drastic action in missionary disputes for the sake of preserving the integrity of the Manchu Empire. There was, however, a tendency among certain British statesmen to regard such loosely controlled areas as China as potential segments of a greater Britain. Once the other Powers began to stake claims in China, strategic necessity combined with this latent imperialism to encourage a forward policy in China.

Sir Claude MacDonald, British minister in Peking from 1896 to 1900, was instructed in Salisbury's policy of restraint, but his very nature must have rebelled against this moderation. The tall and handsomely mustached diplomat had received his training in the military. As a major in the 7th Highlanders in Egypt and as British consul in Zanzibar and the Cameroons, he had helped carve an empire for Britain in Africa. When he arrived in China he could not but measure the scene with an eye to further expansion. In a personal letter to Salisbury, he noted that as one looked down upon Peking from the city wall "one is inclined to weep to think what could be made of the place with two companies of red coats (it would not need more) only half a battery of artillery, but the hand must be free — No 'chers collègues' — but this is only an idle dream." [2] Indeed, French counter-pressure had restrained British ambitions. But such "an idle dream" might be expected from a man who, seemingly, was George Curzon's personal choice for the post. The future viceroy of India was, at that time, a brilliant young undersecretary in the Foreign Office. He was impressed by MacDonald's work in the Niger Protectorate and recommended his "energy and capacity" to Salisbury. [3]

It fell to MacDonald, in large measure, to chart British policy as the Powers began closing in upon China. He was required to navigate the narrows which separated respect for the territorial integrity of China from the strategic requirements of maintaining Britain's position relative to the other Powers in China. MacDonald was not unaware of the unique requirements of higher policy at his new post. He soon acknowledged to Whitehall that international jealousies were much more acute in Peking than he had known them in Cairo. He pointed out that the "whip" employed by the British in Egypt — 13,000 troops — was not to be had in China. [4] However, a study of his handling of general policy as well as the missionary problem may force agreement with A. J. Balfour,

---

[1] MacDonald to Salisbury, Peking, Feb. 13, 1897. F.O. 17/1311.
[2] MacDonald to Salisbury, Peking, May 17, 1896. Salisbury Papers, A/106, No. 3.
[3] Curzon to Salisbury, Priory Reigate, Oct. 2, 1896. Salisbury Papers, Curzon Box.
[4] MacDonald to Foreign Office, Peking, Aug. 30, 1898. F.O. 17/1377.

the first lord of the treasury, who wrote to his uncle, Lord Salisbury, that as regards Chinese affairs MacDonald seemed "very obstinate and not always intelligent." [5]

Germany Defends Christendom

On November 13, 1897, German forces occupied the area surrounding Kiaochow Bay in southern Shantung. This expedition was undertaken in the supposed attempt to obtain settlement for the murder on November 1 of two German Catholic missionaries at nearby Chiach'uang. The upshot of this affair was that on March 6, 1898, the Chinese granted Germany a ninety-nine-year lease to the Kiaochow area and certain railway and mining rights in Shantung. This settlement is generally regarded as the initial strike in the battle for territorial concessions. It also gave vivid evidence of the use which could be made of attacks on missionaries.

Since 1895 Germany had been determined to acquire a port along the China coast as a coaling station and base for commercial exploitation. By the spring of 1897 German aspirations had settled on Kiaochow Bay. It was far to the north of British interests in the Yangtze area, but Russia, it was believed, had a prior claim to the harbor. In the summer of 1897, William II paid a visit to the Tsar of Russia at Peterhof. The German Emperor obtained permission to winter his squadron in Kiaochow harbor in case of necessity and after obtaining the permission of the Russian naval commander in the Far East.[6] Acting on this agreement, Germany notified Russia in September and in October that she felt the need to winter her squadron in Kiaochow, but the Russian reply was vague and evasive.[7] Each Power had interpreted the Peterhof Agreement to its own liking; in any case, it appeared that Germany would not be able to move into Kiaochow without risking rather strained relations with Russia.

Then, as if by some perverse providence, news reached William II, on November 6, of the murder of the two missionaries in southern Shantung. Now it would be difficult to deny that William had need to occupy Kiaochow. He telegraphed the Tsar as follows: "I hope, that in accordance with our personal conversation in Peterhof, you will approve the movement of my squadron to Kiao-chow [Kiaochow], for that is the only port from which it can operate against marauders, and I am under obligation to the Catholic party in Germany to show that I am in a position to come to the defense of their missionaries. Punishment is necessary and it will bring advantages to all Christians." [8]

Seemingly William's conception of the defense of Christendom was not shared by Tsar Nicholas. On November 9, Muraviev, the Russian foreign minister, informed Berlin that, while aid would be given in obtaining satisfaction for the missionaries' death, Russia retained a right of first anchorage (*droit de premier mouillage*) in Kiaochow.[9] This prior claim was supported by notification that Russian ships would go to Kiaochow if the German squadron entered the harbor.

Nevertheless, Germany proceeded to occupy Kiaochow on November 1, acting as the indisputable defender of her missionaries. Under this cover China could be pressed for the desired concessions, while Russia and Britain could be played off against each other for cooperation in the acquisition of a harbor.

In the light of Russia's determined opposition to Germany's permanent occupation of Kiaochow, Hatzfield, the German ambassador in London, was instructed to sound out British opinion. Salisbury was fully aware that his opposition to the Kiaochow occupation would push Germany to seek Russian support in acquiring a port further to the south, so when he received Hatzfield on November 17, Salisbury granted that he would not object to a German stronghold on the China coast, but, he cautioned, the further north that this point lay the better.[10]

Perhaps the Germans believed that Britain was the more pliable foe. At any rate, on November 22, the British admiral in China waters reported that Germany was prepared to occupy Samsa, an inlet which would threaten Foochow where British trade was dominant.[11] But there was no need for Germany to rush to a decision between Kiaochow

---

[5] Balfour to Salisbury, Foreign Office, Aug. 30, 1898. Salisbury Papers, Balfour Box.

[6] Memorandum of Bülow to Foreign Office, Aug. 11, 1897. *G.P.*, XIV, No. 3679, p. 58. Andrew Malozemoff has written the best analysis of the Russian side of these negotiations: *Russian Far Eastern Policy*, pp. 95–98.

[7] Tschersky to Hohenlohe, Oct. 14, 1897. *G.P.*, XIV, No. 3685, pp. 62–64; and Malozemoff, *Russian Far Eastern Policy*, p. 97. The Russians held that by the Peterhof Agreement they retained a "special interest" in Kiaochow. Minge C. Bee, "Peterhof Agreement," *Chinese Social and Political Science Review*, XX, No. 2, (1936–1937), 246.

[8] Malozemoff, *Russian Far Eastern Policy*, p. 97.

[9] Foreign Office to William II, Nov. 10, 1897. *G.P.*, XIV, No. 3693, pp. 73–74. Malozemoff, *Russian Far Eastern Policy*, p. 98.

[10] Hatzfield to Foreign Office, Nov. 17, 1897. *G.P.*, XIV, No. 3708, pp. 92–94.

[11] Commander China Station to Admiralty, Nov. 22, 1897. F.O. 17/1330.

and Samsa; she could bide her time in Kiaochow, offering as excuse the necessity of bringing the Chinese to a satisfactory settlement of the missionary dispute. By the second week of December, MacDonald reported that Russian opposition to the permanent occupation of Kiaochow had led the Germans to shift their claim to certain islands off the coast of Fukien. But the move toward Fukien may have been merely a feint; for, on December 13, the Germans returned to their earlier demands. In their negotiations with the Tsungli Yamen, as reported by MacDonald, they made firm claim to Kiaochow.[12] The following day Russia notified Germany of her intention to occupy Port Arthur; this amounted to virtual acquiescence in the German seizure of Kiaochow.[13] Undoubtedly, advance notice of this Russian move prompted the German claim to Kiaochow on December 13.

As effective as the missionary cause proved to be in this interplay between the Powers, it was perhaps even more useful as a propaganda instrument in diverting the press and world opinion. Had the German seizure of Kiaochow been carried out without the avowed purpose of protecting Christendom, fiery national emotions might have brought the Powers to the brink of war. Indeed objections were raised by the English *Times* and the French *Temps*, but these were tempered by sympathy for the German effort to obtain redress for the murdered missionaries.[14] At the first news of the German move, the Japanese press surpassed itself in violent protest. It was argued that so rapid an occupation after the murder betrayed an ulterior motive. But Sir Ernest Satow, the British minister in Tokyo, was soon able to report that newspaper objections became more moderate once it was learned that an interval of eight days separated German knowledge of the murder from the movement of her fleet.[15]

Finally, some indication of the manner by which Germany forced her territorial claims upon China was given by MacDonald. He patched together his conclusions from an interview with the Tsungli Yamen. Apparently, the basis of German strategy was to make her claim for reparations so stiff that it would be unacceptable to the Chinese. This, of course, would prolong German occupation of Kiaochow, which they ostensibly held pending settlement of the missionary outrage. Particularly irksome to China was the stipulation that Li Ping-heng, the governor of Shantung, be degraded and permanently dismissed from service. Equally distasteful was the demand that the Tsungli Yamen guarantee the prevention of all future attacks on missionaries. Of course, the violation of this guarantee would give the Germans virtual *carte blanche* for any future claim upon China.

Soon it became evident that Germany would modify these extreme demands in exchange for certain territorial concessions. Thus it was that China agreed to the lease of Kiaochow. The initial demand for the guarantee was dropped. The governor of Shantung was removed from office and degraded two ranks, but Germany quietly dropped her demand for his permanent dismissal. While the German minister in Peking claimed that he had received private assurances that Li would never be returned to service, MacDonald regarded these as of "little or no value" as a public deterrent to the further connivance by officials in antimissionary agitation.[16]

[The staunch German defense of missionary interests had served its purpose in winning territorial concessions. But, once the concessions were acquired, Germany demonstrated surprisingly little concern with the articles of settlement for the cause that first brought her into Shantung.]

Whitehall's reaction to Germany's acquisition of Kiaochow was based on realistic political criteria. While Salisbury undoubtedly would have

---

[12] MacDonald to Salisbury, Peking, Dec. 15, 1897. *P.P.*, China No. 1 (1898), No. 70, p. 26. MacDonald reported that the Germans were interested in the islands of "Peikwan" and "Nankwan" off Fukien. I have been unable to discover the proper name or location of these islands.

[13] Muraviev to Osten Saken, St. Petersburg, Dec. 14, 1897. *G.P.*, XIV, No. 3733, p. 121. Malozemoff gives an excellent analysis of the background to the Russian decision, *Russian Far Eastern Policy*, pp. 98–101.

[14] Gough to Salisbury, Berlin, Nov. 19, 1897. *P.P.*, China No. 1 (1898), No. 4, p. 2.

[15] Satow to Salisbury, Tokyo, Dec. 1, 1897. *P.P.*, China No. 1 (1898), No. 36, p. 12.

[16] This interpretation of Germany's negotiations is based on MacDonald's analysis of remarks dropped by the Tsungli Yamen during an interview. MacDonald to Salisbury, Peking, Dec. 15, 1897. *P.P.*, China No. 1 (1898), No. 70, p. 26. The original German terms of settlement as reported by MacDonald were as follows: (1) The Chinese were to erect an Imperial tablet to the memory of the missionaries who were murdered. (2) The families of the murdered missionaries were to be indemnified. (3) The governor of Shantung was to be degraded permanently. (4) The Chinese Government was to defray the cost of the German occupation of Kiaochow. (5) German engineers were to have the preference in the building of any railroads which the Chinese might construct in the Province of Shantung and also in the working of any mines along the track of such railway. MacDonald to Salisbury, Peking, Nov. 22, 1897. *P.P.*, China No. 1 (1898), No. 5, p. 2.

preferred a China free of German encroachments, he had not the power to oppose Germany, as well as France and Russia. Britain particularly feared the possibility of a Russo-German coalition which was likely to result if she took a firm stand on Kiaochow. Salisbury summed up the situation as follows: "My inclination is to think that if they stay where they are, they will act as an irritant to Russia but would not hurt us: but that if they go to Foochow we ought to obtain compensation at Chusan [Chou Shan]. Could we ask MacDonald privately to obtain the views of the Admiral on the Station as to the need for us of another coaling station besides Hongkong in Chinese waters." [17] Salisbury had no intention of joining in the battle for territorial concessions merely because the Germans might occupy Kiaochow. However, this was not a decision based on principle; he appeared to be ready to join the scramble for territorial acquisitions if the other Powers impinged on areas of special British interest.

MacDonald's reaction lacked Salisbury's firmness of mind. MacDonald was, by and large, in sympathy with the German effort to extract ample compensation from the Chinese. Constantly vexed, as he was, by the procrastinations of the Tsungli Yamen in putting down antimissionary risings, he applauded in a dispatch to Salisbury the German occupation of Kiaochow: "The effect on the security of our own people will be of the best. It seems hopeless to expect the Chinese to do their duty in protecting missionaries and discouraging anti-foreign movements unless they are forced thereto by some measure as the Germans have taken for they appear never to understand forebearance, and always interpret it as a sign of weakness." However, MacDonald was not blind to the more material aspects of the German move. His dispatch went on: "If, on the other hand, the German object is to secure Kiaochow as a naval station, under cover of demands for reparations, it is by no means clear that their acquisition of it will prejudice our interests. It is, in all events, evident from the dissatisfaction freely manifested by the Russian legation that such an outcome is resented by Russia as poaching on what she would like to have recognized as her own preserves, and there can be little question that a Shantung port in German hands is far less of a menace to the independence of China than if it were held by Russia." [18]

In short, MacDonald approved of the occupation of Kiaochow both for its usefulness in protecting missionaries and on strategic grounds.

But in the same dispatch he criticized a further German demand for commercial and mining concessions in Shantung. This, he complained, was a "novel precedent"; it would make a commercial concession the price for a missionary murder.[19] This inconsistent attitude in regard to missionary retribution tells us much about British thinking in regard to the missionary problem. Prostitution of the missionary cause might be deplored when this abuse went counter to British interests, as in the exclusive rail and mining concessions. This abuse, however, might be overlooked if it resulted in strengthening Britain's strategic position, as in the Kiaochow acquisition.

Russia and France Join In

Virtually at the invitation of Germany, Russian ships occupied Port Arthur on December 17, 1897. And on March 27, 1898, Russia obtained a twenty-five-year lease to that port as well as to the nearby port of Talienwan and a sizable portion of the Liaotung Peninsula.[20] Whitehall had realistically accepted the German entrance into Kiaochow, but British diplomats were unable to view this Russian move with like equanimity.

Russia required no holy cause to justify her entrance into Port Arthur — or at least none beyond sacred national interest. To China, Russia explained that her acquisitions were compensation for assistance rendered in 1895. To Britain, she pleaded her need for a warm water port. To both, she demonstrated sufficient power to make opposition costly.

The old hands at the Foreign Office were not thrown off balance by this Russian move. On December 23, 1897, Sir Francis Bertie, the assistant undersecretary, noted that there was no real profit in joining in the dissection of China. Salisbury agreed: "I should not take any territory, unless Russia or Germany had avowedly annexed some portion of Chinese soil. If we had to take territory, there are many claimants to our attention whom [sic] we could consider at leisure."[21] But a few days

---

[17] Minute by Salisbury, Foreign Office, Nov. 18, 1897. F.O. 17/1330.
[18] MacDonald to Salisbury, Peking, Dec. 1, 1897. F.O. 17/1312. This same dispatch, with large portions censored out, is to be found in P.P., China No. 1 (1898), No. 53, pp. 19–20.
[19] Ibid.
[20] MacDonald to Salisbury, Tel., Peking, Dec. 17, 1897. P.P., China No. 1 (1898), No. 22, p. 9.
[21] Addition by Salisbury to Minute by Bertie, Foreign Office, Dec. 23, 1897. F.O. 17/1330.

later Salisbury acknowledged that public opinion might force a compensatory acquisition.[22]

Good sense prevailed until late March 1898. Even MacDonald had pointed out that Russian occupation of Port Arthur was insignificant compared to the effect of the long Russian land frontier with respect to influencing Manchu policy in Peking.[23] Salisbury went along with this reasonable analysis; as late as March 22, he cautioned against a "violent revolution" in China policy.[24] But on March 25, MacDonald was instructed to obtain a lease of Wei-hai-wei.[25] This would, it was hoped, balance Russian influence by its position across the Gulf of Chihli from Port Arthur.

The cause of this foolishness was twofold. There was irritation at the Russian tendency to hedge on her promise to respect the treaty rights of others in Port Arthur.[26] Then, too, this decision to demand territorial compensation represented the successful conclusion of a campaign conducted by Curzon through some five cabinet meetings, in which he urged the occupation of Wei-hai-wei.[27] Perhaps it was the absence of Salisbury, who was in southern France for reasons of health, that permitted Curzon to push his policy through. Whatever the motivating factors, by April 3, 1898, China agreed to lease Wei-hai-wei to the British for as long as Russia held Port Arthur.

Now that Britain had ventured her first move in the work of partition, a further step would be difficult to resist. In December 1897, Sir Francis Bertie had laid down a reasonable policy in regard to any extension of Hong Kong: "The acquisition of additional territory at Hong Kong except for a wrong done to us by China would afford France an excuse for taking something. Would it not be sufficient to give instructions to the authorities at Hong Kong to resist by force the landing of any Foreign Naval or Military Force, or any attempt by the Chinese to put up earthworks or place guns on it [the Kowloon Promontory]? On the outbreak of hostilities we can take what we want without compensation." [28] Salisbury had agreed to this policy. But commercial interests in Hong Kong continued to clamor for an extension of territory, and, in April 1898, when France won certain territorial concessions at Kwangchow Bay, Whitehall's arguments for abstinence were weakened. As compensation for this French move, MacDonald was instructed to demand an extension of territory on the Kowloon Peninsula.[29] In June 1898, the Chinese assented to this.

Missionary interests played no real part in the British acquisition of Wei-hai-wei and the Kowloon Peninsula. Both steps were formally undertaken as compensation for the actions of the other Powers. However, these forward moves by the Powers brought interesting comments from various missionaries.

Bishop Scott of the Society for the Propagation of the Gospel reflected mission opinion in general when he welcomed the German move into Kiaochow as a step that would bring change with "wonderful rapidity." And he called for an expansion of mission work in Shantung. On the other hand, he expressed fear that the Russian entrance into Port Arthur might mean the exclusive expansion of the Orthodox Church.[30] When various mission societies raised similar fears, Whitehall could only reply that by treaty right the English missionaries might expect equal treatment in these areas of growing Russian influence.[31]

However, British officials were disturbed by an increasing tendency on the part of the French to profit by attacks on their missionaries, some of whom appeared to be remarkably attracted to martyrdom. Early in 1898, the French issued a virtual ultimatum demanding that the Tsungli

---

[22] J. L. Garvin and J. Amery, *The Life of Joseph Chamberlain* (London: Macmillan, 1933), III, 248–249.

[23] Minute by the Marquess of Salisbury, Foreign Office, March 22, 1898. *B.D.-O.W.*, Vol. I: *The End of British Isolation* (London: His Majesty's Stationery Office, 1927), No. 34, p. 22.

[24] *Ibid.*

[25] Salisbury to MacDonald, Foreign Office, March 25, 1898. *B.D.O.W.*, Vol. I, No. 39, p. 25.

[26] O'Conor to Salisbury, St. Petersburg, March 13, 1898. *B.D.O.W.*, Vol. I, No. 27, p. 19. The Russians, in fact, broke their promise and made Port Arthur a closed military port. This was not done, however, until the British made their bid for Wei-hai-wei. O'Conor to Salisbury, April 4, 1898, St. Petersburg. *P.P.*, China No. 1 (1898), No. 63, p. 151.

[27] Earl of Ronaldshay, *The Life of Lord Curzon* (New York: Boni and Liveright, 1928), III, 285. Curzon to Salisbury, April 11, 1898. Salisbury Papers, Curzon Box.

[28] Bertie to Salisbury, Foreign Office, Dec. 23, 1897. F.O. 17/1330.

[29] Balfour to MacDonald, Foreign Office, April 13, 1898. *P.P.*, China No. 1 (1899), No. 21, p. 19. Later MacDonald wrote privately to Bertie pointing out that for years the Hong Kong colonists had been buying land on the Kowloon Peninsula and that this great speculation was about to pay off. MacDonald to Bertie, Peking, April 29, 1898. Salisbury Papers, A/106, No. 10.

[30] Scott to Standing Committee, Peking, June 16, 1898. S.P.G., Asia, 1898, Vol. II "D," No. 19.

[31] Mathews, General Secretary Alliance of Reformed Churches Holding the Presbyterian System, to Salisbury, London, April 1, 1899; and Minute by Sanderson, Foreign Office, April 4, 1899. F.O. 17/1400.

Yamen settle a case involving the murder the year before of a certain Père Mazel in Kuangsi. MacDonald suspected that this was a ruse to prepare the way for the occupation of the Island of Hainan. But before the French could move the Chinese settled the case.[32]

A year after Mazel's death, a second French missionary, Père Berthollet, was murdered in the same province.[33] There is no indication in the printed French documents that the settlement of this case was linked to the grant of a concession — none beyond the coincidence that separate telegrams of the same date record the settlement of the murder case and the grant of a railway concession between Pei-hai and Hsi-chiang.[34] MacDonald informed Salisbury that he was reliably informed that Pichon, the French minister in Peking, had included the grant of the rail concession among his demands for reparations.[35]

British officials were not unduly disturbed by these maneuvers until a lengthy and destructive rebellion took place in Szechwan. This permitted the French to demand "massive compensation" for riots that undeniably had deeply injured the Christian community. In May 1899, the British chargé in Peking, Bax-Ironside, was informed by reliable sources that the French demand for compensation included a large mining concession in central Szechwan.[36] The British consul in Chungking reported that it was likely that the concession would be granted, as the missionary case gave the French extremely "strong leverage." [37] The China Association, representing British commercial interests, complained that this concession would interfere with rights accorded to the Pritchard-Morgan Syndicate in Szechwan.[38] But Salisbury calmly pointed out that the British could only object to the granting of exclusive mining privileges.[39]

The British consul in Chungking, G. J. L. Litton, summed up British opinion on these new French tactics. French commerce, he felt, was an exotic and exiguous growth; it could not hope to struggle successfully against its more healthy British competitors. As a result, he wrote, the French had resorted to contriving "factitious interests where they have no real ones and on basing political claims on missionary troubles." [40] Litton was right, but his statement was overly rhetorical. Britain, with a free-trade empire already existent in China, saw no profit in resorting to missionary claims to extend its sway. In fact, such attempts amounted to attacks on the *status quo* which they were anxious to preserve. It was, therefore, expedient for Britain to discourage such claims by others and avoid them herself.

British Entanglements

Since Britain had no need to base territorial claims on missionary troubles, here, at least, British diplomats could bolster lagging ties of friendship with China. This would allow British missionaries to demonstrate that their aims were free of political dimensions. Yet such hopes rested on the creation of a firmly guided China policy.

While missionary opinion was, for the most part, repelled by the thought of precipitating the partition of China, many believed that once the disruption of China had begun England could not stand aside. Rev. Griffith John wrote from Hankow in April 1898 that should the Yangtze Valley fall into English hands it would be "a cause of great rejoicing." [41]

---

[32] MacDonald to Salisbury, Peking, Jan. 12, 1898. F.O. 17/1333. Guillien to Hanotaux, Long-tcheou (Liu-chou), Jan. 13, 1898. *D.D.C.*, 1894–1898, No. 57, p. 43.

[33] Guillien to Hanotaux, Long-tcheou (Liu-chou), April 28, 1898. *D.D.C.*, 1894–1898, No. 68, p. 52.

[34] Pichon to Hanotaux, Peking, May 28, 1898. *D.D.C.*, 1894–1898, Nos. 73 and 74, pp. 54–55. Hanotaux had previously telegraphed to Pichon that he would inform him of the demands to be presented to the Tsungli Yamen: demands by which "our interests" would be served. Hanotaux to Pichon, Paris, April 28, 1898, *D.D.C.*, 1894–1898, No. 69, p. 53.

[35] MacDonald to Salisbury, Peking, May 21, 1898. F.O. 17/1334. On receipt of this notice Whitehall simply noted that now the French were mixing "their demands for compensation granted other powers with their own missionary cases." Minute to above dispatch, undated and unsigned.

[36] Bax-Ironside to Salisbury, Peking, May 13, 1899. F.O. 17/1374.

[37] Fraser, Intelligence Report, June Quarter, 1899, Chungking. F.O. 17/1377. Fraser's only solution to this French move was to place a British agent in Ch'eng-tu, the capital of Szechwan, to bring pressure on the Chinese when British rights were infringed. *Ibid.*

[38] Grundy to Campbell, London, May 10, 1898. F.O. 17/1401.

[39] Minute by Salisbury to Grundy's letter, Foreign Office, undated. F.O. 17/1401. One final French missionary case should be mentioned. The murder of Père Chanès in Kwangtung on Oct. 18, 1898, was linked by the French to settlement of the boundary of newly acquired Kwangchow. Pichon to Delcassé, Peking, Oct. 18, 1898. *D.D.C.*, 1898–1899, No. 70, p. 44. Pichon to Delcassé, Peking, July 19, 1899. *D.D.C.*, 1898–1899, No. 81, p. 49.

[40] Litton, Intelligence Report, Chungking, Feb. 14, 1899. F.O. 17/1373.

[41] John to Cousins, Hankow, April 6, 1898. L.M.S./CC/9, 1898. It may be noted that in 1898 there took place an attack on British commercial interests in Sha-shih, near Hankow, which resulted in the Chinese granting a commercial concession as reparation. While the commercial firms of Messrs. Jardine Matheson & Co. and Messrs. Butterfield & Squire were the chief victims, the Swedish mission at Sung-p'u also suffered destruction. Thus there was indirect missionary involvement in the

But there were other concessions aside from territorial grants that might be gained from a weakened China. Sir John Kennaway, president of the Church Missionary Society and a member of the Privy Council, inquired of Salisbury if it were not possible "now that conditions were altered" (that is, now that concessions were being forced from China), to persuade China to allow foreigners to hold land and houses outside treaty ports.[42] Kennaway was informed that missionaries already possessed this right on the basis of the most-favored-nation clause.[43] The Foreign Office chose to overlook Kennaway's obvious intention that this right be formalized and effectively enforced throughout China. Seemingly, mission pressure at home carried little weight in dictating a forward policy in China.

Still, there remained the basic fact that an attack on British missionaries might lead to military intervention which would curtail Chinese sovereignty whatever the avowed policy at Whitehall. Such an occasion had arisen at the time of the Ku-t'ien massacre in 1895. The English-language *China Daily Mail* of Hong Kong raised the cry of vengeance: "Strike deep and sharp, like Cromwell's Ironsides, exterminate root and branch, annihilate the abomination. . . ."[44]

More practical minds in Hong Kong, however, preferred to "strike deep" for territorial concessions. In September 1895, Joseph Chamberlain, the colonial secretary, passed on to Salisbury a letter from Sir William Robinson, the governor of Hong Kong. It advised that the present opportunity be grasped for extending the boundary of Hong Kong and opening the West River to trade.[45] The Foreign Office ignored the suggestion concerning Hong Kong and simply replied that Sir Nicholas O'Conor had the matter of the West River "in hand."[46]

Not until June 1898, was a treaty for the Hong Kong Extension finally signed; it was granted for purposes of defense and as compensation for a French acquisition. But it was not a clearly defined settlement: the exact position of the northern border had yet to be established. And the China Association took this occasion to urge that the border be set considerably deeper than was warranted by the original understanding.[47] Pressure was forming for a further extension of Hong Kong. It was against this background that was played out one of the most involved and bizarre episodes of British diplomacy in China, one that not only proved to be a fiasco in itself but also considerably besmirched the missionary cause in China.

[108]

The first phase of this imbroglio began in April 1899, when the British sought to raise the Union Jack in their newly won Kowloon Extension. The Chinese inhabitants rose to push out the unwelcome intruder. To pacify the area and bring pressure on the governor-general in Canton, who was thought to have secretly organized the resistance, British forces moved beyond their new border and occupied Shum Chun.[48] It was hardly a coincidence that this was the very area coveted by the Hong Kong residents and the China Association.

To the motives of strategy and of avarice there was soon added an additional complicating factor. This involved interest payments which were overdue to English investors on the Chinese-owned Northern Railway. The Chinese Government had guaranteed these payments but now was evasive in fulfilling its pact. There was no obvious connection with the seizure of Shum Chun; none, that is, until certain agile minds at the Foreign Office produced one. Both Salisbury and A. J. Balfour agreed to a proposal apparently put forth by Sir Francis Bertie that Britain should demand settlement of the Northern Railway debt and redress for the ris-

---

demand for compensation. The British included among their terms of settlement a demand that a port in Hunan be opened to trade. After considerable prodding by Pelham Warren, the British consul, the governor-general at Hankow agreed to open a port in Hunan to trade in the near future. But he did this with the understanding that it be formally disconnected with the compensations for the attacks at Sha-shih and Sung-p'u. Warren to MacDonald, Hankow, May 16 and July 13, 1898. *P.P.*, China No. 1 (1899), No. 269, p. 182 and No. 346, p. 259.

[42] Kennaway to Salisbury, Escot, Jan. 18, 1898. F.O. 17/1356.

[43] Bertie to Kennaway, Foreign Office, May 7, 1898. F.O. 17/1358.

[44] Clipping from the *China Daily Mail*, Aug. 5, 1895. F.O. 17/1263.

[45] Meade to Foreign Office, Colonial Office, Sept. 23, 1895. F.O. 17/1263. Governor Robinson took more than one extreme stand with regard to the Ku-t'ien affair. "If I am asked to find a remedy for such frightful atrocities," he wrote, "as have occurred at Ku-t'ien lately, I would point to the successful occupation of Canton from January, 1858, to October, 1861." Robinson to Colonial Office, Confidential, Hong Kong, Aug. 6, 1895. F.O. 17/1263. Finally, Robinson overstepped himself. He associated himself with the residents of Hong Kong in their criticism of Foreign Office laxity. The Foreign Office informed the Colonial Office of this improper connection, and Chamberlain sent a sharp note to Robinson calling him to order. Chamberlain to Robinson, Colonial Office, Aug. 15, 1895. F.O. 17/1261.

[46] Foreign Office Minute, Sept. 23, 1895. F.O. 17/1263.

[47] Bertie to China Association, Foreign Office, Nov. 23, 1898. *P.P.*, China No. 1 (1899), No. 398, p. 302. Bertie noted in this dispatch that the "terms of [the] convention appear sufficiently elastic to permit the rectification as a logical consequence of surveys, which have, presumably, for their object to ascertain the line along which a boundary can be most conveniently drawn."

[48] Foreign Office to Colonial Office, May 29, 1899. F.O. 17/1401. The United States Board on Geographical Names gives Shum Chun as Shen-ch'uan. But, in this case, I have retained the British usage.

ing in Kowloon as a prerequisite for the evacuation of Shum Chun.[49] On June 20, Bax-Ironside, chargé d'affaires in Peking, was instructed to make known to the Chinese this package deal.[50]

It would seem that Salisbury gave his compliance to this maneuver with great reluctance. He was subjected to pressure on all sides. From Peking, Bax-Ironside was urging the much more provocative course of a naval demonstration to secure payment of the overdue interest.[51] In Parliament, St. John Brodrick, the undersecretary for foreign affairs, had managed to postpone debate on the loan question, but pleaded with Salisbury that a time limit be set for Chinese performance.[52] To these calls for action Salisbury replied that "There must be some congruity between the grievance and the remedy." Then he pointed directly to the limitation of Britain's policy of indirect control: "Gunboats cannot . . . make or unmake Ministers. The moment the gunboats are gone the policy recommences." [53] For broader policy reasons, he was wary of this retention of Shum Chun. He cautioned the Colonial Office to occupy no greater tract of land than was necessary to keep order in Kowloon, for "any action sustaining the notion that we are dismembering China is used by the Russians at Peking to persuade [the] Yamen that we are not to be trusted." [54] But, in the final analysis, Salisbury probably reasoned that he could avoid more provocative measures by retaining Shum Chun, tying its return to the payment of the overdue interest.

It was not long before missionary affairs caused further complicated negotiations over Shum Chun. In November 1898, a British missionary, the Reverend Mr. Fleming of the China Inland Mission, was murdered by village militia in the unsettled province of Kweichow.[55] This was the first murder of a British missionary since the Ku-t'ien massacre of 1895, and the British authorities were resolved to make an example of the case. Efforts were underway to capture the village headman, T'an, who had supposedly stood by while the murder was being committed. The British-imposed time limit for T'an's capture elapsed on June 9, 1899, with the culprit still at large. The British therefore demanded the dismissal of the governor of Kweichow, whom they suspected of complicity in the crime and in T'an's escape. This demand met with a flat refusal from the Tsungli Yamen. Missionary groups and the younger officials at the Foreign Office pressed Salisbury to take decisive action. To satisfy these demands, he suggested that Shum Chun would be retained unless the governor were dismissed.[56]

At this point, Britain was occupying Shum Chun ostensibly in recompense for Chinese resistance during the occupation of the Kowloon Promontory; the Foreign Office had declared that its return depended on the payment of a heavy indemnity. However, Salisbury had instructed Bax-Ironside to inform the Tsungli Yamen that the indemnity would be dropped and Shum Chun returned upon payment of the Northern Railway debt and settlement of the Fleming murder.[57] There was a metamorphosis underway which was not as yet complete. On June 27, the Tsungli Yamen gave assurances that the railway debts were about to be paid.[58] This put the British in the position of retaining a segment of Chinese territory for the sole purpose of settling a missionary dispute.

The *raison d'être* for retaining Shum Chun had changed from a military to a financial to a religious one. At the same time, however, the viability of this claim was flaking away. Shum Chun had fallen into a state of anarchy. Strategically it proved impossible to control. Sir Henry Blake, the newly appointed governor of Hong Kong, had initially supported the Shum Chun extension, but now he urged the rapid solution of outstand-

---

[49] Minutes by Bertie and Salisbury, Foreign Office, June 5, 1899. F.O. 17/1439. Minute by Bertie, Foreign Office, June 16, 1899. F.O. 17/1402. Salisbury had previously opposed the use of direct government intervention to maintain commercial or financial concessions. In this case he departed from a statement of policy set down in April when he had indicated that "To use the fleet to collect the Hong Kong Bank's debt will bring down on us all the British capitalists in any part of the world who are being cheated by the local government." Minute by Salisbury, Foreign Office, April 17–22, 1899. F.O. 17/1401.

[50] Salisbury to Bax-Ironside, Foreign Office, Tel., June 20, 1899. *P.P.*, China No. 1 (1900), No. 187, p. 149.

[51] Minute by Bertie, Foreign Office, May 8, 1899. F.O. 17/1400.

[52] Minute by Brodrick, Foreign Office, May 8, 1899. F.O. 17/1401.

[53] Minute by Salisbury, Foreign Office, undated. F.O. 17/1401.

[54] Minute by Salisbury, Foreign Office, undated but between May 21 and 27, 1899. F.O. 17/1341. Salisbury agreed to prolong the Shum Chun occupation on May 13, 1899. Chamberlain to Blake, Colonial Office, undated. F.O. 17/1341.

[55] MacDonald to Salisbury, Peking, Dec. 9, 1898. *P.P.*, China No. 1 (1900), No. 5, p. 4.

[56] Minute by Salisbury to Dispatch by Bax-Ironside, Peking, June 15, 1899. F.O. 17/1381.

[57] Minute by Campbell, Foreign Office, June 22, 1899. F.O. 17/1402. Shum Chun was already top-heavy with claims when Governor Blake of Hong Kong urged that its return be made dependent on China's opening the West River to trade. The Foreign Office noted sharply that Shum Chun was "already fully mortgaged." Minute by Campbell, Foreign Office, June 24, 1899. F.O. 17/1403.

[58] Bax-Ironside to Salisbury, Peking, July 7, 1899. *P.P.*, China No. 1 (1900), No. 291, p. 254.

ing difficulties so that he might be rid of it.[59] Yet, as Blake was soon to observe, even the retrocession of Shum Chun would not end British involvement. Withdrawal was liable to trigger an attack by Chinese brigands on the nearby Basel Mission. If the British did not then return to protect this German mission, Germany herself would have an excuse for intervention. Here lay the danger, for the mission was located in a vitally strategic area between Hong Kong and Canton.[60] Sir Claude MacDonald, on leave in Scotland, commented with a certain sense of satisfaction that "the good people of Hong Kong had bitten off more than they could chew." [61]

But perhaps the Foreign Office had not bitten off enough. Bax-Ironside reported that the Tsungli Yamen showed "a slight indifference" over the loss of Shum Chun, and flatly rejected any action against the governor of Kweichow.[62] The chargé had then reminded the Yamen of the forceful steps that Britain had taken in 1895 to secure the dismissal of the ex-governor-general of Szechwan.[63] And in London, F. A. Campbell, the veteran chief clerk at the Foreign Office, brought to Salisbury's attention the successful use of force in 1895.[64] But, having suffered one setback, Salisbury saw little profit in doubling the stakes. And Campbell admitted that there was no use in setting another time limit for the capture of T'an unless the Foreign Office was determined to take some definite action when it elapsed.[65] Early in July 1899, Salisbury told the Chinese minister in London, Sir C. C. Lo Feng-lu, that he would allow the Yamen more time to secure the capture of T'an.[66]

Salisbury's passivity merely provoked the activists to cry more loudly. Diplomats in Peking and commercial interests in Shanghai blended their voices. Bax-Ironside called for a naval demonstration against Canton or on the Yangtze, and the China Association protested that "When the Chinese find that they can flout us in such matters as reparation for missionary outrages, are they likely to pay attention to us in graver, or rather, bigger questions?" [67] From Parliament and from Foreign Office regulars there came the same advice. Brodrick pointed out that without a naval demonstration the government would be roughly handled in the next session of the House of Commons and officials at Whitehall submitted a long memorandum recounting the successful venture in 1895 against the ex-governor-general of Szechwan.[68] Finally, MacDonald, still on leave in Scotland, wrote recommending that Salisbury present the Chinese with an ultimatum.[69]

[112]

In mid-September, Salisbury bent slightly from his stance of rock-like immobility. He warned the Tsungli Yamen that, if T'an were not captured, measures "not conducive to the independence and stability of China" might be undertaken.[70] But he would set no deadline for compliance. Perhaps this was sufficient, for on October 1, the Tsungli Yamen announced that T'an was captured and simultaneously requested the return of Shum Chun.[71] The feeling of relief at the Foreign Office can best be summed up in Campbell's comment that "We are not likely to have a better moment for handing back Shum Chun."[72] Accordingly, the British withdrew to their original boundary before the end of the year.

The conclusion of this affair was marked by the same ineptitude which marred its inception. Indeed, T'an had been captured — that was all the British had demanded; no requirement had been set down concerning the punishment to be inflicted.[73] But when the time came for his trial, he was brought before the governor of Kweichow; ironically, he was to be judged by the selfsame official who had abetted him in his initial escape. The governor promptly dismissed the charges for lack of evidence.[74] The British had retained Shum Chun and threatened a naval demonstration for the sake of a trial which exonerated the accused. At its best, the

---

[59] Minute by Campbell, Foreign Office, June 21, 1899. F.O. 17/1402. In fact, Blake's opinion on the need to retain Shum Chun shifted several times.

[60] Blake to MacDonald, Hong Kong, July 22, 1899. F.O. 17/1378.

[61] Minute by MacDonald, undated. F.O. 17/1378.

[62] Bax-Ironside to Salisbury, Peking, June 24, 1899. F.O. 17/1381.

[63] Bax-Ironside to Salisbury, Peking, June 27, 1899. F.O. 17/1381.

[64] Minute to Dispatch from Bax-Ironside to Salisbury, Peking, June 27, 1899. F.O. 17/1381.

[65] Minute by Campbell, Foreign Office, July 3, 1899. F.O. 17/1376.

[66] Salisbury to Lo Feng-lu, Foreign Office, July 3, 1899. P.P., China No. 1 (1900), No. 218, p. 172.

[67] Dugeon to Grundy, Shanghai, Sept. 7, 1899. F.O. 17/1406. Bax-Ironside to Salisbury, Peking, Aug. 10, 1899. F.O. 17/1381.

[68] Minute by Brodrick, Foreign Office, undated. F.O. 17/1381. Minute to Salisbury, Foreign Office, Aug. 24, 1899. F.O. 17/1381.

[69] MacDonald to Salisbury, N. Berwick, Aug. 26, 1899. F.O. 17/1381.

[70] Salisbury to Bax-Ironside, Tel., Foreign Office, Sept. 15, 1899. P.P., China No. 1 (1900), No. 334, p. 294.

[71] Tsungli Yamen to Bax-Ironside, Peking, Oct. 1, 1899. F.O. 17/1378.

[72] Minute by Campbell, Foreign Office, undated. F.O. 17/1381.

[73] Bax-Ironside to Salisbury, Tel., Peking, Oct. 2, 1899. P.P., China No. 1 (1900), No. 356, p. 328. Salisbury himself had admitted to the Chinese minister in London that T'an might not have actually taken part in the murder. This opened the door to the dismissal of the charges by the Chinese. Salisbury to Bax-Ironside, Tel., Foreign Office, Sept. 15, 1899. P.P., China No. 1 (1900), No. 334, p. 294.

[74] MacDonald to Salisbury, Peking, Jan. 17, 1900. F.O. 17/1411.

incident showed British policy for the protection of missionaries to be poorly thought out and carelessly executed. At its worst, it involved Britain, even if only indirectly, with Germany and France in the scramble for concessions as a form of compensation for antimissionary disturbances.

The Chinese Reaction

The reaction of the Manchu Government to these territorial claims was in some ways perplexing. The first indication of this curious response came during the negotiations with Germany over Kiaochow.

The Chinese memorial of March 1898, which bowed to the German demands, contained some mystifying passages.[75] For the murder of the missionaries it promised monetary compensation and the punishment of the guilty, including negligent officials. It also granted railway and mining concessions in Shantung in recompense for the missionary murders. But, in apparent contradiction, it noted that commercial concessions would be considered separately, and would be taken up because of the friendship existing between Germany and China. The memorial separated the lease of Kiaochow even more decisively from the missionary atrocity. A German request for a coaling station dating from February 1897 (the missionary murder was in November) was cited. The fact that China owed Germany a certain compensation for aid in the retrocession of Liaotung was mentioned. Having thus obscured the precise motivation for the concession, the memorial granted Germany the lease to Kiaochow.

The memorial satisfied German policy, inasmuch as the missionary case and the grant of concessions were somehow linked. Manchu policy was also served, for Chinese officials and *literati* who would read the memorial closely could see that the connection between the lease and the missionary case was, at best, obscure.

This was no incidental aberration. In later negotiations with France and England, the Tsungli Yamen forcefully insisted that the granting of concessions be separated from missionary outrages. In reparation for the murder of Père Berthollet the Chinese, as we have seen, allowed the French a rail concession between Pei-hai and Hsi-chiang. But these matters were taken up in separate memorials.[76] Later the French obtained mining concessions in Szechwan following the devastations visited on Christians in that province. But the Tsungli Yamen insisted that this concession was based on former demands, not on the missionary trouble.[77] Finally riots at Sha-shih gave the British an occasion to demand the opening of Hunan to trade. In granting this concession, the governor-general at Hankow insisted that it be formally separated from compensation for the riots.[78]

MacDonald's explanation, that the Tsungli Yamen was seeking to avoid the precedent of granting commercial concessions in missionary cases, was reasonable, but perhaps incomplete.[79] After all, the Germans at Kiaochow, in spite of the evasions of the Yamen's memorial, had established that precedent for all Europeans to see. And the ingenuity of the Powers in adopting such justifications was boundless. The key to this puzzle lay hidden in the complex interplay of Chinese politics: certain elements would be sharply offended by news of concessions granted in the wake of attacks on missionaries; still others would hope to profit by fanning this flame of discontent.

The educated class in most immediate contact with the missionaries, the class who were most sensitive of their prestige in relation to the missionaries, and the class from which the antimissionary propaganda sprang was the gentry.[80] They would violently oppose any disposal of Chinese territory, especially if it were done in the name of reparation for injury to missionaries. The Manchu regime was undoubtedly fearful that this class — so essential to the everyday workings of the government — might turn against rulers who would betray the soil of China in so unholy a cause. There was every reason to disguise the actual reason for granting concessions to the Powers.

It must be admitted that any conclusions in regard to the activities of the secret societies enter largely into the realm of speculation; however, a few generalizations may be ventured with a certain degree of confidence. It was evident that the societies frequently instigated antimissionary riots. Unlike the gentry, their primary aim was to create trouble for

---

[75] Memorial as translated in Denby to Sherman, Peking, March 19, 1898. *F.R.U.S.*, *1898*, No. 2884, pp. 187–190.

[76] MacDonald to Salisbury, Peking, May 27, 1898. F.O. 17/1334. However, MacDonald noted that this demand was not excessive when compared to those made by Germany.

[77] Bax-Ironside to Salisbury, Peking, June 5, 1899. F.O. 17/1375.

[78] Warren to MacDonald, Hankow, July 13, 1898. F.O. 17/1335.

[79] MacDonald to Salisbury, Peking, May 27, 1890. F.O. 17/1334.

[80] Paul A. Cohen, "The Anti-Christian Tradition in China," *Journal of Asian Studies*, XX, No. 2 (February 1961), 169–180 *passim*.

the Manchu regime. They would consider themselves especially successful if the riots which they inspired embroiled the Chinese Government in open conflict with the West.

Through much of 1898 there was real fear of rebellion. Long-standing Chinese opposition to their Manchu overlords had risen to a fever pitch because of increasing evidence of governmental incompetence. Indeed, the secret societies had sufficient strength to cause extensive outbreaks in Kwangsi in the summer of 1898.[81] At that time, the secret society rebels were sure to profit by any public display of weakness by the Manchu regime in treating missionary affairs. Even more, it might be expected that the societies would increase their efforts to spark such outbreaks in order to place the regime under one additional form of stress. If the Peking Government, however, could play down in its public declarations the connection of the missionary outrages with concessions to the Powers, the secret societies would have less reason to agitate against the missionaries and the government would be in a stronger position.

There is no attempt here to argue that all the antimissionary outbursts were part of a vast anti-Manchu plot. For example, the Fleming murder was largely a local incident involving rather primitive tribesmen. But the mysterious circumstances surrounding the murder of the German missionaries in November 1897 are worthy of examination.

Interpretations differ on the motivation of the Shantung murders.[82] However, great credibility must be given to the comments of Mgr. Anzer, the Catholic bishop of southern Shantung, who was in close touch with developments in that province. He insisted that the murders were planned and executed by members of the Big Sword secret society. His remarks, as reported in the London *Times*, lacked consistency to a certain degree, but there is no reason to doubt his statement that he had been in direct contact with leaders of the Big Sword society.[83] He argued that the secret society attack on the German missionaries had been encouraged by certain provincial officials. The monsignor's implication was that these officials were willing to run the risk of alliance with an antidynastic society for the sake of opposing the foreigner. It might be added that if this were so, here was a potentially dangerous alliance of the gentry with the secret societies, an alliance to which we will refer again in discussing the Boxer rising. The bishop claimed that some time after the murder, the Big Sword society, in some disgust, broke off its alliance with this group of antiforeign officials and gentry. To fit these facts into our tentative speculations, we may suppose that the Big Sword society had made this temporary alliance with the gentry only in order to damage the dynasty in one way or another.

Whatever the many mixed motives of the Manchu dynasty, it exerted itself through the first half of 1898 as never before to prevent further antimissionary outbreaks. In January 1898, a decree was issued strictly enjoining provincial officials to stamp out antimissionary riots. There had been analogous decrees in 1891 and 1895; but, as McDonald reported, unlike the others this was issued spontaneously.[84] It cast responsibility for enforcement directly upon the heads of the provincial governments and its commands were peremptory in tone. "One false step by local officials in dealing with them [antimissionary risings]," it announced, "gives rise to embarrassment at home and abroad."[85] It warned that small provincial troubles could grow to affect the survival of the entire state and that the latest murders had created "unbearable evils."

Confirmation of the new determination of the Manchu house came pouring in from British consular officials. From Hankow a consul reported that special attention in missionary cases had been ordered to avoid giving the British any pretext for annexing the Yangtze Valley.[86] And from Canton the British consul reported that the Chinese officials were alerted to suppress acts of banditry so that the Kiaochow incident might not repeat itself.[87]

The essential point is that the Manchu dynasty believed that it could

---

[81] L. F. Comber, *Chinese Secret Societies in Malaya*, p. 29.

[82] William L. Langer has cited evidence that the missionaries were not murdered by members of an antiforeign secret society. This contention is based on findings in an unpublished dissertation by Benjamin M. Bee: "The Leasing of Kiaochow" (Harvard University, 1935), pp. 166ff. Langer, *The Diplomacy of Imperialism* (New York: Alfred A. Knopf, 1935), p. 451, n. 14. Bee's argument was based on the reports sent to Peking by Shantung officials which blamed the crime on local bandits. But these officials had long defended the Big Sword society and could not risk accusing it of this provocative murder.

[83] "Crisis in China," London *Times*, June 9, 1900, p. 7. J. H. Laughlin, a member of the London Missionary Society, argued that the killing was the work of the Big Sword society, but attributed it to a long feud with the missionaries involved. Laughlin to Editor, Chi-ning, Nov. 8, 1897. *Chinese Recorder and Missionary Journal*, XXVIII (November 1898), p. 592.

[84] MacDonald to Salisbury, Peking, April 11, 1898. F.O. 17/1368.

[85] Memorial of January 1898. F.O. 17/1368.

[86] Warren, Intelligence Report, Hankow, March Quarter, 1898. F.O. 17/1334.

[87] Pizipios, Intelligence Report, Canton, June Quarter, 1898. F.O. 17/1335.

best preserve itself in 1898 by strict suppression of the antimissionary risings. This policy was no doubt based partly on the belief that the West, particularly Great Britain, would be an ally against dissident elements, just as she had been during the Taiping Rebellion. This essential faith in British support had not yet been dissipated.

It must also be said that strength or support for the anti-Manchu secret societies was not yet so great as to force the Manchu into any sweeping reorientation of values; nor were the bulk of gentry, as yet, the assured allies of the societies. No great tactical maneuvers were necessary to appease or buy off the secret societies and the gentry. The missionary societies could still benefit from the protection of a government which was slowly being gored from without, by the very Powers who had sent the missionaries, and eaten from within, by the antidynastic societies, who most bitterly opposed them.

What was the effect on missionary prospects of these incidents in 1897 and 1898, when the European Powers were excusing their incursions upon the China mainland by relating them to the defense of Christendom? The immediate result was fortunate for the missionaries. Strict orders were sent from Peking to the provinces to prevent antimissionary risings. Most missionaries appeared to regard the increase of European power as beneficial to their cause. Some of the British missionaries looked forward to the time when Britain would incorporate the Yangtze Valley into her empire. Others saw the beginning of partition as the dawn of civilization in China.

In the long run, however, the missionary cause was the loser. The Imperial regime, on whom the missionaries depended for their protection, saw the very group which it shielded being used as a tool against itself. Foes of the regime saw the missionary cause as the symbol of Western advance and of weakness and failure of the Manchus. Chinese of both persuasions saw the missionary cause as a weapon which was being used to shorten the life of the regime.

If these forces continued to weaken the dynasty the happy respite enjoyed by the missionaries could not last. It seemed that the best hope for stability was for Britain to assert herself as the firm friend of the dynasty. In that case the Manchus would be willing to risk much in defending the missionaries against the rising tide of hatred. To follow this course, however, the continuing assurance of the powerful, sustaining hand of the British Government would be necessary.

CHAPTER VII

Reform and Political Involvement

IN THE last two or three years of the nineteenth century relations between Great Britain and China became markedly frigid. The once trusted defenders of China's territorial integrity had joined in the division of spoils — that from a supposed friend was a specially bitter blow. Beyond this, the British, always so cautious to avoid involvement in Chinese affairs, found themselves identified as proponents of reform doctrine; in fact, they appeared to support that most hated enemy of the powerful conservative faction at the Manchu court, the Reform party of K'ang Yu-wei. In addition, Whitehall rejected a sweeping new Chinese proposal to resolve missionary troubles and continued to turn a deaf ear to consular pleas for better control of missionaries. This was not the fruit of positive British policy; rather, it resulted from that retreat from policy which was the perennial Foreign Office attitude in regard to missionary affairs.

Entanglement with the Reformers

By the authority of the young Chinese Emperor, Tsai-t'ien, a sweeping program of political, social, and economic reform was proclaimed through the Empire in the summer months of 1898. This was a belated response to the weakness revealed in the Sino-Japanese War and to China's inability to oppose the recent incursions of the West in the battle for concessions. The West was to be emulated and studied in its commerce and political administration, in its warfare and technology, in its education and social construction. But this was change with pitifully small preparation; the inspired reformer could not overthrow in a day the dead weight of almost a century of decay. Reactionary groups and others of a realistically conservative bent rallied to the Empress Dowager who was convinced that reform had gone too far. Together they threw out the hated innovators. The Emperor himself was imprisoned and his idealistic advisers either fled the country or suffered the executioner's axe. The new regime of the Empress Dowager retained elements of the reform program, including certain of its military features, but the bulk of the innovations were discarded. Even more than in the past China set her face firmly against those forces of change which threatened her traditional values.

The British Foreign Office was, on the whole, a passive observer of these events. It might hope for a modernized and thus stronger China; but it was too well advised to involve itself in the kaleidoscopic events underway in Peking. Nonetheless, British prestige suffered with the collapse of the "Hundred Days of Reform." The Empress Dowager's avowedly conservative regime had special reason to hate and fear the British along with her special enemies, the more extreme reformers. To understand this strange connection, one must examine the background of the Chinese reform movement.

The reform movement was basically Chinese in origin; in fact its philosophy was rooted in Confucianism.[1] The guiding spirit among the more radical reformers was K'ang Yu-wei. As a member of the scholar-gentry class his education was based upon the Confucian classics, but he was able to combine a continued reverence for the Chinese classics with an appreciation of the techniques and culture of the West. Beginning in 1895, he converted the *Ch'iang hsueh-hui*, known to Europeans as the "Reform Club" or the "Mutual Improvement Society," into an instrument for the propagation of his belief that without self-strengthening the country could not be saved. Affiliated societies were established in certain key cities to urge the necessity of reform based on the example of the West. Still, neither the content of the society's program nor the history of its development can be understood apart from the impact of the British missionary movement. This influence centered in and can best be seen by an examination of the role played by Rev. Timothy Richard of the Baptist Missionary Society.

Richard's relation to the reform movement was by way of propaganda literature and personal contact. He was keenly aware of the effectiveness of written works in spreading the Gospel and of the priority that should be given to reaching those on the upper rungs of society. In 1891 he became secretary of the Society for the Diffusion of Christian and General Knowledge in China. Through it he hoped to influence the ruling classes as the first step toward his ultimate goal of elevating the lot of the people of China and bringing them to God. He was quite conscious of the task before him: to mold the opinions of a group of perhaps 44,000 Chinese, composed of mandarins, high examiners, educational inspectors, and professors.[2]

The translation of significant Western works formed part of the society's activity. Richard himself wrote *The Historical Evidences of Christianity* and translated into Chinese Mackenzie's *History of the Nineteenth Century*. It is difficult to judge the influence of these works upon the reform movement, but a British Supreme Court justice passed on a telling anecdote: Count Cassini, the Russian ambassador, asked Prince Kung, president of the Tsungli Yamen, if he had read the translation of Mackenzie's book. Kung replied that he thought it was a useful book for China. Cassini's rejoinder was sharp: "Then I am afraid you have not grasped the moral of it. . . . It teaches democracy versus autocracy. If those views became current throughout China your 6,000,000 Manchus will be outvoted by the 400,000,000 Chinese, and you will have to go."[3]

In distributing this literature the society sought primarily to influence the influential. Its literature was sold at a central depot in Shanghai, but provincial capitals and examination centers were treated as other key dispensing areas. Civil servants became the recipients of special publications. Students were offered prizes for the best essays on such well-contrived topics as the advantages of railways, improved currency, and friendly foreign relations.[4]

Most influential of all was the society's monthly publication: *Wan-kuo*

---

[1] Joseph R. Levenson, *Liang Ch'i-ch'ao and the Mind of Modern China* (London: Thames and Hudson, 1959), p. 18.

[2] William E. Soothill, *Timothy Richard of China* (London: Seeley, Service and Co., 1924), p. 175.

[3] *Ibid.*, p. 214.

[4] *Ibid.*, p. 178; and Paul A. Cohen, "Missionary Approaches: Hudson Taylor and Timothy Richard," *Papers on China*, XI (1957), 50.

kung-pao (the *International Gazette* or, originally, *Review of the Times*). Under the editorship of Young J. Allen, it ran articles of general interest, with an accent on reform.[5] When the Chinese reformers established their own review in Peking, they often carried articles taken directly from the *Review of the Times*.[6] Then in February 1898, on the very eve of the "Hundred Days" the Mutual Improvement Society published its *New Collection of Tracts for the Times*. The renowned reform leader K'ang Yu-wei was represented by thirty-eight essays and his colleague Liang Ch'i-ch'ao by forty-one. Significantly, Richard was included among these Chinese reformers with thirty-one essays.[7]

Richard, of course, was never a member of the Mutual Improvement Society, but the society was receptive to his ideas and his personal contact with its members was significant. K'ang Yu-wei called on Richard in Peking in 1895. Already his great memorial to the Emperor of that year had embraced many of Richard's ideas. Now he came to ask Richard's aid in the work of regenerating China. Through that year and into 1896, Richard and his companion, Rev. Gilbert Reid, frequently dined with the reformers and discussed ideas and methods of action.[8] Later in 1896, the Emperor's tutor, Weng T'ung-ho, who was to be instrumental in paving the way for the period of reform, called on Richard. He requested that the missionary prepare for him a brief summary of his reform program.[9]

When K'ang Yu-wei rose to a position of power during the summer of reform (1898), he continued to consult Richard about appropriate measures. The missionary suggested that Marquis Ito, the great Japanese reformer, be invited to become the Emperor's adviser. Later Richard himself was called to Peking by K'ang as adviser to the Emperor. But his arrival coincided with the coup which returned the reactionaries to power in September 1898.[10] Richard's hopes of leadership were shattered.

The missionary's erstwhile colleagues K'ang Yu-wei and Liang Ch'i-ch'ao had become exiled fugitives with a price on their heads; in fact, they were regarded by the Empress Dowager as the chief criminals of the Empire.[11] But Richard, with his immunity as a British subject, remained untouched and continued to correspond with the exiled K'ang, who resided in Japan.[12] Another reformer, Ch'ing Lien-shan, transferred to Richard the title deed of his Shanghai Girls' School; thus, the missionary's immunity was extended to this reformist school.[13] Perhaps most offensive of all was the fact that the missionary journal, *Review of the*

Times, continued publication, continued, that is, to spread the same virus of reform that had necessitated the violent coup of the reactionaries. How sharply the connection between the Baptist missionary and the reform movement was felt was made clear when in 1899 the Manchu official Kang-i called on Richard in Shanghai and soundly berated him for supporting K'ang and his Mutual Improvement Society.[14]

If Britain was to preserve whatever element of understanding still existed in her relations with China, she had to take some clear and decisive action in regard to Richard's activities. But the British minister, Sir Claude MacDonald, offered neither explanation nor excuse; he neither justified nor condemned the near subversive activities of the British missionary.

MacDonald's reticence was not due to his failure to perceive the association of missionary ideas with the reform movement. He informed Salisbury that "The Manchu party evidently considers foreigners are responsible for K'ang Yu-wei's views, and consequently distrusts all those who have associated in any way with foreigners." [15] But MacDonald, perhaps unavoidably, undertook a series of moves which must have strengthened the conviction of the Manchu court that Britain had chosen to support, even if only indirectly, the hated reformers. The first occurred when he aided K'ang Yu-wei to escape from the pursuing reactionaries by flight to Hong Kong on a British vessel.[16] Another re-

---

[5] Cohen, *Papers on China,* p. 48.

[6] Soothill, *Timothy Richard of China,* p. 219.

[7] *Ibid.,* p. 242. A recent study has shown that the reform movement included various political factions, as well as moderate and extreme advocates of reform. Weng T'ung-ho represented a much more moderate approach to reform than did K'ang Yu-wei. The Empress Dowager supported some of the ideas of Weng, but she opposed K'ang Yu-wei due both to his extreme reformism and to his association with a faction supporting the Emperor. Kung-Ch'uan Hsiao, "Weng T'ung-ho and the Reform Movement of 1898," *Tsing Hua Journal of Chinese Studies,* I, No. 2 (April 1957), 112 and 140–141.

[8] Soothill, *Timothy Richard of China,* p. 219.

[9] *Ibid.,* p. 220.

[10] *Ibid.,* p. 238.

[11] Levenson, *Liang Ch'i-ch'ao and the Mind of Modern China,* p. 31.

[12] Soothill, *Timothy Richard of China,* p. 242.

[13] *Ibid.*

[14] *Ibid.,* p. 246.

[15] MacDonald to Salisbury, Peking, Oct. 13, 1898. *P.P.,* China No. 1 (1899), No. 401, pp. 306–307.

[16] Hosea B. Morse, *The International Relations of the Chinese Empire* (London: Longmans, Green and Co., 1918), III, 146.

former was saved from execution on the direct plea of MacDonald; indeed, the minister's semiofficial intervention probably helped save the life of the Emperor himself.[17] But the worst offense was yet to come. In January 1900, the reactionary court sought to raise the son of Prince Tuan, P'u-chün, to the position of heir apparent to the throne. Fearing that this might be a move toward making Emperor Tsai-t'ien expendable, the foreign representatives as a body withheld their approval, a decision which forced postponement of the reactionary plot.[18]

How is one to explain MacDonald's refusal to take notice of Richard's involvement in the cause of reform, and, later, his neglect in failing to make clear that the British Government in no way supported the reform movement? The answer may rest, in part, in certain attitudes that were prevalent among Foreign Office officials. Whitehall refused to regard the missionaries as a serious political factor; here was a failure to see that what was often to them an amusing element was a threatening force to the Manchu regime. Then too, there was the basic liberal ideology behind informal empire: others, China included, must simply accept the fact that the missionaries, as free agents, were, in most of their actions, beyond British governmental control.

The Foreign Office was aware of the sweeping plans of reform fostered by certain missionaries. But so long as the government was not involved, such conceptions were thought of as harmless, if not laughable. This was brought out with clarity in a rather exceptional exchange between Timothy Richard and George Curzon; no better confrontation of the idealist and the realist is to be found.

In 1897, Richard was on leave in England. He took the opportunity to approach the Foreign Office with his suggestions for an entirely revamped China policy. In a detailed correspondence, he outlined the achievements of his literary campaign. Yet, he pointed out, if the Chinese upper classes were to be drawn to full enlightenment an extensive program was required; a concerted effort by the consular, customs, merchant, and missionary community was essential. Already, he argued, the Reform party had accepted his program, and it had the secret allegiance of certain leading statesmen. All these forces were in sympathy with the Anglo-American influence. The Foreign Office must lead the way in ending nationalist competition and in adopting a "universal" policy for the benefit of China. Chinese tariffs should be raised and the profits used for education (which to the Chinese, he claimed, meant an English education). Grants should be given for lecture facilities. Britain had the chief responsibility in all of this, for Britain was the nation with the largest China trade. "By some such means, British influence, which notwithstanding its faults, is the best I know of in the world, may again become paramount in China." [19]

This program was placed before George Curzon, considered the Foreign Office expert on Far Eastern affairs. The tough-minded Curzon saw no relation between higher policy and this idealistic reform program. He sent the proposals on to Sanderson with the comment: "Here is a letter . . . from the cracked missionary who wanted to see you. His suggestions [reflect] his capacity to advise." [20] Richard, however, was persistent. A second letter warned that the present China policy would lead to a "frightful catastrophe." He urged the creation of a society to help China in reforming her society. Curzon greeted this as the ravings of a "mad mullah." [21]

Again in 1899, Whitehall's distaste for all-encompassing schemes of reform was made manifest. A colleague of Richard's, Rev. Gilbert Reid, approached the Foreign Office with plans for an "International Institute of China," a diversified educational institution propounding Western ideas.[22] At once low comedy seemed to replace high policy at the Foreign Office. The onerous task of conferring with Reid was gaily passed from level to level in a bumptious scramble to avoid the meeting. Finally, the irksome duty was thrust upon a senior clerk, Eric Barrington, who, it was felt, was at comparative leisure, and, as Sir John Brodrick put it, might find amusement in the meeting.[23]

It would have been too much to hope that some all-knowing policy body might combine the idealism and foresight of certain missionaries with the tempering effect of cautious political realism. Nevertheless one must attribute a certain amount of irresponsibility to the Foreign Office. No attempt was made to contact MacDonald in Peking concerning Richard's proposals, nor was the British minister instructed to assume

---

[17] Chester C. Tan, *The Boxer Catastrophe*, Columbia Studies in the Social Sciences, No. DLXXXIII (New York: Columbia University Press, 1955), p. 27.
[18] *Ibid.*, p. 57.
[19] Timothy Richard to G. N. Curzon, Aug. 4, 1897. F.O. 17/1330.
[20] Curzon to Sanderson, Foreign Office, Aug. 4, 1897. F.O. 17/1330.
[21] Richard to Curzon, London, August 1897; and Curzon to Bertie, Foreign Office, Aug. 21, 1897. F.O. 17/1330.
[22] Reid to Villiers, London, April 4, 1899. F.O. 17/1400.
[23] Minute by Brodrick, Foreign Office, undated. F.O. 17/1400.

any particular attitude with respect to the reform movement. As it happened, MacDonald was ignorant of the identity of the reform leader, K'ang Yu-wei, until the duty of saving him from the reactionaries was thrust upon him in September 1898.[24] Whitehall had rejected formal involvement in a reform program; but nothing was done to correct the impression that the work of British missionaries toward reform was a manifestation of official policy. This reform program grew apace. Its supporters temporarily gained power only to be overthrown and branded as revolutionaries and outlaws. The hate of the Empress Dowager for the more extreme reformers was matched by her suspicion of the British. The Foreign Office could ill afford to offend further the Manchu court by way of an insensitive missionary policy.

A Chance for Understanding

What might the Western powers expect with a reactionary, avowedly antiforeign government now entrenched in Peking? When the answer came it was firm and certain. No more concessions or leases would be granted. And to back up this policy proclamations were issued calling for a strong military build-up.

This new period might be characterized as one of "conservative reform."[25] A strict and constructive policy of taxation was extended through the provinces. Edicts were published ordering the build-up of the central military forces and calling for the strengthening of local militia units.[26] The liberals had opened the door to a variety of Western ideas; now the conservatives turned the tide, but they retained those reforms which would tend to strengthen China's military potential without disrupting the traditional social order. By these efforts to raise the prestige and dignity of the regime, the Empress Dowager hoped to calm the growing discontent among the masses of China and negate the aggressive designs of the Western Powers.

That this new program was not mere rhetoric became evident in March 1899, when Italy sought to emulate the other Powers in establishing a territorial concession on the Chinese mainland. The Italian minister presented to the Tsungli Yamen demands for the lease of San-men Bay, as his gunboat fleet gathered near the bay. But the Empress Dowager would not yield. In the face of this determined refusal, the minister backed down and his demands were put aside.[27] Here was proof enough that China was no longer to be bullied by the West.

[126]

Yet China could not maintain her prestige and build up her power if the West continued to confiscate her territory in compensation for attacks on missionaries. Such territorial losses might be eliminated if the role of the European Powers in settling claims for compensation following attacks could be reduced or abolished. Here, then, was part of the background of the Imperial edict of March 15, 1899, which established a new administrative procedure for missionary cases. It proclaimed:

That there may be conformity with what had been decided; Respect this!

Churches of the Catholic Religion, the propagation of which has long been authorized by the Imperial Government, having now been built in all the provinces of China, we desire to see the people and the Christian live in peace, and, in order to render the protection more easy, it has been agreed that the local authorities shall exchange visits with the missionaries under the conditions indicated below; —

1. – In the different degrees of the ecclesiastical hierarchy, the Bishops being, in rank and dignity, the equals of Viceroys [governor-generals] and Governors, it is expedient that they be authorized to demand to see the Viceroy [governor-general] and the Governor.

Vicar-General and Archpriest are authorized to demand to see Treasurers, Provincial Judges, and Taotais.

Other priests are authorized to demand to see prefects, sub-prefects, and other functionaries.

Viceroys, Governors, Treasurers, Provincial Judges, prefects of the 1st and 2nd class, independent prefects, sub-prefects, and other functionaries will naturally respond, according to their ranks, with the same courtesies. . . .

[Articles 2 and 3 specify details in regard to the procedure specified in article 1.]

4. – When a grave or important missionary affair arises in any of the provinces, the Bishop and the missionaries in the place should request the intervention of the Minister or the Consuls of the Power to which the Pope has confided the protection of religion. They will arrange and conclude the affair, either with the Tsungli Yamen or with the local authorities.

In order to avoid numerous diplomatic proceedings, however, the Bishop and the missionaries may equally address themselves at once to the local authorities, with whom they may negotiate and conclude the

---

[24] Soothill, *Timothy Richard of China*, p. 240.
[25] G. N. Steiger, *China and the Occident: The Origin and Development of the Boxer Movement* (New Haven, Conn.: Yale University Press, 1927), p. 105.
[26] Tan, *The Boxer Catastrophe*, pp. 27–30.
[27] *Ibid.*, p. 31.

affair. When a Bishop or a missionary comes to see a mandarin on an affair, the latter should negotiate it without delay in a conciliatory manner and seek a solution.

5. — The local authorities should give timely warning to the inhabitants of the place and earnestly exhort them to live in harmony with the Christians: they must not cherish hatred and cause trouble.

The Bishop and priests shall equally exhort the Christians to devote themselves to well-doing so as to maintain the good reputation of the Catholic religion, and so to act that the people may be contented and grateful.[28]

The basic strategy which inspired the Empress Dowager to issue this edict was not difficult to discern. According to the new arrangement, it was no longer the French consul who would handle the everyday Catholic missionary disturbance or dispute; rather, now that the Catholic clergy was given official status, it was the missionary himself who would settle with the Chinese directly (although in cases of grave offenses the representative of the protective power — that is, France — might still be called on for aid). This confirmed an effort to decentralize missionary affairs which was first evident in Imperial edicts published in January and early March 1899. These directed the local authorities to settle certain commercial and missionary cases on the provincial level.[29] Evidently it was hoped that the further the settlement of missionary disputes could be kept from the foreign ministers in Peking the less likely it would be that the ministers would revert to territorial demands in these cases.

G. N. Steiger, in his pioneer study *China and the Occident*, offered a more sweeping interpretation than that just suggested of the significance of the missionary edict of March 1899. He argued that these new procedures for missionary cases constituted a first step toward the absorption of the Christian religion into the framework of the Manchu Empire.[30] He offered a theoretical and a practical foundation for this thesis.

First, Steiger made reference to the historical practice of Chinese dynasties. It had been characteristic of these regimes that new religions were greeted with tolerance. Buddhism, Taoism, and Mohammedanism, he argued, were eventually amalgamated into Chinese society; and Christianity was on its way to becoming a facet of Chinese life until it became a markedly political tool in the nineteenth century.

The court reactionaries, he concluded, were making a last effort to absorb the new religion in the traditional fashion.[31] Next, Steiger pointed to the practical benefits which would accrue to China if Christianity could be detached from its political moorings. No longer would a missionary murder give excuse for the extortion of territory. No longer would anti-Christian riots trigger efforts to force the dismissal of high Chinese officials. No longer would the central government be accused of using its authority for protection of the hated foreigner.[32]

It must be said, however, that the benefits cited by Steiger (as well as elimination of the attacks on missionaries themselves) might have been achieved without the plan of amalgamation which he saw in the background. These were vital objectives for China whether or not she had any grand design. As for the historical precedents cited by Steiger, one can only say that his case is not logically or historically impossible. However, more evidence is required before his fascinating speculations can be accepted as more than a possible representation of the thinking of the Manchu court. What may be asserted with considerable confidence is this: that the edict of March 1899 constituted a practical effort by the Empress Dowager to discourage the disastrous territorial demands which had followed attacks of one kind or another upon missionaries. If such affairs could be settled locally and if the official representatives of foreign Powers were excluded from participating in as many of the settlements as possible, the central government might be free of most of those formidable demands for compensation which in the past had been laid upon it. And even if the foreign Powers demanded and got broad concessions on the local level, the higher level Manchu leaders would, at least, be free of the stigma of subservience to the West.

The reactions of the foreign Powers to this new Chinese proposal were somewhat confused, but critical analysis of these responses is rewarding, for they provide insight concerning the church-state attitudes of the two great missionary powers, France and England.

When Pichon, the French minister in Peking, negotiated the agreement with China which formed the basis of the edict of 1899, he un-

---

[28] G. N. Steiger, "China's Attempt to Absorb Christianity," *T'oung Pao*, XXIV (1926), 215–218. Henceforth referred to as *T'oung Pao*.

[29] Steiger, *China and the Occident*, pp. 93–94.

[30] *Ibid.*, p. 98; and *T'oung Pao*, p. 236.

[31] *T'oung Pao*, p. 236.

[32] Steiger, *China and the Occident*, p. 91.

doubtedly assumed he was fostering the cause of Christianity and of France — and relieving French officials of the irksome duty of endless negotiations. But critics soon appeared who condemned the new regulations as destructive of French power and detrimental to the missionaries. The knowledgeable French authority Henri Cordier believed that the position of the missionaries was weakened, for the threat of French intervention in every dispute was withdrawn.[33] René Pinon, on the other hand, writing in 1900, regarded the new system as a gain, not a retreat, for French power.[34] He emphasized that by the recent agreement there was assurance that in time of distress French, not German, intervention would be called for.

To a certain extent the Catholic missionaries were accommodating themselves to the desires of the Manchu regime. As already noted the Empress Dowager had issued edicts on January 3 and 8, 1899, which urged provincial officials to settle missionary cases on the local level without reference to Peking.[35] And it was the Empress Dowager, according to Mgr. Favier, bishop of Peking, who first proposed that negotiations be opened to give the missionaries the right to settle their own missionary cases.[36] At the same time it must be remembered that the Catholic missionaries had long desired such an arrangement. The French authorities were often lax in aiding their missionaries, and with the proper authority the missionaries might do better on their own. It should be kept in mind too that the Catholic missionary community was not completely throwing off the protection of France. Minor cases would be settled by direct negotiation. But certainly the missionaries would take advantage of the clause allowing the aid of French officials in grave incidents. The significant point is that the Catholic missionaries operated from a position of greater flexibility than their Protestant counterparts. For the Catholics, unity and direction came in large measure from the Papacy; they could undertake more easily the first step in a process which might eventually cut themselves off from their national roots.[37] Also the Catholic concept of church-state relations, wherein the prelates of an international church frequently accepted a political position for their church and themselves in a national state or monarchy, appeared to allow for the ready acceptance by Catholic missionaries of political positions in the Chinese state.

But we should not make too much of these speculations. The motivations of the various parties are still quite hazy. No one really knew what the new arrangements would lead to. More than anything else the trend of events would dictate the interpretation that might be put on the edict. Nevertheless the acceptance of the edict by the French must have raised the hopes of the Empress Dowager. The French were not necessarily entering on a great new experiment in church-state relations; but, at least, the agreement might be an opening wedge for slightly better missionary relations in the future.

When we turn to an examination of Britain's response to these new regulations, we find that G. N. Steiger is, again, virtually the only critic who has seriously analyzed the politics of the episode. He held that there was little hope of inducing the Protestant missionaries to accept similar proposals: "The more nationalistic character of their organizations and the closer ties between the missionaries and their homelands constituted almost an insuperable barrier to such a process of absorption."[38] The Protestants, according to Steiger, were basically English Protestants or American or Swedish Protestants; their nationhood was inevitably and inalienably a part of their concept of mission. They were structurally part of a foreign national movement in China.

There is a certain amount of truth in these generalizations. But, in many ways, the sharp categories of Steiger's analysis ignore the genuine differences of opinion among the British missionaries and the actual details and the flow of events which marked and determined their attitude.

On the basis of his theoretical structure of church-state attitudes, Steiger proceeded to reconstruct the attitude of the British Government and of the British missionary community to the Chinese proposals. He acknowledged that he had not had access to the British documents. But he "ventured" the opinion that the British authorities had, no doubt, "a clear appreciation" that extension of the edict to their missionaries might tend to break the close ties which linked them to the homeland.[39] Furthermore, he speculated that the British missionaries would reject

---

[33] Henri Cordier, *Histoire des Relations de la Chine*, III, 268–269.
[34] René Pinon and Jean de Marcillac, *La Chine qui s'ouvre* (Paris: Perrin et Cie, 1900), p. 142.
[35] *T'oung Pao*, p. 223.
[36] *Ibid.*, p. 222.
[37] *Ibid.*, p. 237.
[38] *Ibid.*
[39] *Ibid.*, p. 245.

any status in the Chinese state, for this would bring with it a certain responsibility to that state, which "might prove to be an opening wedge to separate them from their own national authorities." [40] He even suggested that the Archbishop of Canterbury, when notified of the possible new departures in China, would reflect on the nationalistic origins of his own Church of England and its break from central authority, and see a similar danger in China. [41]

Now that the British documents are available, what light do they throw upon these tangled motivations? They provide no clear illumination; but they offer enough information to enable us to modify, at least to an extent, Steiger's earlier contentions.

Steiger had made much of the fact that the Chinese, after they announced their new arrangements with the Catholics, turned to the British and Americans and offered them the same terms. [42] One is given the impression that there was an eager attempt to push the British into accepting the new procedures. However, the Foreign Office correspondence reveals that this was not the case. The first indication that these rights might be available to the English came in July 1899. At that time the *taotai* of Hankow instructed his subordinates to extend these rights to Protestant as well as Catholic missionaries. [43] In September the Tsungli Yamen explained to Bax-Ironside that its instructions were to extend these rights to Protestants "so far as they desired to obtain them." [44] Why, then, if, as Steiger claimed, these new procedures were beneficial to China, did the Tsungli Yamen not directly approach the British minister with an offer of this new status and its accompanying privileges?

At best, one may only speculate upon the answer. Nonetheless, there are certain leads on which to build a theory. The Tsungli Yamen had learned from experience that if British approval was required for any departure from customary procedures, it was likely that that approval would be gained only at the expense of concessions elsewhere. For example, it was known that British missionaries were desirous of obtaining the *assured* right to acquire property anywhere in China; this might be the *quid pro quo* for a new arrangement involving missionaries. That the Chinese were aware that they would have to pay somehow for British agreement is supported by the pattern of the negotiations in which they were engaged with the French before the issuance of the edict. No direct testimony is available, but it seems clear that the edict was the product of give and take between the French and the Chinese. Since we have no evidence that there was an immediate plan to bring the Christians into close association with the Chinese state, the grant of equivalent rank and status to the missionaries can best be seen as a concession to French demands. In short, what the Chinese wanted — the relegation of as many missionary cases as possible to local settlement — was exchanged for what the French wanted — the granting of official status to their missionaries.

Now the cautious Chinese approach to the British may be more understandable. They may well have thought that they might avoid granting certain painful concessions to the English if the new dispensation were only gradually extended to the missionaries from the local level on up. Moreover, when the British observed the extension of these rights to the French, they might well demand similar privileges on their own initiative. But in this case it would be the Chinese who would be doing the English a favor. In addition, the Chinese may have foreseen, knowing the temper of the English missionaries, that they would decline the offer of equivalent rank; then mission cases might be referred to the provincial level with no concession at all from the Chinese. The British did refuse status; but, unfortunately for the Chinese, in so doing they rejected the entire Chinese program.

Whatever the Chinese reasoning, the conduct of the Foreign Office in this affair evinced no understanding of the missionary mind. When Whitehall was informed that it might obtain for its missionaries rights similar to those granted the French, it took a favorable attitude, which was supported by the advice of its minister to Peking, Sir Claude Mac-Donald, who urged that the new status be sought and who vouched for the fact that it would be eagerly accepted by the British missionary community.[45] The Foreign Office instructed its chargé d'affaires in Peking, Bax-Ironside, to undertake negotiation to obtain these rights.[46] In none of this correspondence was there any evidence that the Foreign Office was fearful of cutting what Steiger referred to as the subtle

---

[40] *Ibid.*, p. 242.
[41] *Ibid.*
[42] *Ibid.*, p. 223.
[43] Taotai of Hankow to Hurst, Hankow, July 18, 1899. F.O. 17/1379.
[44] Bax-Ironside to Salisbury, Peking, Oct. 20, 1899. F.O. 17/1379.
[45] Minute by Bertie, Foreign Office, Aug. 16, 1899. F.O. 17/1375.
[46] Bax-Ironside to Salisbury, Peking, Oct. 20, 1899. F.O. 17/1379.

alliance between Britain and her missionaries. Nor did the correspondence between the Archbishop of Canterbury and Salisbury reveal any fear that the new rules would destroy the links between church and state. It was Canterbury's concern that his missionaries be kept free of Chinese political affairs [47] that prompted dropping of the negotiations with China.

The archbishop's reaction was similar to that of the majority of British in China, who voiced opposition to the proposal for official status. Their motivation seems to represent a blurred combination of self-interest and idealism. No doubt there was some truth to the view that the assumption of status in the Chinese Empire would imply a certain responsibility to that Empire.[48] This would mean allegiance to a regime which most missionaries regarded with contempt. Then, too, a remark which Steiger quoted from an American missionary applied to the English missionaries as well: that so far as the rights of status in China went, they preferred to consider themselves all bishops.[49] That is, they already had taken upon themselves, contrary to treaty, the privilege of visiting Chinese officials of the highest rank; the edict would confirm this right only for bishops. Finally, as one British missionary frankly put it, the threats or promises which were required in negotiation with the Chinese when they came from a missionary would not carry the same weight as those coming from a British consul.[50]

This, however, was not the central reason given by the British missionaries for their refusal to take part in the proposed administrative arrangements. As the British consuls began to sound out missionary opinion and as letters from missionaries appeared in the English-language press in China, it was evident that their refusal was based on principle. Missionary opinion in general agreed with the contention of the Archbishop of Canterbury that it was not the function of those engaged in spiritual work to take on political responsibilities. They felt that the assumption of such powers by the Catholic missionaries was an abuse; Protestant ecclesiology would not allow such a mingling of the temporal and the spiritual.[51] This and not any selfish consideration was the primary motivation which led the Protestant missionaries to reject the Chinese offer.

There would seem to be a basic similarity in the criteria of conduct of the British Government and their missionaries. Whitehall stood aloof from involvement in Chinese affairs; its liberal political and economic philosophy dictated a policy of informal empire. The missionary community declined to accept formal status in Chinese society; its liberal religious philosophy could not encompass such association with the political. But both diplomat and missionary appeared to be indirectly and unwillfully tending toward what they sought to avoid. This drift toward political entanglement might have been checked by acceptance of a formula specifying limited political rights. There is considerable truth in Steiger's comment concerning the edict of March 15: "Instead of being a step toward the creation of an *imperium in imperio*, as most of the Protestants have contended, it was actually designed to prevent that development." [52]

Indeed, there was tragedy here as men unwillingly encouraged what they sought to avoid. Not a grand tragedy in which a full-scale attempt to assimilate Christianity was rejected, but a smaller if no less real tragedy in which one more attempt to solve the problem of missionary relations was unsuccessful. This was not the final affront which turned the Manchu court, in desperation, to the support of the Boxer movement. But it was one of the many evidences of lack of understanding which contributed to the impression at the court that in time of crisis the British could not be counted on.

The Edge of Crisis

The wound which the edict of March 15 sought to heal bled on, until, inevitably, the infection grew deeper and spread. The refusal of missionaries to assume responsibility intensified direct Foreign Office involvement. And, at the same time, there were increasing indications that opposition to the missionaries was becoming, in some cases, overtly associated with opposition to the Manchu regime. Both these developments were evident in June 1899, as an antimissionary riot broke out in Chien-ning City in Fukien.

The missionaries there became overly excited. Dr. John Rigg, of the

---

[47] Canterbury to Salisbury, London, Feb. 16, 1900. F.O. 17/1437. For the attitude of other missionaries in China see pp. 80–81.

[48] *T'oung Pao*, p. 242.

[49] *Ibid.*, p. 240.

[50] Warren to MacDonald, Hankow, Jan. 19, 1900. F.O. 17/1411.

[51] Foster to *North China Daily News*, Wu-ch'ang, Aug. 21, 1899. F.O. 17/1379. Similar missionary comment is found in F.O. 17/1379, *passim*.

[52] Steiger, *China and the Occident*, p. 98.

Church Missionary Society, told Whitehall that he had seen the dead bodies of three missionaries floating head down in the river.[53] In fact, Rigg's fellow missionaries had escaped death, but Anglo-Chinese relations were tense until the British consul telegraphed a hasty correction to Whitehall a few days later. Though no lives had been lost, the missionaries made it clear that monetary compensation was expected for the other losses they sustained during the riots. However, the relations between the Chinese authorities and the acting British consul, G. M. Playfair, were not improved when Rigg included the cost of his erroneous telegrams concerning his murdered colleagues in his rather exorbitant demands for compensation.[54] The final exasperation came when the missionaries declined to accept the terms of a settlement arduously achieved by Playfair. So irritated was the consul that he abruptly informed the missionaries that it was not within their province to accept or reject a political arrangement worked out between Her Majesty's Government and the Chinese officials.[55]

Not only had the missionaries proven themselves to be unusually obstinate, but British authorities managed to involve themselves more deeply than ever before in Chinese affairs. Playfair had taken an unprecedented step. He forced the gentry of Chien-ning to sign a bond pledging responsibility for any future attacks upon the missionaries.[56]

This entrance into Chinese affairs might have been beneficial if it had brought with it an awareness of general responsibility for the missionary movement. Playfair pointed to this wider responsibility in his report to Lord Salisbury. He noted that in spite of the weight of British demands the Chinese authorities simply could not eliminate attacks on missionaries which might suddenly break out in any part of China.[57] The implication was that Britain should rethink its responsibility to its missionaries and to the Chinese. Agreement with Playfair's contention might have indicated that in order to protect the missionaries Britain would have to set up her own police force in China or, reverting to the opposite extreme, remove her missionaries to the safety of the treaty ports. Salisbury refused to face such a formidable challenge; he simply added his commentary: "Better not approve." [58]

Another aspect of the Chien-ning riot was that it gave evidence of mounting tension in Chinese politics. In origin the riot was thought to have resulted from an implicit understanding between the local gentry and the Ko-lao hui secret society.[59] Such antiforeign pacts were nothing new; but this time there was a marked antigovernmental flavor to the riot. In fact, Playfair asserted that the attack on the missionaries was really an attempt to embarrass the Manchu regime.[60] The riot, however, had no chance to spread; the governor-general at Foochow rushed 500 Imperial troops to the scene and crushed all resistance.[61]

Here were all the ingredients which were to come together in the following year in the Boxer rising. But at this point the mixture was not combustible. The Imperial forces still stood as the protector of the barbarian intruder; this alone prevented a major massacre. Nevertheless this was an unpopular posture for the government to assume, especially in light of the bitter anti-Manchu feeling which already pervaded the provinces. The question was how long the Imperial Government would stand firm as the guardian of the missionaries.

---

[53] Playfair to Bax-Ironside, Kienning (Chien-ning), Nov. 24, 1899. F.O. 17/1379.
[54] Ibid.
[55] Ibid.
[56] Playfair to Bax-Ironside, Foochow, Aug. 22, 1899. F.O. 17/1378.
[57] Playfair to Bax-Ironside, Foochow, Aug. 31, 1899. F.O. 17/1378.
[58] Minute by Salisbury, Foreign Office, undated. F.O. 17/1378.
[59] Playfair to Bax-Ironside, Kienning (Chien-ning), July 18, 1899. F.O. 17/1376. While Playfair claimed that the Ko-lao hui was behind the riot others differed with him. Dr. Rigg held that it was the work of the Vegetarian secret society. For our purposes this confusion is not significant, for the secret societies were all connected in various ways. What is important is that there is a good basis for regarding the riot as secret-society inspired. Rigg to Fraser, Kienning (Chien-ning), June 17, 1899. F.O. 17/1376.
[60] Bax-Ironside to Salisbury, Tel., Peking, July 2, 1899. P.P., China No. 1 (1900), No. 213, p. 171.
[61] Ibid.

CHAPTER VIII

British Policy and the Boxer Rising

A S THE nineteenth century drew to a close the major area of competition between the European Powers shifted overseas; in fact, from 1897 until 1905 the future of China, in large part, determined the relations of the Great Powers.[1] This development was not difficult to understand. The Austro-Russian agreement of 1897 had, for the moment, settled affairs in the stormy Balkans; and Russia turned away from Europe to concentrate on establishing a greater empire in the Far East. By 1897, Germany was driven by interest and ambition to venture into "world policy"; but since the partition of Africa was virtually complete, William II was obliged to cast his eyes eastward. Likewise, France, whose African dreams were cut short by the British at Fashoda in 1898, was determined not to lose a second empire in China.

Britain, obviously, could no longer have it her own way in the Far East. And worse, just as the European Powers turned toward China, Britain, in October 1899, became fully engaged in a costly war in South Africa. Britain's "splendid isolation," her disdain for European alliances, suddenly seemed less grand. Late in 1899 and again in 1900, reports circulated concerning a continental alliance which would pit Germany, Russia, and France against Britain. This combination did not prove to be feasible in Europe; but, with Britain committed elsewhere, each of these nations sought to bolster its claim in China at Britain's expense. Russia, especially, was in a position to exert heavy pressure upon China from her broad northern frontier. It was this competition between Britain and Russia which set the tone for the China policies of the other powers at the end of the century.

As is not uncommon in world affairs, crisis breeds crisis; or, at least, there is a tendency for crises to coincide. So it was in China; for, at that moment, increasing Western aggression gave momentum to a movement of revolutionary potential arising from vast internal discontent. International politics and domestic upheaval merged in the tragedy of the Boxer rising.

The Court Faces the Boxers

The Boxer movement arose in the midst of great social and international turmoil. In the last three years of the nineteenth century portions of the provinces of Chihli and Shantung in northeastern China endured prolonged floods followed by drought. Soon the twin scourges of hunger and banditry beset the area. The Imperial Government appropriated large sums of money to relieve the suffering; but, in large part, these were dissipated by corruption and administrative inefficiency.[2]

This immense social dislocation was aggravated by increasing foreign aggression. Into famine-stricken Shantung the German interloper had sent raiding parties from his enclave in Kiaochow. On the basis of relatively minor provocation these raiders set several Chinese villages to the torch. Near Port Arthur, resistance to Russian expansion resulted in the slaughter of nearly a hundred Chinese.[3] In Wei-hai-wei and Kowloon the British clashed with local villagers who opposed the lease of their land.

The most disruptive factor of all, or at least the factor leading most directly to the initial Boxer outbursts, was the violent conflict which broke out in numerous places along the Chihli-Shantung border between Christian converts and the Chinese villagers. Similar outbursts had pockmarked the last decade; now, however, they reached a new intensity. Chinese officials were almost unanimous in attributing them to interfer-

---

[1] A. J. P. Taylor, *The Struggle for Mastery in Europe, 1848–1918*, Oxford History of Modern Europe (Oxford: Clarendon Press, 1954), p. 372.

[2] Tan, *The Boxer Catastrophe*, p. 34.

[3] *Ibid.*, p. 35.

ence by missionaries in lawsuits involving their converts.[4] Supposedly the villagers would have no more of this and they struck out to correct the abuse. Such reports would hardly ingratiate the missionaries with the Imperial court where they were already regarded as extremists who had sought to use the Reform party to destroy China's unique culture.[5]

These assaults on converts were led by mysterious groups known as Boxers, and historians have not ceased to dispute concerning the nature of these bands. Until recently, the generally accepted thesis was that put forward by G. N. Steiger in his *China and the Occident.* Steiger claimed that the proper Chinese name for the Boxers was "I Ho Tuan" (I-ho t'uan) which in English would be "Righteous and Harmonious Band [or Militia]." Those who referred to the society as "I Ho Ch'uan" (I-ho ch'üan) or "Righteous and Harmonious Fists" were, according to Steiger, merely perpetuating a pun based on the similarity between the rites of the society and the movements involved in boxing.[6] Deriving his conclusion partly from this interpretation of the name, Steiger declared that the Boxers were loyal bands of village militia who were first organized by Imperial decrees of November 5 and December 31, 1898.[7]

However, Steiger's thesis was demolished by Chester Tan in *The Boxer Catastrophe*, the first full-scale study of the movement based primarily on Chinese sources. That the "I Ho Ch'uan" (I-ho ch'üan) was a secret society existing as early as 1815 and even then engaged in the rites of boxing Tan proved by reference to a well-documented study written by Lao Nai-hsüan in 1899.[8] That Boxer activity had broken out well before the proclamation of the Imperial edicts establishing the militia he substantiated by reference to the official records of the Ch'ing dynasty.[9] Finally, he clinched his case by noting that the rites and mysteries of the Boxers constituted the usual secret society ritual, and that some of the Boxer leaders captured in 1899 confessed their membership in the notorious parent secret society, the Eight Diagram Sect.[10] In conclusion Tan drew certain careful distinctions:

It is difficult to say to what extent the Boxer movement was instigated by the heretical sects. For if they played an important role in organizing the movement, their illegal status made it impossible for them to reveal themselves. . . . It is quite possible that the secret societies operated in the background. But whoever the initiator may have been, it is beyond argument that the Boxer movement was dominated by heretical elements. This of course did not prevent the movement from becoming a popular front against the foreigners and the Christians. That was a time when the Chinese hatred of the foreigners was intense and widespread. The Boxer slogan of "upholding the Ch'ing Dynasty and exterminating the foreigners" caught the imagination of the people, and the antiforeign sentiment of the people must at the same time have inspired the direction of the Boxers. . . . At any rate the movement soon galvanized the populace of the northern provinces and spread like wildfire. It absorbed various elements of society and infiltrated various organizations, whether secret or official. At last it recruited the high officials and princes of the blood in the Imperial Court and thus precipitated the great catastrophe.[11]

Tan made no more than passing reference to the stages by which secret society agitation merged into a vast popular front opposed to all things foreign and finally received the formal support of the Manchu court. However, in order to aid understanding of the complex Boxer problem as it presented itself to the diplomats in Peking, some tentative suggestions concerning the development of that movement might be set forth.

In the first stage, from 1895 until the end of 1897, antiforeign activity was not on a mass scale; usually it was confined to the work of secret society agitators. For example, Li Ping-heng, the violently antiforeign governor of Shantung, promoted an alliance between the secret societies and the gentry official class, so as better to harass the missionaries and converts.[12] Such an understanding, according to Mgr. Anzer, the Catholic bishop of southern Shantung, paved the way for the attack by the Ta-tao hui (Big Sword society) which resulted in the murder of two German Catholic missionaries in November 1897.[13]

---

[4] *Ibid.* Here Tan comments that interference by Roman Catholic missionaries in legal disputes was much more common than such interference by Protestant missionaries. This was probably true since the Catholic converts far outnumbered the Protestant converts. But Tan probably underestimates the interference by Protestants. The British ministerial and consular reports reveal frequent, almost continuous, involvement of Protestant missionaries in legal disputes concerning their converts. F.O. 17 and F.O. 228, *passim.*

[5] Tan, *op. cit.,* p. 35

[6] Steiger, *China and the Occident,* p. 134.

[7] *Ibid.,* p. 146.

[8] Tan, *The Boxer Catastrophe,* p. 44.

[9] *Ibid.,* p. 47. Tan's reference was drawn from *Ch'ing te tsung shih lu* (True Records of the Ch'ing Dynasty), 418/2b.

[10] Tan, *The Boxer Catastrophe,* p. 44.

[11] *Ibid.,* p. 45.

[12] Li Chien-nung, *The Political History of China, 1840–1928,* p. 173.

[13] "Crisis in China," London *Times,* June 9, 1900, p. 7.

A second phase extended through 1898 and into the first part of 1899. Now the movement against the foreigners and the converts began to take on a mass appeal. The Ta-tao hui played a diminishing part in antiforeign activity, and some of its leaders approached the Catholic vicar-general in Shantung to announce that their attacks on Christian converts would cease.[14] But the slack was taken up as the I-ho t'uan began to recruit volunteers for action against the Christians in May 1898. This, in fact, was the first notation of Boxer activity in the official Chinese records.[15] Although the Boxer attacks were directed against the converts, there was no doubt that, like the Ta-tao hui, the I-ho t'uan was anti-Manchu in inspiration. During this phase it would seem that there were two possibly antithetical orientations that this burgeoning movement might take. It might become a peasant revolution representative of Chinese resistance to the Manchu, or it might turn all its strength against the hated foreigner and his works.

The third and decisive phase of the Boxer movement dated from the appointment of Yü-hsien as governor of Shantung in March 1899. Mgr. Anzer claimed that Yü was forced to call in certain dissident sects from the adjoining provinces to carry on the attacks against converts, since the Ta-tao hui refused to do this.[16] At any rate, the movement spread rapidly, ostensibly dedicating itself to antiforeignism. The anti-Manchu aspect of the movement was either dropped or momentarily subdued. According to an analysis of the Manchu records made by Jerome Ch'en, it was some time in the first half of 1899 that the Boxers adopted the slogan "support the Ch'ing dynasty."[17] Li Ching-nung, in his *Political History of Modern China*, claimed that it was Yü-hsien who changed the last character of the Boxer title from Ch'uan (Fist) to the more respectable T'uan (Militia). Finally, a study by Victor Purcell has indicated that it was in October 1899 that Boxer support of the Ch'ing became dominant and that the reactionaries at court came to support the Boxers.[18] Whatever the details of the transformation, after mid-1899 the Boxers were expanding rapidly as an avowedly pro-Manchu and antiforeign movement.

The Imperial Government was confronted by a great dilemma. Hatred of the missionary and of all things foreign ensured the popularity of the Boxer movement, which was spreading like wildfire through the key metropolitan provinces of Chihli and Shantung. Yet, the Boxers were suspect in origin, and no one could be sure to what extent they were controlled by the secret societies whose opposition to the regime was beyond dispute. The Manchu authorities could not, without grave risk, blatantly oppose so popular a movement. Nor would it be prudent to stifle a force which might eventually be needed in combating the West. The solution was to ride both horns of the dilemma. The Boxers must be allowed to continue to harass the Christians and recruit volunteers; only in the most extreme cases would Imperial troops be allowed to move against the Boxers. The foreign Powers must be compensated for any injury sustained by their missionaries owing to Boxer activity; but

---

[14] *Ibid.*

[15] Tan, *The Boxer Catastrophe*, p. 47. Apparently, the Chinese records referred to the rebel band as a T'uan in this case. At least that is Tan's translation.

[16] "Crisis in China," *loc. cit.*

[17] Jerome Ch'en, "The Nature and Characteristics of the Boxer Movement — A Morphological Study," *Bulletin of the School of Oriental and African Studies,* XXIII, Part II (1960), 295.

[18] Li Chien-nung, *The Political History of China*, p. 173. Li credited three forces as encouraging the Boxer rising: first, the Empress Dowager and powerful nobles who, when the European Powers frustrated their plans to dethrone the Emperor, turned to the Boxers to drive out the foreigners (with the Empress Dowager only giving gradual assent to their plans); second, the scholar-officials with their traditional distaste for the intruding missionaries; third, the unemployed mobs among which swept a violent antiforeign hatred. P. 164.

For Jerome Ch'en the movement represented the first stirring of Chinese nationalism. "The movement itself," he claimed, "was a manifestation of the inability of officials to repel foreign influence in China. The Boxers wanted to take over the duty of defending the country from higher officials, who were supposed to be the pillars of the Empire . . ." Ch'en in *Bulletin of the School of Oriental and African Studies,* p. 294.

Hu Sheng's work represented a current Marxist interpretation of the rising. He saw the Boxer movement as a revolt of the peasants against the feudal aristocracy. But the court officials and the gentry "tried to incite the masses to xenophobia in order to do away with the anti-feudal and anti-governmental nature of the movement. The political immaturity of the peasants prevented them from resisting such an influence. More and more the movement swerved from the right course and lost itself in a labyrinth of frantic, irrational and anti-modern activities which finally reduced it to a tool and victim of the ruling forces." Hu Sheng, *Imperialism and Chinese Politics* (Peking: Foreign Language Press, 1955), p. 136.

Tan emphasized several factors behind the rise of the Boxers. The social crisis, economic chaos, foreign aggression, and abuses by the missionaries were especially mentioned. He also pointed to the importance of the anti-Manchu secret societies in supplying the movement with an organizational framework. Tan, *The Boxer Catastrophe*, pp. 43–45.

Victor Purcell has compiled the most recent and detailed study of Boxer origins based on Chinese source materials. His excellent study supports the findings of Tan, and argues that by October 1899 the Boxers shifted to a pro-dynastic orientation. Victor Purcell, *The Boxer Uprising* (Cambridge: Cambridge University Press, 1963), pp. 194–222.

only the most stringent and unified pressure by the Powers would move the Manchu to act against the Boxers.

This was a time of great peril for Western diplomacy. To oppose the Imperial court with the usual threat and bluster might be to force it to join hands with the Boxers. To ignore the plight of the missionaries and converts would be to shirk an obligation.

Initial Antimissionary Outbursts

The first Boxer attack reported to a British consul took place at Hsian-ch'ang along the Shantung border of Chihli in May 1899.[19] Having been alerted by members of the London Missionary Society, W. R. Carles, British consul in Tientsin, took the affair in hand.[20] He protested to Yü-lu, the governor-general of Chihli, who sent an emissary to resolve the dispute.[21] A second L.M.S. outpost was victimized in August. This time Yü-lu acted with greater determination. Imperial troops were sent to the scene and "One hundred robbers and malcontents" were executed.[22]

But tension persisted. Although an uneasy peace was maintained by Imperial troops, by October the Boxer ringleaders had shown themselves again.[23] The missionaries claimed that the local officials offered theatricals and feasts to appease the Boxers.[24] But the converts observed the gathering clouds which foretold the coming storm; they buried their few precious belongings and prepared for flight.

Consul Carles was confused by the fact that one magistrate would refer to the outlaws as "good citizens on bad terms with the Christians," while another would denounce them as "treasonable Boxers."[25] He raised this point with Yü-lu, but the governor-general was evasive. First, he told Carles that the Boxers were merely local natives aroused by restless spirits from Shantung; then he acknowledged that they were "a branch of the 'White Lotus' (secret society) and had long been denounced as treasonable."[26]

If the governor-general's explanation was contradictory, his conduct was more so. Missionaries reported that General Mei Tung-ling, whom Yü-lu had ordered to the area, was instructed to protect them but not to attack the Boxers.[27] On December 18, Carles brought this up with the governor-general who assured him that he had given General Mei strict orders to crush the Boxers.[28] Indeed, a few days later Imperial troops captured the Boxer leader Wu Hsui-mu and seventy of his followers. But the picture was again confused soon after when missionary reports indicated that local officials had received no orders to arrest or punish the brigand bands.[29] This news came in the face of the governor-general's claim that many officials lax in their treatment of the Boxers had been removed or transferred.[30]

According to Chester Tan, who based his interpretation on an examination of the official Manchu records, it was part of Imperial policy to pacify rather than to repress the Boxers. He noted that the acting governor of Shantung, Yüan Shih-kai, was warned that he would be held responsible for the consequences if he carried out his policy of ruthless suppression.[31] Consul Carles came largely to the same conclusion. He argued that Yü-lu was earnestly trying to put down the attacks, but was impeded in his task by local officials who favored the Boxers and were unwilling to put an end to harassment of Christians. These officials, he claimed, were supported by men of influence, "such as the late governor of Shantung, Li Ping Hêng [Li Ping-heng], and Yü Hsien, [Yü-hsien], the recently suspended governor of Shantung], and the present financial commissioner of the province."[32]

Bishop Charles Scott of the Society for the Propagation of the Gospel added his observation that "It was commonly reported that the Governor of Shantung (Yü Hsien [Yü-hsien]) has openly said that the marauders had better not molest foreign missionaries, but that the more

---

[19] The diplomacy of this period has been the subject matter of works by G. N. Steiger and R. Stanley McCordock, but they have failed to give sufficient attention to the disunity caused by international rivalry in Peking. Steiger, *China and the Occident*, pp. 173–200; and McCordock, *British Far Eastern Policy, 1894–1900* (New York: Columbia University Press, 1931), pp. 309–330.

[20] Arthur H. Smith, *China in Convulsion* (London: Oliphant, Anderson and Ferrier, 1901), I, 165.

[21] McFarlane to Cousins, Chichou (Ch'i-ch'un), May 29, 1899. L.M.S./NC/10. McFarlane called the outbreak a secret society rising of the I-ho ch'üan. For an additional reference to the I-ho ch'üan see Meech to Cousins, Hsian-ch'ang (Hsia-chang), June 23, 1899. L.M.S./NC/10.

[22] Cochrane to Cousins, Pei Tai Ho (Pei-tai-ho), Sept. 2, 1899. L.M.S./NC/10.

[23] Rees to Cousins, Chichou (Ch'i-ch'un), Oct. 13, 1899. L.M.S./NC/10.

[24] Rees to Carles, Chichou (Ch'i-ch'un), Dec. 14, 1899. F.O. 288/1330.

[25] Carles to MacDonald, Tientsin, Dec. 11, 1899. F.O. 288/1330.

[26] *Ibid.*

[27] Rees to Carles, Chichou (Ch'i-ch'un), Dec. 18, 1899. F.O. 288/1330.

[28] Carles to MacDonald, Tientsin, Dec. 18, 1899. F.O. 288/1330.

[29] Carles to MacDonald, Tientsin, Dec. 21, 1899. F.O. 288/1330.

[30] Carles to MacDonald, Tientsin, Dec. 27, 1899. F.O. 288/1330.

[31] Tan, *The Boxer Catastrophe*, pp. 50–51.

[32] Carles to MacDonald, Tientsin, Dec. 24, 1899. F.O. 288/1330.

they persecute native Christians (short of killing them outright) the better, for that was the way to drive out the Missionaries." [33]

With such propaganda of hate in the air there was much danger for all Europeans. On December 31, 1899, Rev. S. M. Brooks, an S.P.G. missionary, was traveling between missionary stations in a lonely part of Shantung. He was set upon by a gang of vagabonds who proved to be members of the Ta-tao hui (Big Sword society). Fired by antiforeign feeling, they seized Brooks, forced a rough cord through his nose, and led him off. Still, they were unsure just what to do with their captive. They were considering the possibility of ransom when Brooks broke from them and fled. The pursuit was determined. In the heat of the chase Brooks was tripped up. The brigands leaped upon him and brutally hacked him to death. [34]

Now that a British life had been lost, Boxer activity became the direct concern of the British minister in Peking. On January 4, 1900, Mac-Donald, supported by his American, French, and German colleagues, made vigorous protest to the Tsungli Yamen. [35] He demanded that all the antimissionary riots be quelled, that Brooks's murderers be captured and the case properly settled. MacDonald warned that if this was not done "international complications" would ensue. [36] Disturbed perhaps by visions of an English version of the German action in Kiaochow in 1897, the Yamen was quick to reply. On January 5, an Imperial decree was issued which insisted that missionaries be given the rights ensured them by treaty, and orders were out for the speedy capture of the murderers and the punishment of lax officials. [37]

It was evident from MacDonald's report to Whitehall that he expected the affair to be quickly terminated. He pointed out that, just before the murder, General Yüan Shih-kai had been called to become acting governor of the turbulent province of Shantung. The general had asked for his 8000 European trained troops, and MacDonald expected him to make short work of the rebels. MacDonald emphasized the accidental nature of Brooks's death and his insistence on traveling without escort while most of the missionaries were well guarded and safe. [38]

Nor was MacDonald disturbed on January 11 when the Tsungli Yamen sought to impress upon him the great difficulties which it faced in putting down the riots. The Yamen insisted that the basic cause of the trouble lay in the bad feeling which existed between the Christian converts and the ordinary natives. This had become so acute, it was

[146]

insisted, that bands of marauders had formed "who harassed the Christians and other natives alike. . . ." [39]

That same day a decree concerning the riots appeared in the *Peking Gazette*. It contained the government version of the cause of the riots, designed for the consumption of the official-gentry class. It was a masterpiece of equivocation which could be read as either favoring or condemning the outbreaks. It instructed local officials that the "societies" causing the disturbances should not be condemned en masse; some were formed for self-preservation and rural protection, while others were mere confederacies of vagabonds. It insisted on strict justice in missionary cases, and it urged the common people not to give ear to those who would unsettle their minds. [40]

Some of the foreign ministers claimed that the decree excused the existence of the Boxer societies. But MacDonald informed Salisbury that he would not raise any protest unless the Tsungli Yamen was lax in acting against the Boxers. [41] Neither did MacDonald give credence to

---

[33] Scott to Tucker, Peking, Jan. 11, 1900. S.P.G., 1900, series D, Vol. II, No. 82.

[34] MacDonald to Salisbury, Tel., Peking, Jan. 4, 1900. F.O. 17/1418. At this point, British diplomats grouped together in their dispatches the disturbances caused by the I-ho t'uan and the Ta-tao hui, regarding them both as Boxer outbreaks. Only future research on the difficult subject of Chinese secret societies can bring out the undoubtedly meaningful interplay between the secret societies and the Boxers. Until such time as this is done it will be impossible to regard our knowledge of the Boxer rising as definitive.

[35] MacDonald to Salisbury, Peking, Jan. 5, 1900. F.O. 17/1411.

[36] MacDonald to Salisbury, Peking, Jan. 4, 1900. F.O. 17/1418.

[37] MacDonald to Salisbury, Peking, Jan. 5, 1900. F.O. 17/1411.

[38] *Ibid.*

[39] MacDonald to Salisbury, Peking, Jan. 17, 1900. F.O. 17/1411. On January 20, the prefect of T'ai-an-fu issued a proclamation which also blamed the Christians for the outbreaks. It said that "the church-people constantly relying on their 'harbour of refuge' insult people unbearably and the ordinary people suffer so that they are less and less able to live in peace: at first they cultivate the Boxer Societies with a view to protecting their homes and then come to use (borrow) the Boxing Society to retaliate." Campbell to MacDonald, T'ai-an-fu, Jan. 20, 1900. F.O. 17/1412. According to Campbell, Yüan Shih-k'ai, the governor of Shantung, expressed the same views during an interview. The governor said that the intervention of Roman Catholic priests in secular disputes was at the bottom of the trouble, but he praised the conduct of English missionaries. Campbell to MacDonald, T'ai-an-fu, Feb. 4, 1900. F.O. 17/1412.

[40] MacDonald to Salisbury, Peking, Jan. 17, 1900. 17/1410. English translation of decree enclosed in dispatch.

[41] *Ibid.* Edwin Conger, the American minister, admitted that he had some anxiety over the strange wording of the decree of January 11. Still he agreed with his English colleague on the need to give the Chinese a reasonable chance of successfully suppressing the rebellion before raising new objections. Conger to Hay,

the report by missionaries that secret orders from the throne encouraged such risings. He confidentially noted to Salisbury that there was usually "some exaggeration" in the reports that missionaries passed on from their converts.[42]

In this early stage of Boxer activity, MacDonald was content to let the situation mend itself. Neither unsettling reports from Consul Carles and the missionaries nor the ambiguous decree of January 11 disturbed him. With Britain at war in South Africa, MacDonald knew that it was necessary to avoid unnecessary involvement in China. To this extent restraint was justified by reason of higher policy. But there is no evidence that MacDonald was aware of the real problem confronting him. He was ignorant of the massive movement of discontent underway in China. He knew nothing of the great forces which were pushing the Manchu regime toward an overt antiforeign policy. The situation became worse, however, as MacDonald drifted from a policy of complacency to a policy of threat.

The Missionary Coalition

The mounting terror and increased frequency of attacks on Catholic converts finally impelled the French minister, Stephen Pichon, to action. On January 23, he called for a meeting of the ministers of the United States, Germany, and Britain.[43] They assembled two days later, and it was decided that they should send identical notes demanding a new decree suppressing the Boxers.[44] This demand was presented to the Tsungli Yamen on January 27. Pichon thus inaugurated what we shall henceforth refer to as the "missionary coalition." At this stage, MacDonald's role was still a passive one. His intelligence from Carles and the British missionaries had become fairly optimistic, but he had no objection to joining in the action of the French minister.[45]

Not until February 25, after the Powers had reiterated their demand of January 27, did the Chinese reply. The Tsungli Yamen explained that the governor-general of Chihli and the governor of Shantung had been ordered by a secret decree to issue proclamations prohibiting the outlaw societies. The missionary coalition, now joined by Italy, found this reply vague and evasive. They decided to demand an interview with the Tsungli Yamen in order to insist that a new decree be published in the *Peking Gazette*, giving it equal status and publicity with the ambiguous decree of January 11.[46]

But the Chinese and the Western Powers soon reached what seemed to be an absolute impasse. The Powers were not placated when on March 1, the Tsungli Yamen sent their representatives a proclamation issued by the governor of Shantung which condemned the Boxers in unambiguous terms.[47] Nor did the Yamen offer further concessions when they received the ministers in audience the following day. The missionary coalition stood firm in demanding that a decree explicitly condemning the Boxers appear in the *Peking Gazette*; this, insisted the Yamen, was impossible, for it would violate certain administrative procedures.[48]

Now the heretofore passive MacDonald was stirred to action. Perhaps he was enraged by the unbending attitude of the Yamen. Perhaps he was excited by the fact that the Boxers were enlisting recruits in the neighborhood of Peking and Tientsin.[49] Whatever his motive, MacDonald was ready to support drastic measures as the missionary

---

Peking, Jan. 15, 1900. *F.R.U.S., 1900*, No. 312, p. 88. The German minister, Baron von Ketteler, felt that the decree was designed to encourage the Boxers, and he made an immediate verbal protest to the Tsungli Yamen. *Ibid.* The French minister, Pichon, regarded the decree as being "singularly vague and elastic." D'Anthouard to Delcassé, Peking, March 13, 1900. *D.D.C.*, 1899–1900, No. 6, pp. 7–9.

[42] MacDonald to Salisbury, Peking, Jan. 17, 1900. F.O. 17/1412.

[43] D'Anthouard to Delcassé, Peking, March 13, 1900. *D.D.C.*, 1899–1900, No. 6, pp. 7–9.

[44] MacDonald to Salisbury, Peking, Jan. 31, 1900. F.O. 17/1411.

[45] A missionary reported from Ch'i-ch'un that Boxer activity had ceased in those areas where Chinese troops were stationed, but that activity elsewhere was growing. Meech to MacDonald, Hsia-chang, Jan. 13, 1900. F.O. 228/1343. Carles reported that the situation was improving and that the converts were returning to their homes. MacDonald to Salisbury, Peking, Jan. 16, 1900. F.O. 17/1411. And on January 20, Meech, the missionary at Hsia-chang, reported that the "rebellion is in abeyance." Meech to Cousins, Hsia-chang, Jan. 20, 1900. L.M.S./NC/10.

[46] MacDonald to Salisbury, Peking, March 5, 1900. F.O. 17/1411.

[47] *Ibid.*

[48] *Ibid.* The missionary coalition was also dissatisfied that the proclamation by the governor of Shantung condemned only the I-ho ch'üan while the Ta-tao hui was not mentioned.

[49] MacDonald to Salisbury, Tel., Peking, March 10, 1900. F.O. 17/1418. Seemingly, Boxer activity was on the rise early in March after a comparatively quiet February. At any rate, early in February refugees were reported returning to their homes at Ch'i-ch'un in Chihli, and all was quiet there. Rees to Cousins, Chi-Chou (Ch'i-ch'un), Feb. 11, 1900. L.M.S./NC/10. In Shantung, at Wei-hsien the Boxer threat was checked as troops from Cheng-ting engaged the Boxers, killing seven and executing two of their prisoners. Bridges to Cousins, Wei Chen (Wei-hsien), March 1, 1900. L.M.S./NC/10. Governor Yüan, while he refused to compensate converts for their losses, pressed forward with the capture and trial of Brooks's murderers and captured twenty Boxer ringleaders. Campbell to MacDonald, T'ai-an-fu, Feb. 4, 7, and 9, 1900. F.O. 17/1412.

coalition assembled at his residence on March 10. They agreed to send final identical notes to the Tsungli Yamen. These would demand again that the anti-Boxer decree be published in the *Peking Gazette*, but this time the notes would warn that unless their demand was promptly met the ministers would advise their governments to consider "other measures" for the protection of their nationals in China.[50] Most significant of all, the ministers agreed what these measures should be if the Chinese rejected their demand and if the disturbances continued. They would recommend that a joint naval demonstration be directed against China.[51]

The possibility of a threat of naval demonstration raised the problem of the antimissionary riots to the level of world politics. Each nation was forced to consider just what effect such an overt act would have upon its power position in China.

No nation retreated from this proposed display of force with greater speed than England. News of MacDonald's participation in this proposal shocked the Foreign Office. Lord Salisbury agreed with his assistant undersecretary, Francis Bertie, that England should not take the lead in the affair, and the prime minister went on to comment: "Stupid of him [MacDonald] to do this without asking me. One of the demonstrating powers will take the opportunity of appropriating something nice. And with our engagements in South Africa — [we] will hope to grin and look pleasant."[52] As a result, MacDonald was sent instructions to be very quiet at present, and to delay the matter, lest it lead to any naval action.[53]

France, the other great missionary Power, was equally reluctant to commit itself to action in China. M. d'Anthouard, chargé d'affaires at Peking, indicated to Delcassé, the French foreign minister, that he had gone along with this threat so as not to separate himself from the action of his colleagues. But his own opinion was that it was premature to consider a naval action.[54] Later d'Anthouard, almost apologetically, sought to minimize his action. It would never come to the point where a naval demonstration was necessary, he insisted, for the Chinese were convinced of the necessity of action and their delays were only to save face.[55]

When first informed of the decision of the missionary coalition, Delcassé seemed to evince a readiness for action. On March 12 he told Sir Edward Monson, the English ambassador, that while he would have to consult his colleagues for a definitive decision, he did not think he could avoid the advice of the five representatives in China on the naval demonstration.[56] Two days later the French ambassador in London reported that Salisbury told him that a naval demonstration was a dangerous step and that the English preferred to let the situation develop first.[57] Then on March 16, Monson reported to Salisbury that Delcassé had modified his position; the Frenchman now declared that a demonstration was a very serious step and that he was telegraphing his minister in China for more information.[58]

The cause of the French reversal of opinion is not difficult to identify. Freedom of action for France in China was limited to actions which would not overly displease its Russian ally.[59] It was, of course, Pichon who had initiated the missionary coalition with his call for a meeting of the four Powers on January 23. No doubt, Russia did not begrudge France this initial move, but later the threat of joint action by the Powers against China, with whom Russia always sought to ingratiate herself, could not be so easily tolerated. Henceforth all negotiation concerning Boxers was conducted in the shadow of the ambiguous figure of Russia.

---

[50] MacDonald to Salisbury, Tel., Peking, March 10, 1900. F.O. 17/1418.

[51] *Ibid.*

[52] Minute by Salisbury, Foreign Office, March 11, 1900. F.O. 17/1418. This is the initial indication that the Foreign Office exerted continuous pressure on MacDonald to keep things quiet in Peking and to attempt no strong protest lest it provoke a crisis. Such evidence, available in the China file at the Public Record Office, definitely disproves the thesis put forth by McCordock in his *British Far Eastern Policy, 1894–1900.* McCordock's thesis, based on the printed British documents, was as follows: "Although the Foreign Office had in March deprecated a naval demonstration, they readily acquiesced when the request was repeated. Authority to call up the guards [at the end of May] was given immediately. In fact, during the whole crisis, the Foreign Office encouraged him [MacDonald] to aggressive action." P. 328.

[53] Minute by Salisbury, Foreign Office, March 11, 1900. F.O. 17/1418.

[54] D'Anthouard to Delcassé, Peking, March 11, 1900. *D.D.C.,* 1899–1900, No. 5, p. 6.

[55] D'Anthouard to Delcassé, Peking, March 13, 1900. *D.D.C.,* 1899–1900, No. 6, pp. 7–9.

[56] Monson to Salisbury, Paris, March 13, 1900. F.O. 27/3494.

[57] P. Cambon to Delcassé, London, March 14, 1900. *D.D.C.,* 1899–1900, No. 11, p. 12.

[58] Monson to Salisbury, Paris, March 16, 1900. F.O. 27/3494.

[59] On March 13, 1900, Delcassé had requested that his ambassador in St. Petersburg inform the Russian Government about the possible naval demonstration. The Russian reply was not printed. However, one may assume that it firmly objected to such a move. Delcassé to de Montebello, Paris, March 13, 1900. *D.D.C.,* 1899–1900, No. 8, p. 10.

Russian policy in China was shrouded in secrecy; even her French ally was largely kept in the dark about her intentions. Partly because of this, incriminating stories circulated in diplomatic circles concerning Russian encouragement of the Boxers. For example, when Sir Ernest Satow came to replace MacDonald as minister in Peking late in 1900, he reported that there was a good deal of personal feeling against the Russian minister, M. de Giers, in the diplomatic corps there. This ill feeling, he continued, originated at the time when MacDonald and his colleagues were urging the Tsungli Yamen to put down the Boxers. Giers was supposed to have told the Chinese that they need not obey the Western coalition which was powerless to harm them.[60] The Japanese foreign minister also joined in this indictment of the Russians. He informed Satow that Giers had not used his influence in urging the Chinese Government to put down the Boxers. He claimed that Prince Tuan, whom he accused of being the Boxer chief, was in Russian pay, and that the Russians intended to let the Boxers devastate northern China and then step in themselves.[61]

There is no documentation to support these extreme charges. But something can be said about Russia's general attitude during the Boxer devastations. For as long as possible the Russian minister opposed naval demonstrations or the use of force against China. The first indication of this came about the middle of March. Giers approached MacDonald privately and deprecated naval demonstrations and the landing of guards for the legations. Such actions, he said, could lead to unknown eventualities.[62] Basically, the Russians had little sympathy for the missionaries and regarded them as responsible for the outbreaks. Tsar Nicholas II himself contended that the masses of China hated the European missionaries. He called the missionaries the "root of all evil," and instigators of "commercial tyrannies" screened by the "holy name of Christ." [63] The Tsar was amazingly frank with Sir Charles Scott, the British ambassador. After a dinner at Tsarskoe Selo, he warned Scott against those who sought to reform China's Eastern ways; such things, he said, provoked local outbreaks like the Boxer disturbances.[64]

It would be difficult to prove that Russia had any Machiavellian plot in league with the Boxers, and such a plot was unlikely. Her policy of restraint was based on several realistic considerations. She saw no reason to risk her assumed position as China's friend by bringing pressure on the Tsungli Yamen about the Boxers. In fact, Russia sympathized with what she thought were the understandable grievances of the Boxers. Finally, it was in her long-term interest to avoid the intrusion of foreign Powers in the north of China, even for the limited purpose of suppressing the riots.[65]

The missionary coalition, then, proved impotent in this its first attempt at forceful action against China. The home governments of the leading missionary Powers rejected an active policy. England was fully engaged in South Africa and France was sensitive to the wishes of her Russian ally.

MacDonald, in his first active leadership of the coalition, had committed the worst of diplomatic sins. He had engaged in a policy of threat and bluster without the force or unity to back it up. The results were twofold. First, the fact that Britain's representative had led the way in proposing a naval demonstration helped convince the Manchu court more than ever before that it could not look to Britain for understanding and support in its moment of crisis. Britain, who once supported the regime in the face of the Taiping Rebellion, had now been at the forefront of the Powers threatening what might have been the first move in the partition of China. Second, the collapse of the proposed naval demonstration revealed to the Imperial court that the Powers would not hold together once they sought to implement their threats. Henceforth any demands by the Powers would carry less weight.

The Collapse of the Missionary Coalition

Although the attempt by the Powers to bring joint pressure on the Chinese ended in failure, there was a chance that the same end might be achieved by the independent action of one or more of them. But

---

[60] Satow to Salisbury, Peking, Nov. 1, 1900. Salisbury Papers, Satow Box.

[61] Satow to Salisbury, Tokyo, June 25, 1900. Salisbury Papers, Japan Volume, 1895–1900, No. 84.

[62] MacDonald to Salisbury, Peking, May 21, 1900. F.O. 17/1418.

[63] B. A. Romanov, *Russia in Manchuria, 1892–1906*, trans. Susan W. Jones (Ann Arbor: University of Michigan Press, 1952), p. 179.

[64] Scott to Salisbury, St. Petersburg, May 25, 1900. F.O. 65/1599.

[65] Malozemoff, *Russian Far Eastern Policy*, p. 125. Russian policy suffered from inaccurate intelligence concerning the Boxers. Giers's reports concerning the danger of a Boxer rising were overly optimistic; in fact, the more realistic warnings of Colonel K. A. Vogak, a Russian military agent, were labeled as "alarmist" by Giers. *Ibid.* The Tsar put his trust in Giers and thought him to be "prudent." Scott to Salisbury, St. Petersburg, May 25, 1900. F.O. 65/1599.

such a move would call for deft diplomacy, as fear and jealousy among the Powers were rising.

MacDonald still believed that the Boxer attacks could only be stifled by a display of force. He was further incited by a personal affront. Yü-hsien, whose punishment MacDonald had demanded if the Brooks case was not properly settled, was appointed governor of Shansi.[66] The British minister's irritation was evident in his report of March 14 to the Foreign Office. It was useless, he declared, to protest Yü's appointment without taking adequate measures to back up the protest.[67]

MacDonald now seems to have taken it upon himself to bring that pressure on the Manchu government which Whitehall declined to authorize. Such a conclusion is difficult to avoid after examining his conduct between the last days of March and April 7.

On March 23, MacDonald formally requested that the Foreign Office send two warships to Ta-ku, the nearest port of Peking. The ships were required, he explained, for the protection of British missionaries, since new disturbances were breaking out in Shantung. He supported this appeal by pointing out that the United States was sending one ship to Ta-ku, that Italy had two ships ready to send, and that Germany had the use of her Kiaochow squadron.[68] Lord Salisbury acceded to this request. But he cautioned that no force should be employed, except in defense of British lives or property, without reference to him.[69]

What followed was, in effect, a British operation. Secretary of State John Hay of the United States had authorized a warship exclusively for the protection of American citizens and their interests. Even then it did not arrive until April 7, just after the more crucial days of the crisis.[70] The Italian ships arrived about the same time. Apparently, the German ships never left Kiaochow.[71]

On March 29, MacDonald had two British warships standing off Ta-ku. He then appealed to the Foreign Office for action in the Brooks case. He lamented that two guilty officials had escaped punishment. Justice would never be done, according to MacDonald, unless the former governor of Shantung, Yü-hsien, who was chiefly responsible for Brooks's death, was punished.[72]

These arguments fell short of impressing Whitehall. Francis A. Campbell, chief clerk at the Foreign Office, noted that Yü-hsien's appointment to Shansi demonstrated either that he had influential friends at court or that, as many people believed, the secret societies were favored by the government. In either case, he concluded, only the threat of force would remove him from office, and without force it was useless to press for his punishment.[73] Salisbury agreed and gave vent to his general irritation over such examples of justice at long range: "They [his representatives in China] never tell us how they are so cocksure of the complicity of the person they name. If they would lend us some of these detectives to this land [England] it might be of use." [74]

MacDonald was therefore denied support for his plan to have Yü-hsien punished. However, the two British ships were still off Ta-ku, and the five-nation missionary coalition decided to take advantage of their presence to bring pressure on the Chinese Government. On April 4 the coalition met. The ministers agreed to send separate but identical notes to the Tsungli Yamen, demanding that a forthright anti-Boxer decree be published in the *Peking Gazette*. They insisted on an answer in forty-eight hours; this was a virtual ultimatum.[75]

The Chinese reply was again evasive. It explained that it was impossible to publish the decree in the *Gazette*. But in partial fulfillment of the demand the ministers were shown a proclamation by the governor of Shantung, embodying an Imperial edict, which condemned the Boxers.[76]

The missionary coalition met on April 7 to consider the Yamen's reply. Clearly the Chinese had rejected its demand, and unless forceful action were forthcoming the threats of the Powers would appear to be mere bluff. But, in a reversal of position, the ministers agreed to accept the reasonableness of China's objections to publication in the *Gazette*. In fact, they decided to consider the whole issue as closed and they agreed to terminate any further cooperative action on the matter.[77] At its moment of testing the missionary coalition had collapsed.

Previous accounts of the diplomacy of the period have failed to em-

[66] MacDonald to Salisbury, Tel., Peking, March 14, 1900. F.O. 17/1418.
[67] *Ibid.*
[68] MacDonald to Salisbury, Tel., Peking, March 23, 1900. F.O. 17/1418.
[69] Minute by Salisbury, Foreign Office, March 23, 1900. F.O. 17/1418.
[70] Conger to Hay, Peking, May 3, 1900. *F.R.U.S., 1900*, No. 367, pp. 119–120.
[71] P. Cambon to Delcassé, London, April 4, 1900. *D.D.C.*, 1899–1900, No. 17, p. 14.
[72] MacDonald to Salisbury, Tel., Peking, March 29, 1900. F.O. 17/1418.
[73] Minute by Campbell, Foreign Office, March 29, 1900. F.O. 17/1418.
[74] Minute by Salisbury, Foreign Office, undated. F.O. 17/1418.
[75] MacDonald to Salisbury, Peking, April 16, 1900. F.O. 17/1412.
[76] Conger to Hay, Peking, April 12, 1900. *F.R.U.S., 1900*, No. 356, p. 113.
[77] *Ibid.*

phasize the importance of this sudden about-face. Indeed, certain vital documents concerning the story appear to be missing from the Foreign Office files at the Public Record Office. But that an abrupt reversal of diplomacy took place is evident. The explanation of this change of policy is to be seen in the violent reaction which the threatened use of force had caused in the chancelleries of Europe.

On March 31, Pichon telegraphed to Delcassé that three English ships had arrived off Ta-ku and that American, German, and Italian ships were expected.[78] Here was a movement of armed power into the turbulent north of China, with the Franco-Russian bloc distinctly excluded, and led by Britain who previously denied any intention of initiating a naval demonstration. Delcassé immediately telegraphed his ambassadors in Berlin, Washington, and London, asking them to find out for what purpose these governments arranged this demonstration.[79]

Denials of any purposeful naval demonstration came flooding into Paris. Count Bülow, the German foreign secretary, protested ignorance of the English and American move at Ta-ku.[80] The United States replied that the move amounted to a precautionary measure, and that it was not to be regarded as a demonstration in common with the other Powers.[81] The lengthiest explanation came from Britain. Salisbury insisted that it was a simple measure of precaution, designed to reassure the English nationals and to make the Chinese reconsider their antiforeign policy. The permanent undersecretary for foreign affairs, Sir Thomas Sanderson, added his assurances that the move was merely taken on the advice of the British representative in China. He argued that analogous moves were undertaken by other governments, and noted that it was two, not three, warships that Britain had ordered to Ta-ku.[82]

There is no record of the sharp rebuff which the Foreign Office most certainly sent to its adventurous minister at Peking in early April, warning him not to trifle in matters affecting higher policy. But such a dispatch would explain MacDonald's willingness to accept the demise of the coalition. For when the ministers assembled on April 7 and Pichon suggested that the Powers accept China's reply as adequate, there is no evidence of any protest from MacDonald.[83]

MacDonald's bungled attempt to bring pressure on the Chinese had frayed the nerves of the Powers. Britain, having caught a hint of the militant counteraction with which any affirmative policy in China would be met, tended to revert to her traditional policy of drift.

France was driven to align her policy more closely with that of her Russian ally in China. Pichon emphasized in his dispatches to Paris that his efforts to gain suppression of the Boxers would henceforth be taken only in closest cooperation with the Russian minister.[84] French loyalty to her protectorate of the Catholic missionaries had brought together the missionary coalition; now French loyalty to her Russian ally helped split the coalition. The tragedy was that henceforth neither Britain nor France would willingly bring into play the force and initiative necessary to cope with the mounting crisis. The fear of instigating a crisis between the European blocs in China would inhibit any negotiation with the Manchu regime.

Once more the Manchu court received a doubly unfortunate impression. The Western Powers, Britain in particular, took on the appearance of aggressors, determined to press their demands upon the Yamen in ignorance of, or regardless of, the possible repercussions in domestic Chinese politics. But simultaneously the Powers appeared impotent, prevented by disunity and hesitation from implementing their threats.

Before the Storm

Although cooperative action against the Chinese Government had failed, an unexpected turn of events enabled the diplomats to lapse into their accustomed state of complacency. On April 14, a memorial from the governor-general of Chihli appeared in the *Peking Gazette*. It was accompanied by an Imperial rescript urging action against the Boxers.[85] MacDonald had previously dropped the hint that if such a memorial appeared in the *Gazette*, embodying the secret anti-Boxer edict, it would fulfill the demands of the Powers. In this manner the demands of the missionary coalition were unexpectedly satisfied.

---

[78] Pichon to Delcassé, Tel., Peking, March 31, 1900. *D.D.C.*, 1899–1900, No. 15, p. 13.

[79] Delcassé to Ambassadors at Washington, London, and Berlin, Tel., Paris, April 3, 1900. *D.D.C.*, 1899–1900, No. 16, p. 14.

[80] De Noailles to Delcassé, Tel., Berlin, April 4, 1900. *D.D.C.*, 1899–1900, No. 18, p. 15.

[81] J. Cambon to Delcassé, Tel., New York, April 5, 1900. *D.D.C.*, 1899–1900, No. 19, p. 15.

[82] P. Cambon to Delcassé, Tel., London, April 4, 1900. *D.D.C.*, 1899–1900, No. 17, p. 14.

[83] Pichon to Delcassé, Peking, April 20, 1900. *D.D.C.*, 1899–1900, No. 22, p. 17.

[84] *Ibid.*

[85] MacDonald to Salisbury, Tel., Peking, April 16, 1900. F.O. 17/1418.

The reason for this belated compliance is difficult to discern. Perhaps the fact that the British ships were still at Ta-ku had its effect in moving the Manchu court to action. Perhaps, as Pichon reported, this sudden compliance was due to the intercession of the Russian minister, who desired to avoid a renewed diplomatic crisis.[86] Whatever the motivation, it restored the confidence of the Powers.

MacDonald was exuberant. He wrote to Salisbury that while the danger had not yet passed, he felt that the Chinese Government was at last beginning to give evidence of a genuine desire to suppress the anti-Christian organizations.[87] Pichon reported that while he was uncertain concerning the future, the situation seemed to be improving.[88] Conger, the American minister, notified Secretary of State Hay that the Chinese "in their own way and time" had answered the identical notes of the five Powers.[89]

Such was the paper victory which the Powers congratulated themselves on winning over the Boxers. It was happily received, for it eased the tensions growing up among the Powers themselves. But a paper victory can be canceled by the issuance of a new paper. On April 17, the day after MacDonald ordered the British ships to return to their regular duties, a new Imperial decree appeared in the *Peking Gazette*. It approved the formation of rural trained bands which "kept watch and rendered mutual assistance to each other."[90] It warned that good and bad tended to mix in these bands, but it admonished those who caused trouble for the Christians to return to their own callings. This decree, in fact, renewed the ambiguity of the January 11 decree which first brought together the missionary coalition.

Apparently publication of the Chihli governor-general's memorial was only a momentary departure by the Empress Dowager from her basic policy. Efforts were to be made, as before, to pacify the Boxers, but no wholesale condemnation of their activity, as urged by the missionary coalition, was contemplated.

MacDonald refused to believe that his victory could so easily be snatched away. He even argued that the purpose of the new decree was merely to correct the effect of the January 11 decree.[91] Soon, however, the evidence began to mount against MacDonald's contention. On May 2, Consul Carles at Tientsin offered a different interpretation of the decree. He noted that a magistrate at Tung-a Hsien, who formerly offered rewards for the capture of the Boxers, had withdrawn his offer in the face of the new decree.[92] Elsewhere the Boxers openly expressed their gratitude for the decree and claimed that it gave them protection.[93] Rumors were current that the Empress Dowager and Prince Tuan favored the Boxers.[94] The antiforeign Manchu Kang-i was given the leadership of several key ministries.[95] And by April 24 Pichon abandoned his earlier expression of optimism; he sent word to Delcassé that villages were being burned near Pao-tung-fu and that disorder might spread rapidly.[96]

MacDonald's unrelenting optimism was based partly on his ignorance of the mounting unrest throughout China. He failed to indicate to Whitehall the magnitude of the outbreaks, just as he failed to comprehend the dilemma facing the Manchu Government. But it was also an optimism encouraged by the realization that Whitehall did not want a crisis in China. He was aware that, as one Foreign Office official put it, "in the present crisis remonstrance seemed futile — it is only strong action on the spot that commands attention." [97] But the difficulty was that the Foreign Office felt that it was in no position to take strong action. Nevertheless the fault was primarily MacDonald's. On May 14 he sent his current observations on to Francis Bertie at the Foreign Office. While he objected to British inaction there was no indication that he was aware of the destructive upheaval underway: "The Chinese are getting mulish and obstructive. I have spoken to them like a father. Of

---

[86] Pichon to Delcassé, Peking, April 20, 1900. *D.D.C.*, 1899–1900, No. 22, p. 17. By April 12, the two British ships at Ta-ku were joined by two Italian, one American, and one French ship. While the French ship may well have been there primarily to check British action, this gathering of naval power may have carried the same weight with the Chinese as a purposeful naval demonstration. Conger to Hay, Peking, April 12, 1900. *F.R.U.S., 1900*, No. 356, p. 113.

[87] MacDonald to Salisbury, Peking, April 16, 1900. F.O. 17/1412.

[88] Pichon to Delcassé, Peking, April 20, 1900. *D.D.C.*, 1899–1900, No. 22, p. 17.

[89] Conger to Hay, Peking, April 16, 1900. *F.R.U.S., 1900*, No. 360, p. 117.

[90] MacDonald to Salisbury, Tel., Peking, April 16, 1900. F.O. 17/1418.

[91] MacDonald to Salisbury, Peking, April 18, 1900. F.O. 17/1412.

[92] Carles to MacDonald, Tientsin, May 2, 1900. F.O. 17/1413.

[93] Tan, *The Boxer Catastrophe*, p. 54. Tan stated that the decree of April 17 was the same in substance as the decree of January 11.

[94] Meech to Cousins, Hsiao Chang (Hsia-chang), April 17–21, 1900. L.M.S./NC/ 10. But Meech went on to note that these rumors were "difficult to reconcile with the action which the officials ultimately take in killing and imprisoning so many of them [Boxers]. I can put the muddle down to the Chinese way of doing things."

[95] Pichon to Delcassé, Peking, April 20, 1900. *D.D.C.*, 1899–1900, No. 22, p. 17.

[96] Pichon to Delcassé, Peking, April 24, 1900. *D.D.C.*, 1899–1900, No. 25, p. 19.

[97] Unsigned Minute, Foreign Office, May 8, 1900. F.O. 17/1418.

course I am keeping things quiet on account of South Africa and I stand a deal which I shouldn't have done two years ago — I doubt whether the policy is a sound one for the bill will be a big one when we put it in." [98]

We have now traced British diplomacy to the very eve of crisis. Nothing as yet was inevitably lost; no point-of-no-return had been reached. As danger built up rapidly in late May and June wise diplomacy might still have forestalled a catastrophe. But the diplomacy of the preceding five months, principally British diplomacy, had created an ominous precedent. MacDonald's conduct had been erratic. In January, in spite of Brooks's murder, he had been content merely to follow the lead of the French minister in raising a joint protest. In March he sought to unite the missionary coalition in a naval demonstration the threat of which only weakened the coalition. In April he sought to draw Britain into what amounted to a naval demonstration which backfired in the destruction of the missionary coalition. In late April and through most of May he reverted to a passive policy.

The result of all this was that a particular fear and distrust of Britain took possession of the Empress Dowager and her advisers. It was unlikely that the Manchu regime would look to the British minister for understanding and support in its moment of danger; rather, having nowhere else to turn, it would trust the tenacious spirit of the Boxers to expel the foreign aggressor. The British minister had threatened and the threat had proved to be empty; he had attempted to create an alliance against the Manchu regime and the alliance had fallen apart in its moment of testing. Unless MacDonald developed a new grasp of the crisis confronting him, or, at least, gave some evidence of that sense of balance imperative to the diplomat, little could be done to dispel the gathering storm.

---

[98] MacDonald to Bertie, Peking, May 14, 1900. F.O. 17/1413.

CHAPTER IX

European Politics in Peking

B Y THE spring of 1900, the Boxer rising had spread swiftly through northern China, creating a particularly uneasy situation for the diplomats, merchants, and missionaries in Peking. The victims of the deadly Boxer devastations continued to be the Chinese Christian converts, but the foreign ministers in Peking chose to slough off any real responsibility for them. At that moment, more than ever before, it was the struggle between the great Powers for dominance in China which absorbed the diplomats. As it became possible that the apparently uncontrollable Boxer insurrection might in its rampage crush the Manchu regime, the European Powers readied themselves to move in upon China. If partition were to come each sought to gain a dominant strategic position from the outset.

The principal antagonists in the looming confrontation were England and Russia; once either was convinced that the Boxers posed a substantial threat to its legation or that the time was ripe to move in upon a power vacuum in Peking, then the other could ill afford to stand aside in the race. This determination not to be left behind created a situation of unusual tension in the capital, made even more intense by rumors of Boxer plans to exterminate all foreigners. Given a sudden heightening of these fears, one of the Powers might summon troops in large numbers to Peking. Here the danger lay in creating a chain reaction: one that could bring troops of other nations to the capital and then unite the Empress Dowager and the Boxers in overt opposition to all the Europeans.

The Renewal of the Missionary Coalition

Toward the end of May diplomatic activity regarding the Boxer trouble entered a new and decisive phase. Boxer outbursts were gaining in frequency and moving closer to Peking. But no special prescience of danger alerted the diplomats; rather, it was renewed pressure by the missionaries that led the diplomatic corps to reassemble on May 20. The French minister, Pichon, had called the meeting in response to the frantic pleadings of Mgr. Favier, the Catholic bishop of Peking. Many regarded Favier as the best informed European concerning Chinese affairs. The bishop spoke Chinese fluently and had permanently assumed Chinese dress with his hair in a queue.[1] Now his converts were facing massacre all around Peking, and refugees were streaming into the city. Most disturbing of all, the bishop warned Pichon that the Boxers intended the extermination of all foreigners.[2]

Pichon, convinced of the danger, reiterated Favier's warning before the assembled diplomatic corps. MacDonald also had been informed of the growing peril. Two days before he had received news of the destruction of a London Missionary chapel, just forty miles from Peking.[3] And he acknowledged that Favier's years of experience in China and his well-informed sources of information could not be dismissed lightly.[4] Still, MacDonald remarked that he could not yet justify the bringing up of legation guards, as Pichon had suggested, and he seemed to reflect the consensus of the group. The upshot was that the reunited missionary coalition decided to send identical notes demanding that the Manchu Government issue a new anti-Boxer edict. But, if they had no satisfactory answer by the time they met five days later, they would consider calling up legation guards from Tientsin or ordering a naval demonstration.[5]

Pichon's warnings at the May 20 meeting did little to impress MacDonald. This was evident in his report to Salisbury: "As regards my own opinion as to the danger to which Europeans in Peking are exposed, I confess that little has come to my knowledge to confirm the gloomy anticipations of the French Fathers." [6] MacDonald also telegraphed Whitehall that he did not expect it would be necessary to bring guards to Peking. The Powers might resort to a naval demonstration; but even this, he thought, was unlikely, for the Chinese Government now seemed to be sufficiently alarmed.[7] Even the threat of such bold joint action disturbed Salisbury who commented on receipt of MacDonald's telegram: "He must of course be supported: but I regret that he has done this. I do not look forward with pleasure to a 'Concert of Europe' in China."[8]

On May 25, the various Powers received China's reply to their demands of May 21. The Tsungli Yamen promised that a new decree would be issued against the Boxers, but the reply was vague concerning certain other demands.[9] MacDonald immediately telegraphed Salisbury that this reply was unsatisfactory.[10] However, Whitehall rushed back instructions to MacDonald: "Keep in the background as much as possible and let any suggestion for further action come from others."[11]

The following day, May 26, the diplomatic corps met to consider the Tsungli Yamen's reply. Pichon was as vocal as MacDonald was quiet. The French minister declared that China was on the eve of a great outbreak which would endanger the lives of all Europeans in Peking.[12] He urged decisive action. But opinions were divided, and the diplomats could only compromise. They called on the Yamen to produce a detailed statement of the measures taken against the Boxers along with a copy of the new decree. At the same time they agreed that, failing a satisfactory reply, they would send for legation guards.[13] This attitude of wait-and-see apparently received its reward. The following day MacDonald's optimism was increased by an encouraging interview with Prince Ch'ing, chairman of the Tsungli Yamen.[14] And, on May 28, the Yamen met all the demands of the diplomats with a decree which directed forceful action against the Boxers.[15]

[1] Henry Norman, *People and Politics of the Far East*, p. 279.
[2] Pichon to Delcassé, Peking, May 20, 1900. *D.D.C.*, 1899–1900, No. 30, p. 21.
[3] MacDonald to Salisbury, Tel., Peking, May 18, 1900. F.O. 17/1418.
[4] MacDonald to Salisbury, Peking, May 21, 1900. F.O. 17/1413.
[5] MacDonald to Salisbury, Tel., Peking, May 21, 1900. F.O. 17/1418.
[6] MacDonald to Salisbury, Peking, May 21, 1900. F.O. 17/1413.
[7] MacDonald to Salisbury, Tel., Peking, May 21, 1900. F.O. 17/1418.
[8] Minute by Salisbury, Foreign Office, May 21, 1900. F.O. 17/1418.
[9] MacDonald to Salisbury, Tel., Peking, May 25, 1900. F.O. 17/1418.   [10] *Ibid.*
[11] Foreign Office Minute, May 25, 1900. F.O. 17/1418.
[12] MacDonald to Salisbury, Tel., Peking, May 27, 1900. F.O. 17/1418.   [13] *Ibid.*
[14] MacDonald to Salisbury, Peking, May 28, 1900. F.O. 17/1413.
[15] Pichon to Delcassé, Peking, May 28, 1900. *D.D.C.*, 1899–1900, No. 36, p. 27.

However, on May 29, the situation again became ominous. The Boxers had burned to the ground certain railway stations — one of them at Feng-t'ai, six miles from Peking.[16] Traffic between Peking and Tientsin was halted, and the Imperial troops did nothing. Without consulting his colleagues Pichon telegraphed for his legation guards. Later in the day the diplomatic corps met and agreed to follow the lead of Pichon in calling for guards.[17]

Here we must closely examine MacDonald's motivation. His telegram to Consul Carles in Tientsin calling for guards emphasized that European lives were in danger and that no limit should be put on the number of troops sent.[18] But, in spite of mounting reports of Boxer atrocities, MacDonald's attention was riveted on the struggle for position among the Powers. He sent confidential instructions to Carles that the number of British guards must be equal to those of Russia or France, and he ordered the consul to keep him informed of the number and strength of the foreign guards preparing to go to Peking.[19] By June 1, this force of over 300 legation guards arrived in the capital; it was a detachment composed of British, American, French, Italian, Japanese, and Russian marines. Apparently the arrival of the legation guards reassured MacDonald, for on June 3 he informed Admiral Seymour that no more troops would be needed unless the collapse of the Manchu Government brought on a struggle with Russia and France for spoils. Whatever happened, he assured the admiral, the legations would be the last place attacked.[20] It was not the primitive violence of the Boxer which obsessed MacDonald; rather, it was the familiar calculations of the European power struggle.

Perhaps Pichon was more accessible to the missionaries who began to limp into Peking, shocked and terrorized by the sights of savage brutality which they had witnessed. Perhaps he was simply better informed concerning the plots and counterplots underway behind the walls of the Forbidden City. At any rate, the excited Frenchman rallied the foreign diplomats to face the real peril of the Boxer rising.[21] On June 3, to a meeting of the diplomatic corps, he carried the suggestion that each representative should telegraph his government advising that, if telegraphic contact were cut, their naval commanders at Ta-ku should be ordered to take concerted measures to relieve the legations.[22] MacDonald, however, was skeptical. To the prescribed telegram, he added his own confidential postscript. He granted that things were "very serious"; still, he observed, it was difficult to say if the situation was as grave as Pichon assumed.[23]

Events in the next two days shocked MacDonald into a full realization of the Boxer danger. On June 4, news reached Peking of the Boxer murder of the Reverend Mr. Robinson of the Society for the Propagation of the Gospel.[24] The following day news reached MacDonald that Robinson's companion, the Reverend Mr. Norman, had also been murdered. The British minister went immediately for an interview with Prince Ch'ing and the Tsungli Yamen. Ch'ing acknowledged that he could not ensure the safety of Peking, and he doubted that the 6000 Imperial troops which were being summoned to the defense of the city would fire except in defense of government property. MacDonald telegraphed Whitehall that the Yamen was unable to impress the Empress Dowager with the danger in allowing the Boxer devastations to continue unopposed.[25]

With MacDonald at last alert to the growing chaos about him, it might be well to survey Whitehall's reaction to their minister's danger signals. On June 5, the Foreign Office received an unequivocal request from MacDonald that once his communications were cut the British admiral should be instructed to rescue the legations.[26] But Whitehall clung to its passive policy. Francis Bertie, the assistant undersecretary, noted that it would be best to simply follow the lead of the other Powers in military matters. Otherwise, he added, Britain might be left in the lurch to carry out unassisted some policy involving the use of force. Salisbury agreed.[27] But he cautioned that the British admiral in China waters should be given a free hand to meet any emergency.[28]

---

[16] Steiger, *China and the Occident*, p. 202.

[17] MacDonald to Salisbury, Tel., Peking, May 29, 1900. F.O. 17/1418.

[18] MacDonald to Carles, Tel., Peking, May 30, 1900. F.O. 228/1338.

[19] MacDonald to Carles, Tel., Peking, May 29, 1900. F.O. 228/1338.

[20] The MacDonald Papers as quoted in Peter Fleming, *The Siege of Peking* (London: Rupert Hart-Davis, 1959), pp. 69–70.

[21] MacDonald to Salisbury, Tel., Peking, June 4, 1900. F.O. 17/1418.

[22] *Ibid.*

[23] *Ibid.*

[24] MacDonald to Salisbury, Tel., Peking, June 4, 1900. (This was a second telegram of the same date.) F.O. 17/1418.

[25] MacDonald to Salisbury, Tel., Peking, June 5, 1900. F.O. 17/1418.

[26] MacDonald to Salisbury, Tel., Peking, June 5, 1900. (This was a second telegram of the same date.) F.O. 17/1418.

[27] Minute by Bertie, Foreign Office, June 5, 1900. F.O. 17/1418.

[28] Minute by Salisbury, Foreign Office, June 5, 1900. F.O. 17/1418.

On June 6, MacDonald's report to Whitehall pointed to the possibility of a rising in Peking encouraged by the sympathy of the Empress Dowager and certain conservative elements at court for the Boxers. It warned that one or more of the Powers would then be forced to occupy the Imperial City. But MacDonald offered a last-ditch proposal which he hoped might avert foreign intervention. He suggested that the diplomatic corps demand a special audience with the Empress Dowager.[29] There the Empress Dowager might be brought to see the imminent danger of foreign intervention and of European armed intrusion in the Imperial City. But, if the Empress Dowager should refuse to grant this audience, MacDonald advised that strong measures should be taken.[30]

Bertie's comment on MacDonald's proposals testified to the ignorance at Whitehall concerning the drift of Chinese affairs. The assistant undersecretary pointed out that it was doubtful that the ministers would be granted an interview. This was, of course, true but at that point anything was worth a try. The navy, he went on, might be able to protect European lives in Peking and keep the railway open, but it could hardly drag the Empress Dowager to an audience. But Bertie's solution was even more fantastic: Britain, he thought, should shift her support to the Reform party, overthrow the Empress Dowager, and restore the Emperor.[31] Such an abrupt reversal of traditional policy might have been feasible as a long-range goal, but to have adopted it at that point would have sealed the doom of the ministers in Peking and would have plunged Britain into a prolonged conflict with China.

Fortunately, Salisbury's sense of balance prevailed. He approved MacDonald's suggestion, and informed Bertie that "We cannot take the tiller safely out of his [MacDonald's] hands."[32] At the same time, on June 7, Salisbury alerted MacDonald to the particular requirements of his diplomatic task: "Take precisely what measures you think expedient. The situation is difficult and your discretion must be quite unfettered. There are many possible dangers: the most serious is that Russia should move to occupy the whole or part of Peking. It would be very difficult to move her out. We must therefore if possible avoid making her wish to occupy Peking but if she shows signs of tending to do so we should occupy some important part simultaneously so far as our resources enable us to do so. Arrangements of course would be made with the other Powers but they are less important."[33] That Salisbury was determined to permit as little as possible of China to fall to Russia was also evident in his rejoinder to a second suggestion by Bertie. The latter had urged that if Russia took Peking and the Ta-ku forts, then the British should take the island of Chou Shan and the forts at Nanking, thus controlling the Yangtze Valley. Salisbury's blunt reply was that he hoped Britain would never allow Russia to take all the Ta-ku forts which were so vital for the control of Peking.[34]

Salisbury's determination to retain Britain's position at Peking, in spite of Russia's growing power, evidently eclipsed his concern over the danger of Boxer attacks. On June 9, the Queen informed him of her anxiety for the safety of MacDonald and the legation personnel. She suggested the removal of the foreign minister from Peking. Salisbury's reply was revealing: ". . . It would be imprudent to interfere with Sir C. MacDonald's entire discretion as to his movements. If he left Peking, Russia backed by France would remain supreme. . . . Russia not China, seems to me the greatest danger of the moment." [35]

The Impact of European Rivalry

Just as Britain's apprehensions centered on Russia and not the Boxers, so the conduct of the other key Powers in Peking can best be understood in the context of the power struggle. Pichon, in particular, by his efforts to rally the Powers to action over the Boxer outrages, was running

---

[29] MacDonald to Salisbury, Tel., Peking, June 6, 1900. F.O. 17/1418.

[30] *Ibid.*

[31] Minute by Bertie, Foreign Office, June 7, 1900. F.O. 17/1439. This statement by Bertie is the first evidence that I have found that the Empress Dowager was partially correct in fearing that the British might swing their power behind the Emperor and a reform regime. Bertie, as we shall see, returned to this theme at a later stage. This is no evidence, however, that the British ever moved to implement such a scheme.

[32] Minute by Salisbury, Foreign Office, June 7, 1900. F.O. 17/1439.

[33] Salisbury to MacDonald, Tel., Foreign Office, June 7, 1900. F.O. 17/1439.

[34] Minutes by Bertie and by Salisbury, Foreign Office, June 7, 1900. F.O. 17/1439. On the same day Salisbury suggested that troops be sent to the Peking area from Hong Kong, Wei-hai-wei, and Singapore. Salisbury to Bertie, Hatfield, June 7, 1900. F.O. 17/1439.

[35] J. D. Hargreaves, "Lord Salisbury, British Isolation and the Yangtze Valley, June–September, 1900," *Bulletin of the Institute of Historical Research*, XXX (1957), 63. This article emphasized the fear which gripped the Foreign Office that a Continental European bloc would oppose Britain in China. In spite of such a threat Salisbury attempted to uphold a policy of isolation for Britain. For our purposes the article is useful in showing how considerations of world policy overshadowed domestic Chinese disturbances in the formation of British policy.

counter to French policy which sought to ingratiate itself with Russia by avoiding the threat of intervention in northern China. In mid-April, the Russian minister, Giers, agreed to aid Pichon in urging the Chinese to suppress the Boxers. But in return Pichon was to reject any alliance with the other Powers who, according to Giers, were merely protesting the Boxer danger in order to advance their own acquisitive designs.[36] As the crisis grew in intensity, however, Giers was obliged to associate himself with the diplomatic corps, called together by Pichon on May 20.[37] For the Russian minister this was a distasteful duty. In fact, immediately after, he confided to MacDonald, who was also eager to avoid drastic measures, that he did not think that a naval demonstration was called for.[38]

Thereafter, St. Petersburg sought to impress upon the other Powers that the situation in China was improving. On May 25, the Tsar told the British ambassador, Sir Charles Scott, that Count Muraviev had received good news from Peking. China, he said, was now moving against the Boxers and the need for European pressure was removed.[39] The Tsar contended that, in any case, extreme measures, such as a naval demonstration, should not be considered unless the lives of missionaries or of Europeans in general were in imminent peril. In an obvious jab at Pichon, the Tsar added that while MacDonald and Giers were in agreement certain other ministers were a little too impulsive.[40]

The divergence between France and Russia was evident when the ministers assembled on May 26 to consider the Chinese reply. Pichon, as we recall, led the way in demanding action. Giers agreed that there was a certain danger from the Boxers, but he argued that the Chinese Government would take effective measures against them.[41] But when Pichon instigated the call for legation guards on May 29, Giers could do little else but call for Russian guards as well, for it would not do for Russia to be undermanned militarily in Peking.

At this point Paris and St. Petersburg sought to bring their policies together again. It was the Russian policy which prevailed. On May 30, the Tsar assured Scott that the Chinese were about to send a reliable force against the Boxers.[42] And on the same day Delcassé told the English ambassador, Sir Edward Monson, that he expected no drastic turn of events in Peking.[43] However, differences now developed between French policy in Paris and in Peking. On June 5, just after Pichon had led the diplomatic corps in sending home warnings that intervention by European naval detachments might be necessary to rescue the legations, Delcassé told Monson that for the moment all danger had passed in Peking.[44] But the same day the French Government found it necessary to deny officially a report in a Paris newspaper that there was a divergency of views between Delcassé and Pichon.[45] This might explain Monson's comment that Delcassé seemed reluctant to discuss recent events in Peking.[46]

However difficult it may have been to maintain the Franco-Russian alliance, it was the intense rivalry between that bloc and the British which

---

[36] Giers to Foreign Office, Peking, April 18, 1900. U.S.S.R., *A Digest of the Krasnyi Arkhiv*, compiled, translated, and annotated by Leonid S. Rubinchek and edited by Louise M. Boutelle and Gordon W. Thayer (Cleveland: Cleveland Public Library, 1947), p. 130.

[37] MacDonald to Salisbury, Tel., Peking, May 21, 1900. F.O. 17/1418.

[38] *Ibid.*

[39] Scott to Salisbury, St. Petersburg, May 25, 1900. F.O. 65/1599.

[40] *Ibid.*

[41] MacDonald to Salisbury, Tel., Peking, May 27, 1900. F.O. 17/1418.

[42] Scott to Salisbury, St. Petersburg, May 30, 1900. F.O. 65/1599.

[43] Monson to Salisbury, Tel., Paris, May 31, 1900. F.O. 27/3495.

[44] Monson to Salisbury, Paris, June 5, 1900. F.O. 27/3495.

[45] *Ibid.*, enclosed report on news item.

[46] *Ibid.* It is certain that Russia, aided by France, sought to delay firm action against the Boxers. Britain was, perhaps, just as guilty in her refusal to face the growing crisis. Nonetheless, a rumor grew up in diplomatic circles during the summer of 1900 in regard to the special negligence of Russia and France. The story was connected with the sudden death of Count Muraviev, the Russian foreign minister in June 1900; some looked on this death as more likely a suicide. Sir Edward Monson reported on these rumors from Paris as follows: "I hear so much of the 'comedy' played by France and Russia during Muraviev's life in regard to the situation in China that I have not been able to refrain from including it officially. Delcassé will probably escape an interpellation in regard to M. Pichon's warnings, because the Chambers are about to adjourn: but lots of people in Paris who were in constant correspondence with the [minister] at Peking know that he gave timely warning to the Ministry of Foreign Affairs. I am assured on the other hand, on very good authority, that the Russian Minister at Peking did not send home so strong a warning as the Frenchman did. If this is really true, it would to a certain extent excuse Muraviev's optimism. At the same time I expect that if the Russian telegrams, which were shown[,] were less pessimistic there must have been private ones which told the truth. It is terrible to think that so awful a catastrophe has been partly caused by the intriguing and deceit of a great power; but appearances are so strong that there are many people here who [estimate] that such is the case. At any rate, Delcassé seemed to me the day before yesterday perfectly miserable; and [he harped] so much upon the absence of all *arrière pensée* on the part of the French Government as to make me more suspicious than ever." Monson to Salisbury, Paris, July 6, 1900. Salisbury Papers, Vol. CLXXVII, No. 50.

Only access to the French and Russian archives can reveal the culpability of France and Russia in delaying in the face of the rising Boxer crisis. At the same time one may estimate that these Powers were no more guilty than the English. All the European Powers were absorbed in the world power struggle in China; and all the Powers regarded such domestic troubles as the Boxers as being of secondary concern.

overshadowed all events in China. One would be justified in attributing any new and drastic move by one of the Powers to that competition. Keeping this in mind we must now examine the nature of that fateful decision made by the Peking diplomats between June 9 and 10. This was the decision to order the admirals at Ta-ku to send a relief force to Peking.

Up to the time of this decision preparations were carried forward for the proposed interview with the Empress Dowager, although the decision to demand the audience was postponed until June 9. This was done on the apparently sincere plea of the Tsungli Yamen that rail communications would be restored by then and that this evidence of the regime's ability to restore order would make the audience unnecessary.[47] Judging by the willingness of the diplomats to put off their demand, the situation had at least not taken a turn for the worse. Then, suddenly, on June 9, MacDonald sent an urgent telegram to Tientsin ordering Consul Carles to instruct Admiral Seymour to send reinforcements immediately.[48] MacDonald later explained that he had taken this step after having been secretly informed by Lien Fang, an emissary of the Tsungli Yamen, that the Empress Dowager planned to exterminate all foreigners in Peking.[49]

This call for troops was taken without the consent of the other diplomats. When the diplomatic corps assembled later in the day on June 9, MacDonald was persuaded to withdraw his call for reinforcements. Most startling of all, it was Pichon who led the way in rejecting MacDonald's move. The Frenchman claimed to have information that the situation was improving, and this led the diplomats to put off any decisive action for another day.[50]

How is one to explain this amazing reversal of roles between MacDonald and Pichon? The answer must lie in the maneuvers between the Powers for positions of strength in Peking.

By June 9 both the French and the Russians were convinced that the crisis had become so formidable that only European intervention could prevent certain catastrophe. A strong Russian force had already been assembled at Port Arthur; and, on June 9, Giers telegraphed St. Petersburg that only its prompt arrival could save the lives of the foreigners in Peking.[51] Nevertheless, Pichon, representing the Franco-Russian bloc, put off the call for reinforcements from Tientsin. He urgently desired armed intervention; but, even more, he hoped that this force would be dominated by the large Russian detachment on its way from Port Arthur. The delay of a few days was vital.

The British documents do not reveal if MacDonald was aware of the dispatch of the Russian force from Port Arthur. But it was highly probable that he, at least, possessed information that a large Russian force was grouping. In fact, MacDonald was sufficiently alarmed so that, later in the evening of June 9, he renewed his call for troops from Tientsin.[52] As news of this order spread through Tientsin, the few Russian and French troops already there opposed the dispatch of a British dominated expedition, even to the point of refusing to accompany it. Of course, at the last minute they dropped this protest since they could hardly allow the British alone to occupy Peking.

MacDonald's excuse for calling the troops was weak beyond belief. Supposedly, he was impelled to action by rumors of the planned slaughter of Europeans in Peking.[53] Such rumors had been commonly reported for the past month and before. If this suddenly incited MacDonald to action, it was a case of sheer panic. If, however, it was his intention to bring a contingent of troops to Peking before the arrival at Tientsin of the 4000 Russian troops, he was merely following Salisbury's instructions to checkmate any Russian advance. Indeed, it must have been MacDonald's hope to restore order in Peking with a force in British command and largely British in number. If outbreaks were quickly put down, Russian troops might be denied their excuse for marching on Peking; this, of course, constituted a wild and, as events proved, foolish gamble.

This last diplomatic episode, as the crisis entered a new stage, bore a tragic but paradoxical similarity to the diplomacy of the previous six months. In the past the decision to intervene to block persecution of the

---

[47] MacDonald to Salisbury, Peking, June 10, 1900. F.O. 17/1413.

[48] *Ibid.*

[49] *Ibid.*

[50] *Ibid.*

[51] Malozemoff, *Russian Far Eastern Policy*, p. 127.

[52] MacDonald to Salisbury, Peking, June 10, 1900. F.O. 17/1413. By June 9, the Tsungli Yamen was aware that Russia was about to bring a large force to Peking. "Crisis in China," London *Times*, June 13, 1900, p. 5.

[53] At this stage the expedition which marched on Peking was to be under a British admiral, Sir Edward Seymour; and the British in the expedition outnumbered the combined French and Russian force. Specifically, of the 2129-man international force, 915 were British, 312 were Russian, and 157 French. The contribution of other nations was as follows: Germany, 512; the United States, 111; Japan, 54; Italy, 42; Austria, 26. Fleming, *The Siege of Peking*, p. 75.

converts had been rejected, since intervention would provoke a dangerous interpower conflict. Now that same rivalry among the Powers
speeded up the process of intervention, since once the first move
was made to bring in troops no Power could afford to be left behind. In
both cases diplomatic decisions based on the requirements of the domestic Chinese scene were given secondary consideration.

Diplomacy on the Brink of Siege

The gravity of the dispatch of a military expedition, 2000 strong,
through the seventy miles which separated Tientsin from Peking must be
fully understood. This was an area inflamed by Boxer activity. No mission compound had escaped destruction, no convert was safe along the
route. Now the actual presence of foreign troops galvanized the fanatic
villager to even greater works of devastation. There is no evidence that
the foreign ministers were aware of the grave consequences of their call
for troops; they had complete confidence in the ability of the force of
Britain's Admiral Seymour to push aside all Chinese opposition. And,
just as they had underestimated the fighting ability of the enraged Chinese masses, they miscalculated the effect of this call for troops on the
Imperial court.

The court was stunned by the news of Seymour's departure. There
was no precedent for the dispatch of a military force against a foreign
capital in time of peace. It was disturbing enough that legation guards
had been called to Peking, but guards had come and gone in 1894–1895
and 1898–1899. Now an additional force was on the way to protect the
apparently secure legations, and an even larger Russian force was at sea
bound for Ta-ku. How could the Imperial court avoid the conclusion that
the long-feared and much-discussed partition of the Chinese Empire
was, at last, underway?

Undoubtedly incited by Seymour's advance, the pro-Boxer party assumed a firm hold on the Imperial administration on June 10. The antiforeign Prince Tuan was named president of the Tsungli Yamen, suc-
ceeding Prince Ch'ing.[54] Hope for a peaceful solution was not abandoned, and members of the Tsungli Yamen called on MacDonald on
June 11 and 12, urging that he order Seymour back to Tientsin.[55] But
MacDonald refused to countermand his instructions. Apparently the
British minister was so intent upon checking any Russian move upon

Peking that he was blind to the almost inevitable reaction which would be provoked by this power play.

As efforts at persuasion had failed, the Imperial court almost inevitably turned to the use of force. On June 13 a decree was issued, addressed to the governor of Chihli, Yü Lu, and to General Nieh. They were to resist the advance of the Seymour expedition, and to block the landing of any additional allied troops.[56] As if by command, Boxer activity increased in intensity. A Boxer force flung itself at Seymour's well-armed contingent; so great was the fury of the assault that the European expedition was unable to continue its advance.[57] And, soon after, Seymour's communications with Tientsin were severed. Henceforth, the fate of the expedition was in doubt. At Peking, the Boxers were no less active. On the afternoon of June 13, a large force of Boxers was permitted to pour through the city gate. And there began a massive slaughter and pillage directed principally against the Christians of the city.[58]

As yet, General Nieh had found it unnecessary or inexpedient to turn his Imperial Army against the stalled Seymour expedition. Up to this point it was simply "rebels" who had attacked the European force. There was still time for conciliation. The Imperial Council met on June 16. There was every indication that the Empress Dowager was prepared for war with the Western Powers. But, if war came, it would be the doing of the foreigner, for she dispatched envoys to meet Seymour and dissuade him from continuing his advance.[59] On the following day there was a second meeting of the Imperial Council. The Empress Dowager was furious; she announced the receipt of four demands from the foreign legations. To assent to these demands would, in effect, place China's financial and military power under European control. The Empress Dowager took further steps to ready China for war. She ordered troops up from the provinces, and she commanded three Chinese officials to proceed to the legations and inform the ministers that if they desired to open hostilities they must depart from China.[60] It has now been established

---

[54] Tan, *The Boxer Catastrophe*, p. 69.
[55] *Ibid.*, p. 71.
[56] *Ibid.*, p. 70.
[57] MacDonald to Salisbury, Peking, September 20, 1900. *P.P.*, China No. 4 (1900), No. 2, p. 20.
[58] *Ibid.*
[59] Tan, *The Boxer Catastrophe*, p. 72.
[60] *Ibid.*, p. 73.

that these "demands" by the foreign Powers were falsified by the court reactionaries, who hoped thereby to move the Empress Dowager to an act of war.[61] However, the foreign Powers themselves managed to blunder into an act even more provocative than the supposed "demands."

Since June 14, Seymour had lost contact with the allied squadron anchored off Ta-ku. Fearing that a Chinese build-up of military strength, underway at the Ta-ku forts, would render it impossible to re-establish contact with Seymour, the European admirals decided that it was essential to occupy the Ta-ku forts.[62] An ultimatum was delivered to the Chinese commander of the forts on June 16; it demanded their surrender in twenty-four hours. And on the following day the allies took the forts by force.

This attack on China proved to be both unnecessary and disastrous. It was unnecessary according to the best possible authority, Colonel G. F. Brown, the British military attaché for China, who was then on leave in London. He informed Whitehall that the capture of the forts was not essential since "troops can be landed at Rocky Point near Pei-ta-ho [Pei-hai-ho] whence there is a railway to Tientsin." [63] And according to a missionary on the spot the attack had disastrous consequences: "The taking of the forts has precipitated matters still further, as now all Chinese forces, including Manchus and Imperial troops as well as Boxers will be turned against the foreigners. Interior [missionary] stations will be given up to the mercy of the mob." [64]

Indeed, the consequences of the attack mounted rapidly. The news reached the Chinese military commanders in Tientsin on the same day, and immediately an attack on the foreign settlement was unleashed. By June 18, the word reached General Nieh, and for the first time he threw his Imperial troops into the battle against the stranded Seymour expedition. Not until the following day was the Imperial court informed of the attack.[65]

Meanwhile, an attempt at mediation had been underway in Peking. The delegation which the Empress Dowager had sent to the legations to reject the supposed foreign "demands" was intent on restoring friendly relations. During their interview with MacDonald, it became evident that the British minister was ignorant of the "demands" he and his fellow ministers had supposedly made. But he remained adamant in refusing to order the Seymour expedition to return to Tientsin.[66]

At this point events had reached a standstill; neither side seemed willing to undertake a move which might result in open hostilities. But on June 19, news of the Ta-ku attack ruptured the prevailing calm. Such an affront could not be tolerated, and the Empress Dowager moved to sever diplomatic relations with the foreign Powers. Late that afternoon the legations received identical notes from the Tsungli Yamen. They were notified of the attack at Ta-ku, and they were requested to depart from Peking within twenty-four hours. Their safety, it was explained, could not be guaranteed in the Imperial City, but they would be granted an escort for their journey to the coast.[67]

This threw the legations into instant turmoil. The diplomatic corps, meeting late into the night, finally formulated a reply to the Tsungli Yamen. It signified a readiness to depart from Peking, but a meeting with the Tsungli Yamen was requested for the following morning at nine o'clock.[68]

---

[61] *Ibid.*

[62] Commander Gaunt to Admiralty, Tel., Luu-kun-tao (Liu-kung Tao), June 17, 1900. *P.P.*, China No. 3 (1900), No. 148, p. 61.

[63] Minute by Brown, Foreign Office, June 16, 1900. F.O. 17/1440. Peter Fleming argued that it was necessary to occupy Ta-ku since a giant trap was about to be closed by the Chinese who would cut the rail line to Tientsin and mine the channel before the Ta-ku landing area. He held that "Once the trap was sprung by the closing of the Pei Ho the naval squadron riding twelve miles out to sea beyond the Taku [Ta-ku] Bar would be impotent." He may be right that the rail line was about to be cut. But the European forces did not attempt to defend the rail line; they occupied Ta-ku. Fleming, *The Siege of Peking*, p. 79.
Steiger also discussed this question; but he, too, was unaware of the Minute of Colonel Brown. Steiger assumed that it was a military necessity to take the Ta-ku forts, and that this was brought on by the foolish dispatch of the Seymour expedition by the aggressive Western Powers. Steiger, *China and the Occident*, p. 233.

[64] Murray to Cousins, Taku (Ta-ku), June 18, 1900. L.M.S./NC/10.

[65] Steiger, *China and the Occident*, p. 225.

[66] MacDonald to Salisbury, Peking, Sept. 20, 1900. *P.P.*, China No. 4 (1900), No. 2, p. 22. The delegation which visited MacDonald went on to see Edwin Conger, the American minister. Here their reception was even less encouraging. Conger not only refused to oppose Seymour's advance, but he warned that American troops were on the way from Manila, a thousand of which "could kill every Boxer in Peking." And, as for the Seymour expedition, it would be composed of thousands of equally efficient European troops, Conger warned the Chinese. To say the least this was inept diplomacy; such rhetoric could only drive the Chinese to desperate action. Conger to Hay, Peking, June 18, 1900. *F.R.U.S.*, *1900*, No. 393, pp. 152–153.

[67] The Tsungli Yamen to MacDonald, Peking, June 19, 1900. *P.P.*, China No. 4 (1900), Enclosure 6 in No. 2, p. 26.

[68] Cologan to the Tsungli Yamen, Peking, June 19, 1900. *P.P.*, China No. 4 (1900), Enclosure 7 in No. 2, p. 27.

The diplomats reassembled early on the morning of June 20. No answer had been received in regard to the requested audience, and it was decided that it would be useless to visit the Yamen. However, Ketteler, the explosive German minister, announced that an appointment had been made with the Yamen and that he meant to keep it.[69] Shortly after, Ketteler set out for the Tsungli Yamen. Nearing his destination, he was halted by a group of Chinese soldiers and shot to death. When news of Ketteler's murder reached the legations, the diplomatic corps, fearful for their own lives, dropped all plans for departure.

It has generally been assumed that Ketteler's murder was a spontaneous act, perpetrated by fanatical Chinese soldiers. However, British documents contain a report written just after the relief of the legations by J. W. Jamieson, one of the best informed members of the legation staff. The report concluded that: ". . . No other minister but the German would have been murdered on his way to the Yamen that day. It was the firm hatred towards him cherished by Li Peng Hêng [Li Ping-heng], who fancied that he had been deprived of the Governorship of Shantung owing to German representations that proved fatal to Baron Ketteler." [70] Finally, the report noted that the murderer had received precise orders from his superior officer to kill Ketteler.

Beyond that it was quite probable that there was an additional broad political purpose which motivated Ketteler's assassination. Early on the morning of June 20, Pichon had dispatched two quite conciliatory messages to the Tsungli Yamen. In the first he suggested that Ta-ku might be handed back to the Chinese forces, and in the second he asserted that the legations would be satisfied if Seymour's force merely waited outside the walls of Peking to escort the foreigners to Tientsin.[71] Months later, Chinese officials told Sir Robert Hart that they were about to send a delegation to the legations to establish good relations when Ketteler's murder destroyed that possibility.[72] It may have been that the war party at the Imperial court, fearing a peaceful settlement, quickly arranged for the assassination of Ketteler.

Whatever the machinations behind Ketteler's death, it had settled certain issues. The Imperial court was convinced that it was impossible to avoid hostilities with the Powers. The diplomatic corps discarded any thought of departing the safety of their legations. But all this does not quite explain the decision to attack the legations. For an understanding of that fateful decision, it will be necessary to review the events before Ketteler's death from a different angle, that of the missionaries.

---

[69] MacDonald to Salisbury, Peking, Sept. 20, 1900. *P.P.*, China No. 4 (1900), No. 2, p. 23.

[70] Jamieson to Satow, Peking, Jan. 5, 1901. F.O. 17/1469.

[71] Notes attached to Pichon to Delcassé, Peking, Aug. 28, 1900. *D.D.C.*, 1899–1900, No. 362, p. 199.

[72] Minute by Hart, Peking, Aug. 22, 1900. F.O. 228/1343.

CHAPTER X

The Missionaries and the Siege

EUROPEAN rivalry, sharpened by a sudden fear of the mounting Boxer strength, had led to an urgent call for troops to support the legation guards in Peking. We have seen how the dispatch of this relief expedition brought about forceful opposition to its advance by the Imperial Chinese Army and by the Boxers. This resistance was intensified after the foolhardy assault by the combined European naval forces upon the Ta-ku forts. While the scene was set for the siege of the legations, a negotiated solution was still possible. As long as the legations were not subjected to attack by Imperial military units, the danger of full-scale war and the dispatch of European expeditionary forces to China might be avoided. All hope rested on the working out of a *modus vivendi* in Peking.

One long-neglected issue, however, beclouded efforts at compromise. It was the emotion-laden problem of the relationship of convert to missionary to foreign minister and the chain of responsibility implicit in this grouping. In spite of previous neglect, there remained an undeniable bond between the diplomats and the native Christians, a bond which was reinforced through the efforts of the missionaries. It was insufficient to deny responsibility for the converts; this was merely to ignore the existence of a crucial problem. When diplomacy refuses to recognize the existence of a vital problem it loses control over the solution of the problem. Ironically, in a rapid series of events, the diplomats suddenly found themselves more closely identified with the converts than ever before. This constituted the final causal development which led to the siege of the legations and the dispatch of European armies to the north of China. Now it must be shown how this came about and where diplomacy once again failed in this tragic chapter in East-West relations.

A Refuge for the Converts

The foreign ministers appeared to be relatively safe as compared with the missionaries and their Christian converts who were scattered throughout northern China. With the rising Boxer tide, converts by the thousands streamed toward Peking in hopes that they might find refuge. The large Catholic cathedrals and the Protestant mission compounds were thrown open to them. But with the increasing danger of Boxer risings in the city itself, the safety of the missionaries and their flocks became a matter of grave concern. British policy on this matter was clear. The missionaries were welcome to the safety of the legations; however, the converts, as Chinese subjects, were denied this shelter.[1]

According to treaty this policy was strictly correct, but soon it was apparent that the lives of thousands were at stake. And the missionaries took upon themselves the task of designing some sort of protection for the converts. Most of the Catholics took refuge in the four Catholic cathedrals, especially the heavily walled Pei-t'ang or Northern Cathedral.[2] Sometime early in June representatives of the various Protestant missions assembled at the American Board Mission in Peking. They agreed that the American Methodist Mission, a defensible compound near the legation area, should become their center for Christian refugees.[3] They obtained the cooperation of Edwin Conger, the American minister, who sent some twenty-five American marines — about half his guard — to protect the compound.[4] Yet, it was doubtful if there would be room for all the refugees, so only refugees from the country and the homeless were to be admitted. And the refugees were to be required to show proper cre-

---

[1] Roland Allen, *The Siege of the Peking Legations* (London: Smith Elder and Co., 1901), p. 86.

[2] Fleming, *The Siege of Peking*, p. 92.

[3] Saville to Thompson, Peking, Sept. 9, 1900. L.M.S./NC/10.

[4] Sarah Pike Conger, *Letters from Peking* (London: Hodder and Stoughton, 1909), p. 96.

dentials. The London Missionary Society therefore issued cards reading L.M.S. Christian Please Admit.[5]

Difficulties, however, quickly ensued. On June 8, a group of L.M.S. Christians were turned away at the American compound. The American missionaries issued a circular letter to explain their action: the "British" Christians were to be admitted if the English minister would supply a guard, and if the English missionaries would join in the defense of the compound. But, at that point, the L.M.S. Christians were still without shelter for the night.

A young and determined British missionary, Miss L. E. V. Saville, came quickly to their aid. She hurried to the American compound and won admission for her Christians. But these homeless women and children were admitted on the condition that Miss Saville go personally to Sir Claude MacDonald and beg him to send English guards to help in the defense of the refugee compound.[6] She went quickly to the British legation. Not until late in the evening of June 9 was she received by MacDonald. The British minister was impressed by her straightforward zeal and he promised to send a guard of about ten men. Late the next day, however, MacDonald reneged on that promise. No doubt this was done at the urging of Captain Strouts, the marine commander, who refused to divide his force.[7] Although Conger was irked at what he considered a selfish decision, a compromise was worked out; the L.M.S. converts were to retain their shelter in return for the transfer of ten British rifles for defense of the American compound.[8]

Many of the missionaries were enraged by the general attitude of the foreign ministers; as one missionary put it: "[The] ministers seemed to display an almost cruel disregard for the massacre or suffering of native Christians. . . ." [9] But circumstances were soon to upset this attitude of indifference. On the night of June 13 the Boxers entered Peking; the ensuing twenty-four hours of death and destruction for the converts culminated in the burning of the historic South Catholic Cathedral. A rescue party sped forth from the French legation, and returned at dawn on June 15 with a small group of refugees, including twenty Chinese nuns.[10] They were apparently given shelter in the French legation. This was the first breach of the general prohibition against opening the legations to Chinese refugees.

That same day two unofficial rescue parties set forth from the legations to gather any Christians who might have survived the devastations in the area of the South Cathedral. The first party brought in 230 Chinese, and the second rescued many more.[11] It was Dr. G. E. Morrison, the London *Times* correspondent, and Professor Humberty James of the Imperial University who were the real heroes of the day. They persuaded Prince Su to open his palace (the Fu) to the refugees. It soon seemed, according to Lenox Simpson, who aided in the rescues, that "the whole Roman Catholic population of Peking is pouring in on us." [12] Indeed, estimates were that between 1200 and 2000 native Christians entered the Fu; as yet, the Protestant Christians remained in the American compound.

Since the Fu was basically an enclave in the legation area, the legations, by indirection, had come to offer refuge to an impressively large number of Christians. One witness remarked that the legations were most disturbed by this fact: "They say that this action will make us pay dearly with our lives: that the Legations will be attacked." [13]

It was under these circumstances that the foreign ministers received the ultimatum of June 19 to evacuate the legations in twenty-four hours. Each minister might take his family, his staff, and his guard, but no mention was made of the converts.[14] That was a night of tension, as the diplomatic corps debated a course of action which might involve the lives of thousands. The German minister held that to evacuate amounted to appeasement, but the French and American ministers urged departure. Not until late into the night did the diplomats decide that they must accept the order to leave Peking.[15]

Dr. Morrison of the *Times* was plunged into despair by what he regarded as a cowardly decision. He intercepted MacDonald as the meeting of the diplomatic corps broke up, and begged him to stay for the sake of the converts. Apparently he made little impression on the tired British minister, who may have been more concerned with the lives of

---

[5] Saville, *loc. cit.*

[6] *Ibid.*

[7] *Ibid.*

[8] Biggin to Cousins, Peking, Sept. 24, 1900. L.M.S./NC/10.

[9] Allen, *The Siege of the Peking Legations*, p. 80.

[10] Arthur H. Smith, *China in Convulsion*, I, 237.

[11] *Ibid.*, p. 238.

[12] B. L. Putnam Weale [Bertram Lenox Simpson], *Indiscreet Letters from Peking* (New York: Dodd, Mead and Co., 1911), p. 76.

[13] *Ibid.*, p. 74.

[14] Smith, *China in Convulsion*, p. 274.

[15] Cologan to the Tsungli Yamen, Peking, June 19, 1900. *P.P.*, China No. 4 (1900), Enclosure 7 in No. 2, p. 27.

the women and children under his care than for the Christian refugees.[16]

That night many of the legations busied themselves with packing and gathering transport. Conger alerted his missionaries at the Methodist mission to prepare for a speedy departure. They hastily replied that to leave would signal the massacre of the Christians under their protection.[17] However, had not the murder of Ketteler on the following day halted this preparation for exodus, there is every reason to believe that the converts would have been abandoned to massacre.

Ketteler's murder shattered the illusion that the legations were safe in spite of the bloody devastation which wracked Peking. A last ray of hope shown through on the afternoon of June 20. A note from the Tsungli Yamen extended the deadline for leaving Peking, but it warned the ministers not to leave the legation area since Peking was in a state of unrest due to "the ill-feeling between the people and the converts."[18] Any expectation that the legations might be preserved from the savage attacks of wild-eyed Boxers and the disciplined assaults of the Imperial forces was crushed at four o'clock that afternoon. General Tung Fu-hsiang's fierce Kansu warriors opened fire on the legations.[19] The siege had begun.

The Converts and the Siege

In the history of warfare no more peculiar combat has been recorded than that of the legation siege. From the first shots fired on the afternoon of June 20, the Europeans were embattled for almost two months, an international expeditionary force of 20,000 men finally arriving on August 14 to disperse the attacking Chinese. While our attention centers upon Peking, the death and destruction taking place beyond the legation walls far exceeded the sufferings of the European community. In the northeastern provinces of China an estimated 32,000 Chinese Christians and nearly 200 Protestant and Catholic missionaries were hunted down and exterminated by the Boxers.[20] Only the firm stand taken by the governor-generals in central and southern China, conscious of Western retribution, prevented the eruption of like violence there. But it was the siege in Peking that was particularly rife with political implications and this in part explained its baffling course.

What motivated the Imperial court to authorize the siege? Up to that point only defensive military measures against the West had been permitted. By such means Seymour's advance had been stalled. Although the allies had taken Ta-ku, the ministers indicated a willingness to negotiate its return to Chinese control. With hope for a compromise settlement within grasp of the Imperial court, the attack on the legations appeared to be senseless.

Chester Tan has suggested four possible motives for the court's decision. He argued, first, that by the attack the reactionaries meant to vent their long-suppressed hatred of the foreigner. Second, the attack was to stimulate the zeal and patriotism of the people in opposing the foreign aggressions. Third, there was real fear that the legation guards might menace Peking, and the attack was to eliminate that threat. And fourth, once the legation personnel were disposed of, such violence could be attributed to the action of "rebels."[21] Tan presented ample documentation to support these speculations. Yet it would seem that the attack may have been principally motivated by an even more compelling factor.

The June 20 note from the Tsungli Yamen gave the clue to that factor when it lamented that conflicts between the people and the converts had created the present crisis. The anti-Christian rallying cry had united the various discontented factions in northern China. A movement potentially destructive of the Manchu dynasty had in this manner been turned against the missionary and his converts. Now, if the court proclaimed itself the protector of the detested convert, Boxer hatred would turn against the dynasty once again. This was not all, for at that moment the military aid of the Boxers seemed more vital to the Imperial court than ever before. Already the Boxers had cut off the advancing Seymour expedition; and, with the opening of hostilities at Ta-ku, they were desperately needed on the front line. On June 19, the date of the ultimatum to the legations, the court ordered Yü-lu, who was directing operations against the invading foreigner, to organize the Boxers so as to strengthen Chinese resistance.[22]

---

[16] Fleming, *The Siege of Peking*, p. 105. Fleming apparently discovered a notation of this comment by Morrison in the Morrison diary to which he obtained access.

[17] Smith, *China in Convulsion*, p. 249.

[18] The Tsungli Yamen to Cologan, Peking, June 20, 1900. *P.P.*, China No. 4 (1900), Enclosure 8 in No. 2, pp. 27–28.

[19] Smith, *China in Convulsion*, p. 266.

[20] Columba Cary-Elwes, *China and the Cross* (London: Longmans, Green and Co., 1957), p. 224.

[21] Tan, *The Boxer Catastrophe*, pp. 96–97.

[22] *Ibid.*, p. 93.

At the same time the legations had become a refuge for the Boxers' most constant foe, the Christian converts. Then, too, expeditions had sallied forth from the legations to save the converts, and these forces had, at the same time, taken a heavy toll of Boxer lives.[23]

This explains the attempt by the Imperial court on June 19 to separate the converts from the legations. The foreign ministers would be safely escorted to the coast while the converts would be left to their fate. This would appease the Boxers and their energies would be absorbed in hunting down and slaughtering the Christians. Since the diplomats would be saved, however, a basis for renewed friendly relations with the West would be preserved. But Ketteler's death shattered the hopes of the Chinese peace party. And both the foreign ministers and the converts united in defense of the besieged legations. No longer could the court defend directly the European diplomats for this would be equivalent to defending the Chinese converts, and amid the revolutionary ferment in Peking this would be equivalent to self-destruction.

The converts remained a special object of wrath for the attacking Chinese. The Imperial forces assailed the Fu, where the Christians were sheltered, with particular fury. The Christians were cursed from beyond the lines; stones were hurled at them from over the walls; and the shelling in their area was markedly heavy.[24] The peace party deplored the identification, in the minds of the Boxers, between the converts and the legations. In a memorial of July 20, urging the protection of the legations, Yüan Ch'ang and Hsü Ching-ch'eng explained that the brigands made their hatred of Christianity an excuse for attacking the legations.[25] The missionaries were also special objects of hatred. This is clear from the proclamation issued on June 28 by the Peking Gendarmerie: "Whereas the religious chapels in Peking having been burnt and destroyed, and having no place wherein to conceal themselves, the foreigners must have scattered and fled into hiding . . . All who surreptitiously offer shelter to foreigners of a certainty render themselves liable to legal penalty of death." [26]

Conclusive indications of the central position occupied by the converts appear in the correspondence between the Imperial court and the legations beginning on July 14. MacDonald, who had taken command of the legation defense, regarded these dispatches and the cease-fire which accompanied them as a crudely designed attempt to trap the legations: "When they found they couldn't turn us out by brute force they tried diplomacy, at which, I venture to think, they found us equally their masters." [27]

Here MacDonald was quite wrong. Brute force could have overwhelmed the legations at any time. As Sir Robert Hart, chief of the Chinese Imperial Customs Service, put it: ". . . Somebody, probably a wise man who knew what the destruction of the Legations would cost the Empire and the Dynasty, intervened between the issue of the order for our destruction and the execution of it. . . ." [28] As a result apparently successful attacks were never pushed home; the firing would be heavy and at times continuous but relatively ineffective; and modern artillery, which was available and could have smashed the legations, was never fully employed. There is good reason to believe that it was Jung-lu, the grand secretary of the council and commander-in-chief of the armies during the siege, who restrained the attacks and instigated the correspondence with MacDonald. [29]

The trap which MacDonald felt he had so deftly avoided took the form of an offer in the first letter of July 14. It invited the foreign ministers to proceed under escort with their staff and families to the safety of the Tsungli Yamen. [30] MacDonald's strategy was to show a certain inter-

---

[23] Putnam Weale, *Indiscreet Letters from Peking*, pp. 54–83.

[24] Allen, *The Siege of the Peking Legations*, p. 171. Fleming noted briefly that "To open their gates [of the legations] to those who were the immediate objects of the Boxers' wrath might invite reprisals from the Boxers." *The Siege of Peking*, p. 99. However, he does not enlarge on this consideration. In fact, past studies of the siege of the legations have overlooked the importance of the presence of the converts in the legations as a prime cause, perhaps the basic cause, of the siege of the legations.

[25] Memorial of July 20, 1900. Contained in F.O. 17/1469.

[26] Enclosed in Satow to Salisbury, Peking, Nov. 15, 1900. F.O. 17/1415.

[27] MacDonald to Salisbury, Peking, Sept. 4, 1900. F.O. 17/1413.

[28] Sir Robert Hart, *These from the Land of Sinim* (London: Chapman and Hale, 1901), p. 40.

[29] Tan, *The Boxer Catastrophe*, pp. 89–90.

[30] Prince Ch'ing and others to MacDonald, Peking, July 14, 1900. F.O. 17/1414. The printed British documents incorrectly attribute this letter to the Tsungli Yamen. The Tsungli Yamen to MacDonald, Peking, July 14, 1900. P.P., China No. 4 (1900), Enclosure 1 in No. 3, p. 37.

The source of these letters is a matter of dispute. The probable authors were Jung-lu and Prince Ch'ing. However, one must take into account the following report from Sir Ernest Satow, the British minister in Peking: "I [Satow] then produced certain letters which had been received at the British Legation during the siege, bearing the name of Prince Ch'ing and others, and asked whether they were issued by authority of His Highness. Prince Ch'ing, after examining the documents, replied that they were not in the form used by the Tsungli Yamen, because that body had become disorganized in consequence of the troubles in Peking. Certain

est in these proposals in order to strengthen the hand of the peace party at the court. But he never seriously considered abandoning the security of the legation compound. It must be observed here that it was hardly likely that those, such as Jung-lu, who did so much to preserve the legations while they were under attack would plot the massacre of their personnel on the journey to Tientsin. In addition, Chester Tan informs us, there was every reason to expect that by July 14 the peace party in Peking had gained sufficient strength to open this correspondence. On the previous day the European forces had taken Tientsin. A memorial from the southern governor-generals, dated July 14, had argued the need to protect the foreign ministers. And warnings had come from the Western capitals that the Imperial Government would be held responsible for the fate of the legations.[31] MacDonald, it seems clear, was also quite wrong in thinking he had outwitted the Chinese in diplomacy. He was scarcely aware that diplomacy was underway.

Nonetheless, MacDonald's conduct may add substance to our theory. First of all, he was convinced that the whole thing was a plot by "treacherous orientals." Secondly, he explained: "We could not have abandoned to massacre the native Christians we had been protecting, yet with them we should have formed a convoy of over 3,000 people, nearly 2,000 being women and children. Even leaving the native Christians out of the calculation, a train of over 200 white women and children and 40 or 50 wounded men could not have been guarded by the force that sufficed to hold the Legation defenses." [32] Because of his distrust of the Chinese, MacDonald did not have to confront the decision of whether to abandon the native Christians in order to save the legations. However, the continued correspondence between the Tsungli Yamen and the legations stands as a vital, and relatively untouched, source for understanding the forces which compelled the attack on the legations.

By July 19 this strange correspondence took a new and revealing tack. A letter signed by "Prince Ch'ing and others" offered the following explanation for the attack on the legations. Discord, it was said, had broken out between "the people and the converts." This had grown to the point where there was "a general ferment absolutely beyond control . . . only the destruction of the Legations will satisfy it. . . ." [33] This was a diplomatic way of saying that only the destruction of the legations and the death of the converts sheltered there would satisfy the mob. The letter had implored the foreign ministers to accept a strong escort to Tientsin.

But MacDonald put off the offer by inquiring how the ministers could be safe on the road if they were not safe in the legations.[34]

These overtures from "Prince Ch'ing and others" took another form on July 27. Now it was argued that if the converts were sent out of the legation they would be permitted to pursue their vocations in safety, since feeling against them had become "quiet and tranquil." [35] But MacDonald still would not budge.

Again the court reversed its ground. An August 1 letter supplied MacDonald with numerous arguments for abandoning the converts. First the converts were accused of violating the truce by opening fire the previous evening. Then it was explained that "We have heard of late strong rumors to the effect that the converts have collected together in excessive numbers, and that they are opposed to the departure of the foreign Ministers from the capital, hoping to secure perpetual protection for themselves. . . . If such is the case, we feel sure that the foreign Ministers will have at once seen through the scheme, and will not fall into their trap." [36] The Chinese continued, in this manner, to blame the converts for the continuation of the siege until the relief expedition arrived.

There remained one final possibility for dislodging the foreign ministers. It might be arranged for their respective governments to or-

---

members of the Tsungli Yamen were also members of the Grand Council (Chun-chi-ch'u). Amongst these were Prince Tuan and Chao Shu-ch'iao, who he presumed drafted the letters at the Grand Council, and issued them in his name as President of the Tsungli Yamen." Satow to Lansdown, Peking, Feb. 6, 1901. F.O. 17/1470. At that moment there was every reason for Prince Ch'ing to disassociate himself from any connection with the group in power during the siege. Thus it was to his benefit to deny authorship of the letters. Also it was quite unlikely that the anti-foreign Prince Tuan would have composed these friendly letters.

[31] Tan, *The Boxer Catastrophe*, p. 101.

[32] MacDonald to Salisbury, Peking, Sept. 20, 1900. F.O. 17/1414.

[33] Prince Ch'ing and others to MacDonald, Peking, July 19, 1900. F.O. 17/1414.

[34] MacDonald to Prince Ch'ing and others, Peking, July 20, 1900. F.O. 17/1414.

[35] Prince Ch'ing and others to MacDonald, Peking, undated (received July 27, 1900). F.O. 17/1414.

[36] Prince Ch'ing and others to MacDonald, Peking, Aug. 1, 1900. F.O. 17/1414. MacDonald replied that no interference by the converts would be tolerated in the making of policy. MacDonald to Prince Ch'ing and others, Peking, Aug. 2, 1900. F.O. 17/1414. On August 11, 1900, a letter from the Tsungli Yamen complained that the converts had opened fire on the Chinese lines. Tsungli Yamen to MacDonald, Peking, Aug. 11, 1900. F.O. 17/1414. MacDonald replied that none of the converts were armed. MacDonald to Tsungli Yamen, Aug. 12, 1900. F.O. 17/1414. However, there are indications that at least some of the converts were armed. Concerning the converts moved from the Methodist Mission on June 20, Smith remarked: "Several of the Chinese were furnished with guns. . . ." *China in Convulsion*, p. 258.

der them to the coast. Accordingly, before the end of July, Li Hung-chang, who had been officially designated to negotiate with the Western capitals, offered a compromise: the ministers would be escorted safely to Tientsin, he promised, if the Powers would not march on Peking.[37] This Chinese strategy came to a head on August 4, when a note from the Tsungli Yamen was delivered to MacDonald. The ministers were asked to set a date for their departure; for, it was pointed out, their governments have requested "that safe escort out of Peking should be provided without delay."[38] But the ministers replied that they must receive direct orders from their governments before they would depart; and they enclosed in their reply cipher telegrams to their governments concerning such instructions.[39] The Chinese Government passed on these cipher messages, and instructed its ministers in Europe to press urgently upon the Powers the need of ordering a temporary retirement to Tientsin.[40]

This Chinese maneuver, however, came to nothing. The cipher messages warned the European governments that it was impossible to depart from the legations in safety, and pleaded for quick relief.[41] Salisbury noted that Britain had no recourse but to hasten its effort to relieve the legations.[42] And Britain followed the French lead in informing the Tsungli Yamen that only the removal of the Chinese forces barring the way to Peking would be considered proof of Chinese sincerity.[43]

A final possibility for a compromise solution arose as the new and hastily formed relief expedition neared Peking. Japan proposed, on about August 13, that the Chinese allow an international contingent to enter Peking in order to escort the foreigners back to Tientsin.[44] The Chinese minister in St. Petersburg countered with a proposal that the foreigners be escorted to Tientsin by thirty mandarins of high rank. Salisbury found this unacceptable. But he indicated his willingness to halt the relief expedition just outside the wall of Peking, and there to receive the foreigners who would be returned to Tientsin.[45] The converts had, obviously, been forgotten. However, all such plans were too late; for, even as these discussions were proceeding, the relief expedition had, with a sudden surge, reached Peking on August 14. The legations and the converts were saved.

MacDonald remarked soon after the relief of the legations that the siege had been "very good fun."[46] Indeed, the British minister had happily put aside the perplexities of diplomacy and eagerly assumed the role he loved best, that of soldier. From June 9, when he issued the fatal call for Seymour to march on Peking, until the termination of siege, Mac-Donald had thought strictly in military terms. He had dismissed the temporary truce with its accompanying diplomatic exchange as merely a ruse to entrap the legations. But MacDonald's ignorance was, ironically enough, the salvation of the converts. First, it is doubtful that MacDonald would have opened the legations to the converts, even in the offhand manner in which it was done, had he been aware that this would incite the Boxers and, eventually, the court to attack the legations. Second, if MacDonald had realized that the court was sincere in its offer of a safe escort to Tientsin, he would have been under great pressure to leave the converts to their unhappy fate.

In other words had MacDonald had full knowledge of his situation, he would have been presented with a frightful moral dilemma. Should he remain in Peking and risk all for the Chinese Christians in the Fu? This would bring with it the likelihood of European military invasion and occupation with the prospect of the partition of the Empire among the Powers. To defend the converts also meant that MacDonald would have been required to put aside his supposed first duty to protect the European community gathered about him in Peking. On the other hand, if he abandoned the converts this would have meant the almost certain slaughter of perhaps 2000 Chinese who looked to the legations for sanctuary and to whose protection the Europeans were implicitly bound by religion and association. While it can be argued that the sacrifice of the converts might have avoided the armed European invasion of China with all its indiscriminate bloodshed, to forsake the converts, at that moment, would have constituted a cold-blooded and dastardly act of be-

---

[37] Hay to Porter, Washington, D.C., Aug. 2, 1900. *D.D.C.*, 1899–1900, Enclosure in No. 204, p. 110.

[38] Tsungli Yamen to MacDonald, Peking, Aug. 4, 1900. F.O. 17/1414.

[39] Cologan to Tsungli Yamen, Peking, Aug. 5, 1900. F.O. 17/1414.

[40] Ministre de Chine à Ministre des Affaires Étrangères, Paris, Aug. 9, 1900. *D.D.C.*, 1899–1900, No. 226, p. 120.

[41] Pichon to Delcassé, Peking, Aug. 5, 1900. *D.D.C.*, 1899–1900, No. 212, p. 114.

[42] Minute by Salisbury, Foreign Office, Aug. 10, 1900. F.O. 17/1418.

[43] Delcassé to Yu-Keng, Paris, Aug. 10, 1900. *D.D.C.*, 1899–1900, No. 229, p. 121.

[44] Delcassé to French Ambassadors in St. Petersburg, London, Berlin, Vienna, Rome, and the Vatican, Paris, Aug. 16, 1900. *D.D.C.*, 1899–1900, No. 246, p. 129.

[45] Aide mémoire by Monson, Paris, Aug. 15, 1900. *D.D.C.*, 1899–1900, No. 239, p. 126.

[46] MacDonald to Salisbury, Peking, Sept. 4, 1900. F.O. 17/1413.

trayal. It was too late now to revise past policies and commitments – the fate of the legations and that of the converts were inevitably bound together.

Foreign Office Attitudes

Whitehall, while committing itself to the rapid military relief of the legations, attempted to retain a hands-off attitude in regard to internal Chinese politics. In short, the Foreign Office was still guided by the criteria of "informal empire" which had, up to that time, proved so profitable in China. This attitude was accompanied by a concern for the overriding implications of the struggle between the European Powers for a position of dominance in China. Britain still wanted the best of both worlds; she wished to remain the dominant Power in China, but to do this by means of informal control.

This policy line was reaffirmed early in July when the French attempted to secure the safety of the legations by means of an understanding with Jung-lu and Prince Ch'ing, an understanding which would have guaranteed European support for the Manchu regime. The British would have none of this. A minute by Bertie summarized the Foreign Office attitude:

It is possible that the Chinese as distinguished from their Manchu fellow subjects may wish to get rid of the present dynasty and under some Chinaman succeed in doing so. If so the capital would probably not be in Peking.

The Russians naturally want to maintain Peking as the capital with a Manchu Dynasty under their control.

There will have to be a good deal of fighting between the various factions in China before we can see what is coming out on top. It would be a big job and an unprofitable one to attempt to prop up a discredited dynasty.[47]

Salisbury agreed with his assistant undersecretary, and added the comment that Prince Ch'ing might prove to be on the wrong side.[48] It was just this noncommittal attitude which had incited Manchu suspicions of the British, and was one of the factors which drove them to put their trust in the Boxers.

As for the relationship between the missionaries and the Chinese people, the Boxer rising might best be regarded as a massive antimissionary riot. All the worst aspects of the riots which had marred the previous ten years were repeated in exaggerated form during the Boxer outburst. The missionaries, fearful for their own safety and for that of their converts, pleaded for foreign military intervention. The Chinese officials assumed an ambivalent position, half condemning and half condoning Boxer activity. The Chinese masses, in their evident hatred of the foreign missionary and his minions, gave renewed testimony to the deep gulf which separated the Christian culture of the West from the Confucian culture of China. Finally, it was Western military power that carried the day. The Chinese were, at last, forced to admit the technical superiority of the West. But, more than ever before, the religion and culture of the West were identified with the aggressive invader.

---

[47] Bertie to Salisbury, Foreign Office, July 10, 1900. F.O. 17/1441.
[48] Minute by Salisbury, Foreign Office, undated. F.O. 17/1441.

CHAPTER XI

Conclusion

BETWEEN 1891 and 1900 the working relationship which existed between Britain and China was subjected to an increasing number of threats and strains, despite the basis for solid understanding which existed between the two nations. Even though the extension of British commerce into China was forcibly achieved, the Manchu dynasty regarded this penetration as less threatening than the establishment of foreign political enclaves upon the Chinese mainland. There was, then, greater reason for China to tolerate Britain's "informal imperialism" than to accept the total political claims of the other European Powers.

But for "informal imperialism" to succeed in China certain grave obstacles had to be overcome. There was the difficulty arising from the fact that a weakened China required a degree of political support from allies in order to stand against the threats of foreign Powers. This support Britain would reluctantly supply, even though it tended to bring about the very political commitment which informal empire sought to avoid. Apparently, the forms of informal empire were sufficiently flexible to allow for political aid in time of crisis; for, after all, the disruption of China meant the disruption of British trade. However, it soon became clear that Britain's readiness to support China tended to decrease in proportion to the increasing encroachments of the other European Powers in China. Informal empire could not endure if China remained the central theater of international conflict. One other factor, however, worked relentlessly to draw the Powers toward intervention in China. This was the missionary movement.

Expanding missionary work necessitated the extension of protection for the missionaries; for Britain this meant frequent protests to the Tsungli Yamen on behalf of the missionaries, and, on occasion, a display of naval force. This, of course, was contrary to that attitude of restraint which the Foreign Office sought to foster; but, even worse, it focused the attention and concern of other European Powers upon China. Thus the British themselves might furnish the occasion for some other European Power to take something or some place from China. In 1891, there took place a striking example of the interaction of these forces as the Chinese in various towns along the Yangtze River rose against the missionaries. These riots were suppressed with the aid of the Chinese authorities, but the intervention of a large fleet of European gunboats had been necessary before tranquil conditions were restored.

Certain disturbing portents were discernible in these riots. First, only with the greatest difficulty were the European Powers able to coordinate their efforts in China. Second, Britain showed a great reluctance to precipitate any action which would interfere with the internal workings of the Manchu regime. An examination of the riots themselves reveals an even more ominous undercurrent. It was apparent that a fear and hatred of the missionaries penetrated all levels of China society, and might easily explode into violence. Antidynastic secret societies had evidently inspired some of these riots. This meant that as organized attempts to subvert the regime grew in number the assaults on missionaries might grow as well.

British policy attempted no solution of this problem in the years of grace between the 1891 riots and the flurry of political events which terminated the decade. At most, the Foreign Office took on the role of a somewhat ineffectual "honest broker" between the aggressive missionaries and the obstinate Chinese. But this neither satisfied the missionaries nor pacified the Chinese.

The complaints of consuls on the scene finally roused the Foreign Office to action concerning the conduct of certain missionary groups, but the correctives amounted to politely phrased statements of advice which were circulated to the home offices of the mission societies in London. Promises to heed these cautions were promptly returned from the various mission headquarters; however, by the time the injunctions reached the missionaries in the field, they had lost much of their impact. As another means of control, the Foreign Office permitted their consuls to prohibit the work of missionaries in certain highly disturbed areas. However, such prohibitions were usually of short duration, and there was no consistent standard worked out for all of China as to when mission work should be temporarily suspended. Whitehall was particularly concerned with the risks undertaken by female missionaries in China. Even in this case, however, its rulings were vague and inconsistently applied.

Britain also brought political, and on occasion military, pressure on China to stamp out antimissionary violence. However, these diplomatic measures were fitful, usually following an attack on missionaries, and no consistent policy was developed for coping with such assaults. For example, great energy was at first expended in forcing the Chinese Government to apprehend Chou Han, the author of certain inflammatory antimissionary propaganda. Finally, Chou was reprimanded, but his activities were never completely curbed. The Chinese had simply outwaited the British until their determination had lagged and other issues occupied their attention.

On the other hand, the British could act with great force in defense of their missionaries. In 1895, attacks on missionaries had become especially widespread, culminating in the massacre of a party of British missionaries at Ku-t'ien. As compensation for these crimes the British minister demanded the dismissal of the negligent governor-general of Szechwan. The Foreign Office supported its minister with a naval demonstration, and the governor-general was dismissed.

Action by the British minister in obtaining the removal of a Chinese governor-general amounted to an intrusion into an area where China claimed absolute sovereignty. No other Power had demonstrated the determination to push such a claim to a successful conclusion. Here was ready testimony to the extent that missionary problems could involve British officials in the domestic politics of the Manchu regime. In addition, this particular incident came at an especially unhappy time for Anglo-Chinese friendship. Britain had just declined to help China in the retrocession of Liaotung, while other European Powers had stepped in to aid her. China had simultaneously snubbed England in obtaining a loan from Russia. Like it or not, the missionary problem, because of the animosity it had created and because it had flared up at a time of strained relations, had become as much a factor in international relations as the disputes over alliances and loans.

It was not long before the missionaries became an even more important factor in Britain's rivalry with the other Powers. By the occupation of Kiaochow in 1897, China became the scene of a scramble for territorial grants and economic concessions between the European Powers. First Germany and then France sought to gain concessions under the guise of defending their missionaries. Britain held aloof from such tactics. But finally she blundered into retaining a segment of Chinese territory adjacent to Kowloon until dismissal of the governor of Kweichow Province where a British missionary was murdered. Britain finally returned this area to China in a farcical episode in which the supposed murderer of the missionary eventually escaped punishment. Besides giving evidence of Britain's inept diplomacy, this episode tended to identify the British missionary with the cause of imperialism.

The Kowloon incident proved British diplomacy to be more foolish than dangerous. But Whitehall's laissez-faire attitude toward missionary activity permitted certain missionaries to identify themselves with a cause which came to threaten the very existence of the Manchu regime. In their preaching and teaching and in their literature the missionaries had emphasized the need for social reform; as the missionary saw it, only Western methods and organization could remedy the appalling conditions of disease, dirt, and corruption which were so commonplace in China. These ideas were incorporated in a native reform movement. In 1898, the Emperor appointed certain of the reformers to positions of authority and began a sweeping program of reform. It appeared that with this turning to Western ways the missionary cause would profit as never before. But reform threatened the position of the official-gentry class; and the court reactionaries rallied around the Empress Dowager and overthrew the reformers. Henceforth the Empress Dowager regarded the British missionaries as potential allies of her bitter enemy, the Reform party of K'ang Yu-wei.

By its very policy of noninvolvement the Foreign Office had permitted forces to operate which led the Manchu Government to identify the British with the opponents of the regime. But, apparently, the Foreign Office would accept no policy which might regulate or restrict missionary activity. In 1899, the French Government negotiated a treaty which gave the Catholic missionaries a certain official status in the Chinese bureaucracy; in turn, the French missionaries were to settle disputes on the local level and only in cases of dire need call on the French authorities for assistance. At first Whitehall hastened to obtain similar privileges for its missionaries. But most of the British missionaries were reluctant to accept official status in China, for this would preclude asking for the assistance of the British consul in minor disputes. Then, too, the idea of official status went contrary to the ideals of the English missionaries. By their rejection of this program the missionaries blocked a move which would have been a first step in organizing and controlling missionary activity in China. Again, the door of negotiation was closed upon the Chinese.

Toward the end of 1899, with Britain preoccupied in the South African war, events in China came to a head. In northeastern China, internal unrest and the growing intrusion of the West led to the formation of a grass-roots antiforeign movement. The missionary and his converts were the primary target of this rising of the masses of China known as the Boxer movement. Britain's chief concern was to keep things quiet in China; and, as usual, the Foreign Office relied on the Manchu Government to put down the rising. It was thought that, just as in the past, this disturbance would burn itself out without need of full-scale foreign intervention.

However, on this occasion the Manchu dynasty could not be relied on to cooperate with the West. It was only by the most astute maneuvering by the Imperial court that the hatred of the regime latent in the Boxer movement had been turned aside, and a certain unofficial sympathy was given to the persecution of Christian converts. Any forthright attempt to repress the movement might again turn it against the regime. Also, the Empress Dowager feared that the Western Powers were about to lay their final claim upon China's mainland; she saw in the Boxers a patriotic upsurge which might prove to be the first line of defense against the West. In the past the Manchu regime had looked to England in time of crisis for aid against her foreign and domestic foes. But in the last decade Britain had shown an increased fear of political involvement in China. Even more important, Britain through her missionaries appeared to be allied with the Reform party. The Boxers' enthusiasm seemed to be a more reliable quantity than British friendship.

In its attempt to bring the court to suppress the Boxers, British diplo-

macy shifted from a rather passive stance to a violently threatening attitude only to return to its previous relative passivity. In part, this was because MacDonald's freedom of movement was restricted by Whitehall's
injunction to keep things quiet in Peking. But the British minister was
erratic and ill informed; in fact, he aggravated the situation. Admittedly,
some kind of explosion with respect to the Boxers seemed unavoidable;
but the devastation need not have involved the official community in
Peking, and it was its involvement which brought the great European
expeditionary force to Peking.

Boxer activity spread through the north of China and reached Peking
in June 1900. The foreign legations demanded that the Manchu regime
suppress the Boxer attacks which already had killed many converts and
threatened the lives of missionaries. For their own safety, the legations
had ordered European guards to Peking to protect their compounds. If
the Boxers confined their attacks to converts, however, Western military
intervention was unlikely.

But the struggle between the foreign Powers for strategic position
came to the fore. If the long-expected partition of China was about to
take place, both Britain and Russia desired to be first upon the scene in
Peking. Suddenly and somewhat unexpectedly, the British minister
called for large reinforcements from Tientsin. They were to come as protection against the Boxers, but perhaps their most vital purpose was to
strengthen MacDonald's hand in dealing with the unrest before the arrival of a large Russian force being sent from Port Arthur (no doubt also
coming for the dual purpose of protection and power). This unleashed
a chain of events which culminated in the capture of China's Ta-ku forts
by a combined European naval force. This was an act of war and China's
Imperial Army began its successful opposition to the advance of the expedition MacDonald had called to Peking. But, at this point, there was
evidence that both the Imperial court and the legations were prepared
to come to a negotiated settlement.

However, the foreign ministers had not allowed for the significant
position occupied by the missionaries and the converts. When the official
legation community could not be persuaded by the Tsungli Yamen to
leave the compounds for a safe conduct to Tientsin, the court could no
longer stand in the way of the raging Boxers. Partly in response to the
demands of the missionaries, more than 2000 converts had been given
shelter behind the legation walls. Until that time, it appeared that the

[197]

Imperial forces would protect the legations from Boxer attacks, but to do so now would appear to offer protection to the hated converts. As a result, both the Boxers and the Imperial Army joined in the attack.

During the siege the legations might have been granted relief if the foreign ministers had been willing to surrender their converts to the attacking foe. Humanitarian reasons might well have prevented the legations from cooperating in such a cold-blooded deed in any case. Yet the British minister, who conducted allied strategy during the siege, was unaware of the central position occupied by the converts. In fact, he dismissed as pure deception Chinese overtures to escort the foreigners safely to Tientsin, a plan which implied that the converts would be left in Peking to face their fate. Just as at other crucial points in the preceding decade, the British minister failed to realize how much hatred the missionary and his converts had aroused among the Chinese.

The Boxer rising and the siege of the legations stand as a monument to the failure of a decade of British diplomacy in China. Certainly others shared in the responsibility for this failure. The Catholic missionaries were perhaps a greater source of annoyance to the Manchu regime than the British Protestants; and the French Government was as ready as the British to avenge attacks on missionaries. Also, the Boxer rising was merely a manifestation of a vast internal upheaval; Chinese hatred for their Manchu overlords had been galvanized into active opposition by governmental incapacity in the face of famine and foreign encroachments. The foreigners and the missionaries, however, by their presence permitted the rising to come to a head in a most violent manner. And Britain, as the nation with the largest stake in China and the strongest voice in Chinese affairs, must assume a major share of responsibility for the direction taken by the Boxer rising.

It is one of the primary tasks of diplomacy to ease tension and negotiate disputes between nations. In China, British diplomacy ignored tensions and rejected negotiation, because the informal empire which Britain sought to sustain meant, in practice, the presence of Britishers in China who all too often thought and acted with no sense of responsibility. There was no reason to condemn this policy as being any more vicious than was the outright political aggrandizement plotted by the other European Powers. But, judging Britain's China policy by itself, one cannot avoid noting the contradictions which prevented its successful execution.

Britain's commercial policy sought to extract the most from China with the least commitment to China. But, at the same time, British missionaries pledged themselves, and by indirection their government, to spreading the Christian gospel in China. This involved an enormous commitment with inevitable political implications. Such a contradiction could arise since it was Whitehall's policy to allow free play to all those interests which sought to influence China. But this amalgam of forces, which had brought success to Britain elsewhere in the world, misfired in China.

When judged by the hatred and confusion which it helped to create among the Chinese, Britain's policy of informal empire was a disastrous one. Several factors combined to bring this policy to ruin in the Boxer rising. Among the elements which Britain might have controlled, it was the missionary movement which did most to defeat that policy. By its very nature "informal empire" was subtle policy. The Chinese might resent the commercial inroads made by the British, but there was no immediate fear that these would be followed by political demands. In exchange for economic privileges, the Chinese might even expect a certain amount of British support against the incursions of other Powers. This was a cool, detached, and rational plan of economic penetration; it was hoped that in the long run both Britain and China would profit by this exchange.

But the missionary movement unleashed forces which worked directly against this finely balanced policy. Inevitably, the missionary aroused the opposition of the gentry-official class who saw in the missionary a rival for the esteem of the masses. Then, too, the masses resented the fact that their time-honored institutions were subject to attack, and they were suspicious of the strange ways of the foreigners who penetrated the deepest inland recesses. Almost invariably, missionary work created the need for direct British intervention. Whether it was the simple pressure which a British consul wielded in a legal dispute involving a Chinese convert, or the massive display of force necessary to obtain the removal of a Chinese governor-general, British political and military power came more and more into play. This inflamed the opposition of almost all classes of Chinese, and weakened the basis of friendship necessary for successful commercial operations in China. Still the Foreign Office was content to limp on with this contradictory policy for China.

Such a policy must appear to be absurd; but the "absurd" had worked well for England elsewhere on the globe. The second British Empire had grown up as a result of the operation of just such apparently contrary forces as the selfish trader and the altruistic missionary. Just as the merchant had been allowed his freedom, so had the missionary. To curb the activities of either might be to betray the genius which had already renewed the Empire in Africa and elsewhere in Asia and which promised a greater Empire for the future. However, the difficulty was that Britain no longer possessed the power to exclude her European rivals and, if necessary, incorporate China into her Empire. The best Britain could hope for was a limited prolongation of her informal empire in China.

Finally, it was the intermingling of these forces, economic and altruistic, which reinforced orthodox Confucian opposition to the religion of the West. Given the nature of the nationalistic expansion of Europe at the end of the nineteenth century this was perhaps unavoidable. But this does not erase the fact that China's hatred and distrust of one of the West's most cherished institutions was both confirmed and intensified in the decade we have just reviewed.

BIBLIOGRAPHY AND INDEX

Bibliography

Primary Sources

MANUSCRIPTS

British Foreign Office. Foreign Office correspondence and other documents relating to Anglo-Chinese relations covering the period from 1891 to 1901, filed under series F.O. 17/— and F.O. 228/— and related materials under F.O. 27/—(France) and F.O. 65/— (Russia) in the Public Record Office, London.

The Church Missionary Society. The correspondence and reports of C.M.S. missionaries in China, filed chronologically and by district at Church Missionary House Archives, London.

The London Missionary Society. The correspondence and reports of the L.M.S. missionaries in China, arranged chronologically in boxes at the headquarters of the L.M.S., London.

The Salisbury Papers. The correspondence and other documents of the Third Marquess of Salisbury in bound volumes and boxes in the library at Christ Church, Oxford.

The Satow Papers. The correspondence and other papers of Sir Ernest Satow, filed under P.R.O. 30/33— in the Public Record Office, London.

The Society for the Propagation of the Gospel in Foreign Parts. The correspondence and reports of S.P.G. missionaries in China, arranged chronologically in volumes at S.P.G. headquarters in London.

PRINTED DOCUMENTS

Britain:

Parliamentary Papers. Correspondence Respecting Anti-Foreign Riots in China. China No. 3 (1891), c. 6431. London: H. M. Stationery Office, 1891.

———. *Further Correspondence Respecting Anti-Foreign Riots in China.* China No. 1 (1892), c. 6585. London: H. M. Stationery Office, 1892.

———. *Correspondence Respecting the Affairs of China.* China No. 1 (1898), c. 8814. London: H. M. Stationery Office, 1898.

——. *Further Correspondence Respecting the Affairs of China*. China No. 1 (1899), c. 9131. London: H. M. Stationery Office, 1899.

——. *Further Correspondence Respecting the Affairs of China*. China No. 1 (1900), cd. 93. London: H. M. Stationery Office, 1900.

——. *Correspondence Respecting the Insurrectionary Movement in China*. China No. 3 (1900), cd. 257. London: H. M. Stationery Office, 1900.

——. *Reports from Her Majesty's Minister in China Respecting Events in Peking*. China No. 4 (1900), cd. 364. London: H. M. Stationery Office, 1900.

——. *Further Correspondence Respecting the Affairs of China*. China No. 1 (1901), cd. 436. London: H. M. Stationery Office, 1901.

——. *Further Correspondence Respecting the Affairs of China*. China No. 3 (1901), cd. 442. London: H. M. Stationery Office, 1901.

——. *Further Correspondence Respecting the Affairs of China*. China No. 4 (1901), cd. 443. London: H. M. Stationery Office, 1901.

——. *Further Correspondence Respecting the Affairs of China*. China No. 5 (1901), cd. 589. London: H. M. Stationery Office, 1901.

——. *Further Correspondence Respecting the Affairs of China*. China No. 6 (1901), cd. 675. London: H. M. Stationery Office, 1901.

Gooch, G. P., and Harold Temperley. *British Documents on the Origins of the War, 1898–1914*. Vols. I and II. London: H. M. Stationery Office, 1932.

France:

French Ministry of Foreign Affairs. *Documents Diplomatiques Chine, 1894–1898* ("Livres Jaunes"). Paris: Imprimerie Nationale, 1898.

——. *Documents Diplomatiques Chine, 1898–1899* ("Livres Jaunes"). Paris: Imprimerie Nationale, 1900.

——. *Documents Diplomatiques Chine, 1899–1900* ("Livres Jaunes"). Paris: Imprimerie Nationale, 1900.

——. *Documents Diplomatiques Français, 1871–1914* (1re serie 1871–1901). Vols. VIII, IX, and XVI. Paris: Imprimerie Nationale, 1938–1957.

Germany:

Lepsius, J., A. M. Bartholdy, and F. Thimme (eds.). *Die Grosse Politik der Europäische Kabinette, 1871–1914*. Vols. XIV and XVI. Berlin: Deutsche Verlagsgesellschaft für Politik und Geschichte, 1924.

Russia:

U.S.S.R. *A Digest of the Krasnyi Arkhiv*. Compiled, translated, and annotated by Leonid S. Rubinchek and edited by Louise M. Boutelle and Gordon W. Thayer. Cleveland: Cleveland Public Library, 1947.

United States:

U.S. Department of State. *Papers Relating to the Foreign Relations of the United States, 1891–1901*. 13 vols. Washington, D.C.: Government Printing Office, 1892–1902.

CONTEMPORARY NEWSPAPERS AND PERIODICALS

Chinese Recorder and Missionary Journal. Vols. XXII–XXXI. Shanghai, 1891–1900.

Church Missionary Intelligencer and Record. Vols. XVI–XXV (new series). London, 1891–1900.

Mission Field. Vols. XXXVI–XLVI. London, 1891–1901.

North China Daily News. Shanghai, 1891–1900.

Times. London, 1891–1900.

BOOKS

Allen, Rev. Roland. *The Siege of the Peking Legations*. London: Smith Elder and Co., 1901.

Anti-Foreign Riots in China, The. Shanghai: North China Herald, 1892.

Beals, Z. Charles. *China and the Boxers*. New York: M. E. Nunson, 1901.

Beresford, Lord Charles. *The Break-Up of China*. London: Harper and Brothers, 1899.

Bing, E. J. (ed.). *The Secret Letters of the Last Tsar*. New York: Longmans, Green and Co., 1938.

Bland, J. O. P., and E. Backhouse. *China under the Empress Dowager*. Peking: Henri Vetch, 1939.

Boell, Paul. *Le Protectorat des missions Catholiques en Chine et la Politique della France en Extreme Orient*. Paris: Institut Scientifique de la libre pensee, 1899.

Boxer Rising: A History of the Boxer Trouble in China, The. Reprinted from the *Shanghai Mercury*. Shanghai: Shanghai Mercury, 1900.

Broomhall, Marshall (ed.). *Last Letters and Further Records of the Martyred Missionaries of the C.I.M.* London: Morgan and Scott, 1901.

Casserly, Captain Gordon. *The Land of the Boxers*. New York: Longmans, Green and Co., 1903.

Christie, Dugdale. *Thirty Years in Moukden, 1883–1913*. London: Constable and Co., 1914.

Conger, Sarah Pike. *Letters from Peking*. London: Hodder and Stoughton, 1909.

Cunningham, Alfred. *A History of the Szechuan Riots, May–June, 1895*. Shanghai: Shanghai Mercury, 1895.

Curzon, G. N. *Problems of the Far East*. New York: Longmans, Green and Co., 1896.

Duyvendak, J. J. L. (ed.). *The Diary of His Excellency Ching-shan*. Leiden: E. J. Brill, 1924.

Edwards, E. H. *Fire and Sword in Shansi*. London: Oliphant, Anderson and Ferrier, 1903.

Gammon, Charles. *The Rise and Progress of the Boxer Movement in China*. Yokahama: Fukuin Printing Co., 1900.

Gerard, A. *Ma Mission en Chine, 1893–1897*. Paris: Librairie Plon, 1918.

Hart, Sir Robert. *These from the Land of Sinim*. London: Chapman and Hale, 1901.

Ketler, Isaac C. *The Tragedy of Paotingfu*. New York: Fleming H. Revell, 1902.

Ku Hung-ming. *Papers from a Viceroy's Yamen*. Shanghai: Shanghai Mercury, 1901.

Machie, Alexander. *China and Christianity*. Boston: Knight and Millet, 1900.

———. *The Englishman in China*. 2 vols. London: William Blackwood and Sons, 1900.

———. *Missionaries in China*. London: Edward Stanford, 1891.

M'Intosh, Gilbert. *The Chinese Crisis and Christian Missionaries: A Vindication*. London: Morgan and Scott, 1900.

MacMurray, J. V. A. *Treaties and Agreements with or concerning China, 1894–1919*. 2 vols. New York: Oxford University Press, 1921.

Martin, W. A. P. *The Siege in Peking*. New York: Fleming H. Revell, 1900.

Pinon, René, and Jean de Marcillac. *La Chine qui s'ouvre*. Paris: Perrin et Cie, 1900.

Putnam Weale, B. L. [Bertram Lenox Simpson]. *Indiscreet Letters from Peking*. New York: Dodd, Mead and Co., 1911.

Smith, Arthur H. *China in Convulsion*. 2 vols. London: Oliphant, Anderson and Ferrier, 1901.

Yarmolinsky, A. (ed.). *The Memoirs of Count Witte*. New York: Doubleday, 1921.

BIBLIOGRAPHY

ARTICLES

Allen, C. J. R. "A Layman's Defense of Missions in China," *Mission Field*, XLVI (January 1901), 25–30.

Laughlin, J. H., to Editor, Chi-ning, Nov. 8, 1897. *Chinese Recorder and Missionary Journal*, XXVIII (November 1897), 592.

Masters, F. L. "An Account of Chinese Secret Societies," *Chinese Recorder and Missionary Journal*, XXII (May 1891), 268–273.

"Present State of Troubles in China and Their Cure, The," *Chinese Recorder and Missionary Journal*, XXII (November 1891), 525.

Secondary Sources

BOOKS

Bee, Benjamin Ming-Chu. "The Leasing of Kiaochow." Unpublished Ph.D. dissertation, Harvard University, 1935.

Cameron, Meribeth E. *The Reform Movement in China, 1898–1912.* Stanford, Calif.: Stanford University Press, 1931.

Cary-Elwes, Columba. *China and the Cross.* London: Longmans, Green and Co., 1957.

Chao-kwang Wu. *The International Aspect of the Missionary Movement in China.* Baltimore: Johns Hopkins Press, 1930.

Clements, Paul H. *The Boxer Rebellion.* Columbia University Studies in History, Economics, and Public Law, Vol. LXVI, No. 3. New York: Columbia University Press, 1915.

Cohen, Paul A. *China and Christianity: The Missionary Movement and the Growth of Chinese Antiforeignism, 1860–1870.* Harvard East Asia Series, No. 11. Cambridge, Mass.: Harvard University Press, 1963.

Colquhoun, Archibald R. *Problems in China and British Policy.* London: P. S. King and Son, 1900.

Comber, L. F. *Chinese Secret Societies in Malaya.* Locust Valley, N.Y.: Augustin Incorporated, 1959.

Cordier, Henri. *Histoire des Relations de la Chine avec Les Puissances Occidentales, 1860–1902.* 3 vols. Paris: Ancienne Librairie Germer Bailliere et C', 1902.

Crewe, The Marquess of. *Lord Rosebery.* 2 vols. London: John Murray, 1931.

Dennett, Tyler. *Americans in Eastern Asia.* New York: Macmillan, 1922.

Dugdale, Edgar T. S. *Maurice de Bunsen, Diplomat and Friend.* London: John Murray, 1934.

Endacott, G. B. *A History of Hong Kong.* London: Oxford University Press, 1958.

Fairbank, John K. (ed.). *Chinese Thought and Institutions.* Chicago: University of Chicago Press, 1957.

Fleming, Peter. *The Siege at Peking.* London: Rupert Hart-Davis, 1959.

Garvin, J. L., and J. Amery. *The Life of Joseph Chamberlain.* 4 vols. London: Macmillan, 1932–1951.

Goodall, Norman. *A History of the London Missionary Society, 1895–1945.* London: Oxford University Press, 1954.

Groot, J. J. M. de. *Sectarianism and Religious Persecution in China.* 2 vols. Amsterdam: Johannes Müller, 1903.

Hamer, F. E. (ed.). *The Personal Letters of Lord Rendel.* London: Ernest Benn, 1931.

Hu Sheng. *Imperialism and Chinese Politics.* Peking: Foreign Language Press, 1955.

Hughes, E. R. *The Invasion of China by the Western World.* London: Adam and Charles Black, 1937.

BIBLIOGRAPHY

Hummel, Arthur W. (ed.). *Eminent Chinese of the Ch'ing Period, 1644–1912.* Washington, D.C.: Government Printing Office, 1943–1944.

Jansen, Marius B. *The Japanese and Sun Yat-sen.* Cambridge, Mass.: Harvard University Press, 1954.

Joseph, Philip. *Foreign Diplomacy in China, 1894–1900.* London: George Allen and Unwin, 1928.

Kiernan, E. V. G. *British Diplomacy and China, 1880–1885.* Cambridge: Cambridge University Press, 1939.

Langer, William L. *The Diplomacy of Imperialism, 1890–1902.* New York: Alfred A. Knopf, 1935.

Latourette, Kenneth S. *The Great Century in Northern Africa and Asia, 1800–1914.* Vol. VI of *A History of the Expansion of Christianity.* New York: Harper and Brothers, 1944.

––––––. *A History of Christian Missions in China.* New York: Macmillan, 1929.

Levenson, Joseph R. *Liang Ch'i-ch'ao and the Mind of Modern China.* London: Thames and Hudson, 1959.

Li Chien-nung. *The Political History of China, 1840–1928,* trans. and ed. Ssu-yü Teng and Jeremy Ingalls. Princeton, N.J.: D. Van Nostrand Co., 1956.

Lin Yutang. *A History of the Press and Public Opinion in China.* London: Oxford University Press, 1937.

Lovett, Richard. *A History of the London Missionary Society, 1795–1895.* London: Henry Frowde, 1899.

McCordock, R. Stanley. *British Far Eastern Policy, 1894–1900.* New York: Columbia University Press, 1931.

MacNair, Harley F. *China's New Nationalism and Other Essays.* Shanghai: Commercial Press, 1926.

Malozemoff, Andrew. *Russian Far Eastern Policy, 1881–1904.* Berkeley: University of California Press, 1958.

Maybon, Albert. *La Politique Chinoise.* Paris: V. Guard and E. Briere, 1908.

Michael, Franz H., and George E. Taylor. *The Far East in the Modern World.* Revised edition. New York: Holt, Rinehart, and Winston, 1964.

Moon, Parker T. *Imperialism and World Politics.* New York: Macmillan, 1926.

Morse, Hosea B. *The International Relations of the Chinese Empire.* 3 vols. London: Longmans, Green and Co., 1918.

Newton, Thomas W. L. *Lord Lansdowne.* London: Macmillan, 1929.

Norman, Henry. *People and Politics of the Far East.* New York: C. Scribner's Sons, 1895.

Pao Chao Hsieh. *The Government of China (1644–1911).* Johns Hopkins University Studies in Historical and Political Science (new series), No. 3. Baltimore: Johns Hopkins Press, 1925.

Parker, Edward H. *China Past and Present.* London: Chapman and Hall, 1903.

Pascoe, C. R. *Two Hundred Years of the S.P.G.: An Historical Account of the Society for the Propagation of the Gospel in Foreign Parts, 1701–1900.* London: S.P.G., 1901.

Pelcovits, N. A. *Old China Hands and the Foreign Office.* New York: American Institute of Pacific Relations, 1948.

Purcell, Victor. *The Boxer Uprising.* Cambridge: Cambridge University Press, 1963.

Romanov, B. A. *Russia in Manchuria, 1892–1906,* trans. Susan W. Jones. Ann Arbor: University of Michigan Press, 1952.

Ronaldshay, The Earl of. *The Life of Lord Curzon.* 3 vols. New York: Boni and Liveright, 1928.

Sargent, A. J. *Anglo-Chinese Commerce and Diplomacy.* London: Oxford University Press, 1907.

Soothill, William E. *Timothy Richard of China.* London: Seeley, Service and Co., 1924.

Steiger, George N. *China and the Occident: The Origin and Development of the Boxer Movement.* New Haven, Conn.: Yale University Press, 1927.

Stock, Eugene. *A History of the Church Missionary Society.* 4 vols. London: C.M.S., 1916.

Tan, Chester C. *The Boxer Catastrophe.* Columbia Studies in Social Sciences, No. DLXXXIII. New York: Columbia University Press, 1955.

Taylor, A. J. P. *The Struggle for Mastery in Europe, 1848–1918.* Oxford History of Modern Europe. Oxford: Clarendon Press, 1954.

Teng, Ssu-yü, and John K. Fairbank. *China's Response to the West: A Documentary Survey, 1839–1923.* Cambridge, Mass.: Harvard University Press, 1954.

Thompson, Rev. H. P. *Into All Lands: A History of the S.P.G., 1701–1950.* London: S.P.C.K., 1951.

Thompson, R. Wardlaw. *Griffith John: The Story of Fifty Years in China.* New York: A. C. Armstrong and Son, 1906.

Varg, Paul A. *Missionaries, Chinese and Diplomats: The American Protestant Missionary Movement in China, 1890–1952.* Princeton, N.J.: Princeton University Press, 1958.

Whates, Harry Richard. *The Third Salisbury Administration, 1895–1900.* Westminster: Vacher and Sons, 1900.

Wright, Stanley F. *Hart and the Chinese Customs.* Belfast: William Mullan and Son, 1950.

ARTICLES

Bee, Minge C. "Peterhof Agreement," *Chinese Social and Political Review,* XX, No. 2 (1936–1937), 231–250.

Butler, Kenneth D., Jr. "The Yangtze Valley Riots of 1891." (A seminar paper submitted to the East Asia Regional Studies Seminar at Harvard University, and made available for this study through the courtesy of Professor John K. Fairbank of Harvard.)

Ch'en, Jerome. "The Nature and Characteristics of the Boxer Movement — A Morphological Study," *Bulletin of the School of Oriental and African Studies,* XXIII, Part II (1960), 287–309.

Ch'en Ch'iu. "The Political Thought of the Anti-Reformists during the Time of the Hundred Days of Reform," *Yenching Journal of Chinese Studies,* XXV (1937), 263–65.

Chi-yun Chen. "Liang Ch'i-ch'ao's Missionary Education: A Case Study of Missionary Influence on the Reformers," *Papers on China* (East Asia Regional Studies Seminar, Harvard University), XVI (1962), 66–125.

Chün-tu Hsüeh. "Sun Yat-sen, Yang Ch'ü-yen and the Early Revolutionary Movement in China," *Journal of Asian Studies,* XIX, No. 3 (May 1960), 307–18.

Cohen, Paul A. "The Anti-Christian Tradition in China," *Journal of Asian Studies,* XX, No. 2 (February 1961), 169–80.

————. "The Hunan-Kiangsi Anti-Missionary Incidents of 1862," *Papers on China* (East Asia Regional Studies Seminar, Harvard University), XII (1958), 1–28.

————. "Missionary Approaches: Hudson Taylor and Timothy Richard," *Papers on China* (East Asia Regional Studies Seminar, Harvard University), XI (1957), 29–62.

Dunstheimer, G. G. H. "Le Mouvement des Boxeurs," *Revue Historique,* CCXXXI (April–June 1964), 387–416.

Fairbank, John K. "Pattern behind the Tientsin Massacre," *Harvard Journal of Asiatic Studies,* XX (December 1957), 480–511.

BIBLIOGRAPHY

Gallagher, John, and Ronald Robinson. "The Imperialism of Free Trade," *Economic History Review,* 2nd Series, VI (1953), 1–15.

Hargreaves, J. D. "Lord Salisbury, British Isolation and the Yangtze Valley, June–September, 1900," *Bulletin of the Institute of Historical Research,* XXX (1957), 62–75.

Kawai, K. "Anglo-German Rivalry in the Yangtze Basin, 1885–1902," *Pacific Historical Review,* VIII (1939), 413–14.

Kung-ch'uan Hsiao. "Weng T'ung-ho and the Reform Movement of 1898," *Tsing Hua Journal of Chinese Studies,* I, No. 2 (April 1957), 111–245.

Muramatsu, Yuzi. "The Boxers in 1898–99," *Annals of the Hitotsubashi Academy,* III, No. 2 (April 1953), 236–61.

"O'Conor, N. R.," *Dictionary of National Biography,* Supplement, January 1901–December 1911, III, 37–40.

Ping-ti Ho. "Weng T'ung-ho and the 'One Hundred Days of Reform,'" *Far Eastern Quarterly,* X, No. 2 (February 1951), 125–36.

Rankin, Mary Backus. "The Ku-t'ien Incident (1895): Christians versus the Ts'ai-hui," *Papers on China* (East Asia Regional Studies Seminar, Harvard University), XV (1961), 30–61.

Sheeks, Robert B. "A Re-examination of the I-ho ch'uan and Its Role in the Boxer Movement," *Papers on China* (East Asia Regional Studies Seminar, Harvard University), I (1947), 74–135.

Steiger, G. N. "China's Attempt to Absorb Christianity," *T'oung Pao,* XXIV (1926), 215–46.

Varg, Paul A. "The Foreign Policy of Japan and the Boxer Revolt," *Pacific Historical Review,* XV (1946), 279–85.

Index

Bee, Benjamin M., theory on Shantung murders, 117n82

Belgium, and joint protest, 33

Berthemy Convention, confirms missionary rights, 5

Berthollet, Père, murder linked to rail concession, 106, 114

Bertie, Sir Francis: attitude on partition of China, 103; view on Hong Kong extension, 104; proposal on railway debt, 109; urges passive China policy, 150, 165; receives MacDonald's report, 159; urges overthrow of Empress Dowager, 166, 167n31; on supporting Manchu or Chinese regime, 190

Bible: Chinese view of, 22; Gardner urges regulated circulation of, 50

Big Sword society (Ta-tao hui): and Shantung murders, 116–117, 141; diminishing role in convert attacks, 142; and murder of Brooks, 146; as Boxer society, 147n34

Blake, Sir Henry: reports anarchy in Shum Chun, 111; and opening of West River to trade, 111n57

Bluejackets, British, possible use of, 137

Bock, Mr., Swedish consul-general, criticized at meeting, 74

Boxer Catastrophe, The, reveals nature of Boxer movement, 140–141

Boxer movement and rising: compared with 1895 crisis, 76; and alliance of gentry with secret societies, 116; Manchu and, 135, 141, 142–144, 172, 196; factors leading to, 139–140; nature of movement, 140–141, 196; stages of growth, 141–142; interpretations of, 143n18; first attack reported by British, 144; officials appease Boxers, 144–145; studies of European diplomacy during, 145n19; Western Powers demand decree suppressing, 148–150, 155, 157, 162; influence of Russia on negotiations concerning, 151; and ambiguous edict, 159; rumored extermination of foreigners, 162, 170; railway station destroyed near Peking, 164; Seymour's expedition attacked, 173; reign of destruction in Peking, 180; slaughter of converts and missionaries, 182; role in defense of China, 183, 196; as massive antimissionary riot, 190–191; failure of British diplomacy in, 198

British commercial interest in China, *see* Commercial interest in China, British

British consuls, involvement in converts' lawsuits, 16–17, 61–62, 141n4

Broderick, Sir John: urges action on railroad debt, 110; urges naval demonstration, 112; attitude toward missionaries' reform program, 125

Brooks, Rev. S. M.: killed, 146; settlement of case delayed, 154

Brown, Colonel G. F., on capture of Taku forts, 174, 175n63

Buddhism, Chinese tolerance of, 128

Bülow, Count, denies knowledge of demonstration, 156

Bullock, Consul T. L., reports pursuit of Ko-lao hui, 43

Butterfield & Squire, commercial station, attacked, 107n41

Campbell, Francis A.: suggests naval demonstration, 112; urges return of Shum Chun, 113; on limits of power in Peking, 154–155

Campbell, R. C., calls for punishment of officials, 74

Canadian Methodist missionaries, conduct in Szechwan riots, 84

Candlin, Rev. G. T., analyzes riots, 51–52

Canterbury, Archbishop of: cautions missionaries, 46; consulted by Rosebery, 54; informed of Allen's proposals, 60, 61; rejects official status for missionaries, 81; reaction to missionary edict of 1899, 132, 134

Carles, Consul W. R.: acts to suppress Boxers, 144; analysis of action by Chinese authorities, 145; notes unfortunate effect of new edict, 158–159; ordered to send guard to Peking, 164

Cassels, Rev. W. W., forced from residence by Chinese, 47

Cassini, Count, warns of democracy in China, 121

Chamberlain, Joseph, on request for expansion of Hong Kong, 108

Chanès, Père, murder linked to boundary settlement, 107n39

Chao Shu-ch'iao, probable author of correspondence during siege, 185n30

Chapman, General Edward, on troops available for China, 30

Ch'en, Jerome: analysis of evolution of

Macartney, Sir Halliday: intermediary in *1891*, 32; urges strong China policy, 67

McCordock, R. Stanley: discusses diplomacy of Boxer period, 145n19; interpretation of British policy disputed, 151

MacDonald, Sir Claude: on official status for Protestant missionaries, 80; view of China policy, 97; reports on German negotiations, 100; criticizes German settlement, 101; analysis of Germany in Kiaochow, 102–103; views requested on territorial additions, 102; sees Port Arthur occupation as insignificant, 104; asks Hong Kong extension, 104; critical of Hong Kong residents, 112; urges ultimatum in missionary case, 112; on Manchu attitude on concessions, 115; cites Manchu effort to stop riots, 117–118; aware of missionary-reformer connection, 123; ignores political role of missionaries, 123–124; intervention saves Emperor, 124; urges new missionary rights, 133; and Brooks case, 146; optimistic on Boxer trouble, 147; on court support of Boxers, 147–148; supports drastic action, 149; criticized by Foreign Office, 150; conference with Giers, 152; proposed joint demonstration dropped, 153; urges punishment of Yü-hsien, 154; sets up naval demonstration, 154–155; satisfied by published memorial, 157; optimistic despite ambiguous decree, 158; fails to report magnitude of outbreaks, 159–160; erratic diplomacy traced, 160; unmoved by Pichon's warnings, 162–163; motive in calling legation guards, 164; convinced of danger, 165; alerted to block Russia, 166–167; proposes interview with Empress Dowager, 166; opposes drastic measures, 168; calls for reinforcements, 170, 171; refuses to recall Seymour, 172, 174; promises guard for missionaries and converts, 180; begged not to evacuate, 181–182; role in siege, 184–190, 197

Macklin, Rev. W. E., urges use of gunboats, 30

Malet, Sir Edward, reports on German policy, 40

Manchester Guardian, article on riots, 51

Manchu dynasty: British support of, 7, 192; deterioration of, 7–8; impact of West on, 9; missionaries weaken ties with Britain, 18; stability of desired by Germany and Britain, 40; suppression of riots by, 42–43, 117–118, 137; implicit compromise with Britain, 44; alienation of *literati*, 73; fears partition, 78, 172, 192; forced to acknowledge weakness, 91; and territorial compensation in missionary cases, 114–115; weakened by missionary movement, 118; suspicious of Britain on reform issue, 125–126; purpose of missionary edict of *1899*, 127–128, 135; would relegate missionary disputes to local level, 128–130; opposition to missionaries, 135, 137; dilemma over Boxers, 142–144, 191, 196; ambiguous decree issued on Boxers, 147, 158; loses faith in British support, 153; sees European disunity, 157; endangered by Boxers, 160, 198; MacDonald on possibility of collapse, 164; could not appear as defender of converts, 183; British refuse commitment to, 190–191

Manzel, Père, murder of, 106

Marquis Tseng, friend of Britain, 38

Marshall, Baron von, fears French policy, 40

Methodist Episcopal Missionary Society, operations in China, 14

Ming dynasty, restoration of, 25

Missionary coalition: organized by Pichon, 148; considers naval demonstration, 150; presses for proper decree, 150; accepts compromise, 155; sends ultimatum to Tsungli Yamen, 155; terminates cooperation, 155–156; renewal of, 162

Missionary edict of *1899*: excerpts from, 79, 127–128; reaction of British missionaries to, 80, 134–135; gives status to Catholic missionaries, 127–128, 195–196; analysis of, 128–129, 131–135

Missionary movement: right of inland residence gained, 4–5; toleration of Christianity confirmed, 5; undermines Confucian system, 14; imprudent conduct of missionaries seen as cause of riots, 20; Chinese view of morality of,